Problem Solving In A Dynamic Environment

Problem Solving In A Dynamic Environment

Yan-Hong Ng
Department of Electrical Engineering
Imperial College
London SW7 2BT

Shou-Fong Chin
The Army
The Republic of China

World Scientific
Singapore • New Jersey • London • Hong Kong

Published by

World Scientific Publishing Co. Pte. Ltd.

P O Box 128, Farrer Road, Singapore 9128

USA office: Suite 1B, 1060 Main Street, River Edge, NJ 07661

UK office: 57 Shelton Street, Covent Garden, London WC2H 9HE

PROBLEM SOLVING IN A DYNAMIC ENVIRONMENT

ISBN 981-02-2029-4

Printed in Singapore by Uto-Print

Acknowledgements

We wish to express our gratitude to the Army of the Republic of China, for funding part of this work. Without them, this research would not have been possible. Special thanks also due to Hamlet X. Wang for valuable discussions and advice on the style of writing and presentation of the manuscript.

CONTENTS

CHAPTER ONE

INTRODUCTION

1.1 The Motivation

In a dynamic environment where the state of the domain is constantly changing and evolving, the transformation from one temporal stable state to another is normally caused by an external event, or a chain of events. In such a dynamic environment, it is impossible to model all conceivable external events that may cause changes in the domain. Therefore, it is practical to draw up a plan on an assumption that all the factors which are not taken into consideration here remain unchanged in the course of plan execution. But should it fail, the plan inevitably becomes unworkable. Is re-planning the only course of action following such failure or can modification be brought into the procedure of the plan execution?

Traditionally, planning relies on the "complete knowledge" of the solution space or the ability to conduct an "exhaustive search" of all state variations in the domain. However in a dynamic environment, none of these conditions are available, the methodology, or perhaps more appropriately the strategy, of plan deliberation seemingly enters into a "no thoroughfare" lane. Therefore, reactive planning and Interleaving Planning Execution (IPE) have long been advocated as the methodology for planning in a dynamic environment. Nevertheless, we believe that reactive planning and IPE though useful in coping with uncertainty in the environment, lack the sophistication and strategy in formulating comprehensive plan. In here, we propose a planning methodology that combines both search and recognition paradigms in plan formulation, and applies the idea of reactive planning and IPE only at the plan execution stage to steer the plan through the uncertain environment or unforeseeable counter-operation from the opponent. In other words, the selection and confirmation of the operational plan (plan deliberation) is only half of the story and the successful conclusion of the plan relies on the ability of the plan executor to repair, to modify the operational plan during the cause of execution.

1.2 Some Fundamental Background

In this section, we examine some of the fundamental background in problem solving.

- The problem solving methodology; and
- The architectural platform required to support the methodology.

In the artificial intelligence (AI) literature, the term "problem solving", which stems from the work of Newell and Simon [Newell and Simon 1972], is described as consisting of selecting "sequence of operators" that transform the problem from an initial state into a desired state. Those sequences of operators are also known as "course of actions". The study of problem solving mainly concerns on how to obtain a suitable course of actions by analysing the current state. For instance, in means-end analysis, the course of actions are chosen by the criteria with the minimum distance between the current state and the desired state; while in heuristic search, the course of actions are composed by an evaluator of selecting the best choice among all of the possible alternatives. Both methods are applied at each intermediary state recursively until the desired state is reached.

As far as the problem solving methodology is concerned, there are basically two schools of thought, which could be distinguished by the amount of domain knowledge needed to arrive at a solution. One of them known as "recognition paradigm" examines the current state and attempts to reach the resulting goal state by applying a large amount of domain knowledge and experience to find the best, or every available course of actions that connects the two states together. The second approach, known as "search paradigm", attempts to reason either forward from the current state or backward from the goal state to search for a path or a plan that connects the two states together with very little domain knowledge available at either state. Generally speaking, the recognition paradigm is adopted by the knowledge-rich system; the knowledge could be a set of complicated rules. Whereas the search paradigm is employed mainly by the knowledge-poor system, where the knowledge could sometimes be only a simple algorithm.

Since both paradigms have their strength and weaknesses, it is very difficult to come down firmly on one or the other in the context of problem solving. In the recognition paradigm, the complexity of the problem domain often means that it is very difficult to conduct knowledge acquisition. Therefore, the degree of match required by the system would frequently return with "solution unavailable". On the other hand, with the search paradigm, more algorithms could only move tactically either by breadth-first search or some forms of heuristic search to move towards a solution. However, they do suffer from the "horizon effect" of being unable to foresee and avoid problem along its path without a long-term strategy. In the most practical applications, search paradigm tends to have an edge over the recognition paradigm, as the advance in hardware making the exploration of larger solution space more easier than the encoding of complicated knowledge.

Ideally, a better solution could result if one would be able to combine the best of both worlds (paradigms) which complement each other, since "the further a process can look ahead, the less detailed knowledge it needs" [Berliner and Ebeling 1989]. It means that more knowledge need less search and vice versa. "SUPREM" (Search Using Pattern Recognition as the Evaluation Mechanism) architecture is one of the typical example, which has attempted to investigate the basis where the recognition in the domain knowledge is required to properly evaluate the states likely to be reached by a search starting from the current state. Its architectural figure is as follows:

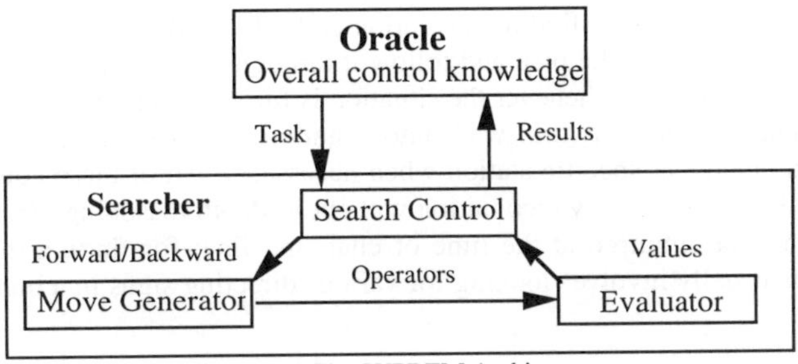

Figure 1.1 The SUPREM Architecture

In the architecture above, the knowledge base (recognition paradigm) is a set of rules about the domain, where each rule takes the form of conditions and related patterns. At the start of each iteration in the processing, the Oracle system analyses the problem, selects and generates the appropriate rule to be down-load onto the evaluator of the searcher. The searcher (search paradigm) then takes the pattern specified to select the depth of search and initiates a visit to any node within its reach for a possible solution. Each node in the search tree is examined by the evaluator with the parameter down-loaded from the Oracle system. At the end of the specified search, the control is returned to the Oracle system with a result, or suggestion of a possible move. Hence, the linkage between these two paradigms is for knowledge base to specify the domain and parameters needed for the searcher to look and evaluate solution. A comparison to illustrate the mapping between the methodology and the architecture in SUPREM is shown as follows:

Methodology		Architectural Platform
Recognition Paradigm	---------------------->	Oracle
Linkage (interface)	---------------------->	Evaluator
Search Paradigm	---------------------->	Search Control and Move Generator

However, from the methodology point of view, the recognition paradigm in SUPREM is only playing a minor role in providing the parameters for path evaluation, with the brute force search being the main "work horse" in the system for finding a solution. Therefore, in order to construct a more effective decision support system, a better balance would have to be achieved where different paradigm could be called upon to advise at a different level or different aspect of the problem in the way similar to the human reasoning process.

Generally speaking, the common strategy adopted in dealing with problem solving in a dynamic environment is by initially going for familiarity. Pattern matching both the current and desired positions associated with a possible and pre-programmed plan. The details of the plan may not be clear or available at the very beginning, but it does provide a framework and direction in finding a solution path. Once the plan is recognised, what one has to do is to activate the plan and follow it through from start to finish. During this period, search is necessary whenever the situation is fuzzy, or unspecified. Travelling on the London underground network: walk into a station, select your destination, take the right train and change at specific station when necessary. All of these course of actions are achieved almost entirely by recognition without in-depth reasoning. However, search in this case may be required at the time of changing line; for finding the appropriate platform. This usually involves looking for various directing signs in a big or unfamiliar station.

It would be slightly different to take a trip outside London. The recognition in this case can only provide a skeleton plan with several important landmarks like towns or junctions along the travelling route. The search is required to find the most convenient roads between those landmarks. Hence, a human-oriented problem solving methodology is using recognition to identify the possible intermediate states, while relying on search to identify the reasonable linkages between these states as shown in the following diagram:

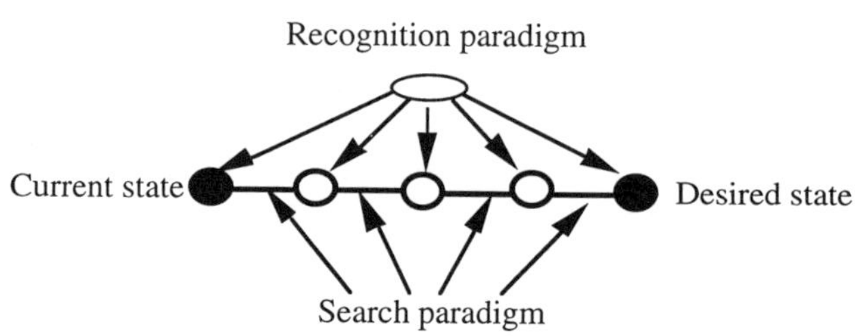

Figure 1.2 A Human-Oriented Problem Solving Methodology

Incidentally, a military decision-making procedure used in the real or simulated battlefield over centuries provides us with such a framework. The recognition paradigm (the experience and know-how of the commander) is relying upon for strategic planning, while tactical implementation or realisation of the strategic plan are the objectives set for staff or local commanders in the light of volatility in the battlefield environment. This book is to study the feasibility of constructing a decision support system based on just such a battlefield management system, better known as the standard operating procedure (SOP) which is usually divided into four related stages:

- **Deliberation**: to understand, study, and analyse the current situation, desired situation, and the environment.
- **Planning**: to find and discover several possible and suitable paths between the current and the desired situation according to the result of the deliberation stage.
- **War meeting**: to examine the quality of each report from the above procedures, and select the best as the operational plan and the rest as the stand-by plans.
- **Plan execution**: to execute the operational plan in an uncertain environment, to alter it when necessary, or replace it with the most suitable stand-by plan, or work out a new plan. When the new plan is needed, the decision-making procedure restarts from the beginning of the deliberation stage.

In the deliberation stage, the problem is presented in the context of current situation as against the desired situation (strategic plan). The Planning stage could establish the fully connected solution path of all intermediate states identified in the strategic plans. When all plans are put forward for consideration, they will be selected under some kind of criteria. All these three stages are conducted in a multi-stream reasoning environment, where several independent agents are invoked in trying to find solutions. Therefore, a protocol of merging and consolidating various proposals would have to be installed to accommodate different points of views. This requirement also applies to the plan execution, known as the "command and control (C^2)" in assuring that the selected plan will achieve its original goal in the light of moving target or changing environment. In this book, we would develop a problem solving methodology based on this SOP and discuss the required architectural platform to support it.

1.3 The Contributions

The aims of this research are at the further understanding in problem solving methodology applied in a dynamic environment and the architectural platform that underpinned this decision support technology. The main contributions of the reported work can be summarised in the following:

- To demonstrate that it is feasible to construct a complex decision support system based on a long standing military decision-making procedure (SOP), by which the traditional recognition and search paradigms are combined to provide a more comprehensive framework for problem solving.

- To develop the methodology for co-operative planning, where all sub-plans are co-ordinated under the view of one strategic plan during planning, as well as during plan execution overseen under the C^2.

- To study the feasibility of constructing a multi-agent platform to support these multi-stream reasoning technology in a dynamic environment, where the solution space is unbounded and resources are limited.

- To develop the foundation, on which a real battlefield decision support system could be constructed.

1.4 The Contents of the Book

There are eight chapters in this book. Of which, Chapters 2 and 3 are devoted to the necessary background material of problem solving in the context of AI, paving the way for the presentation of the proposed methodology in Chapter 4. The proposed platform is then tested and examined in the domain of chess in Chapter 5 and 6. Chapter 7 will compare the finding from the case studies in Chapter 6 to project on gap between the proposed planning methodology and a number of battlefield systems known to the authors. Finally, Chapter 8 will examine the significance of learning in a truly dynamic (volatile) environment.

Chapter 2 will briefly describe the standard operating procedure used as the basis to develop our decision-making methodology.

Chapter 3 will provide an overview of problem solving and decision support technology in the context of Artificial Intelligence.

Chapter 4 will present the design and the implementation of the proposed problem solving methodology and its architectural platform.

Chapter 5 will introduce some background and development of the computer chess, the features of Chinese chess, and the goal-oriented algorithm will also be high-lighted as the basis for our simulation testbed.

Chapter 6 will put forward a six-case study to demonstrate the behaviours and the functionality of our decision support methodology, and evaluate how well the multi-agent platform in supporting the decision-making activity in the context of goal-oriented chess playing. Several issues are also examined in details with the help of these case studies.

Chapter 7 will be draw up a possible functional requirement for the battlefield decision support system based on the methodology and platform we have put forward.

Chapter 8 will examine the issue of learning in the context of a foreign exchange market, assess the adaptivity and enhancement in the light of machine learning, and map out the direction for further research.

CHAPTER TWO

A MILITARY PROBLEM SOLVING METHODOLOGY

2.1 The Command Post Exercise

For centuries, military commanders have been seeking ways to train their staff in peacetime and prepare them for a war. The Command Post Exercise is such a system that is designed to serve the purpose, by which a commander can guide his staff in a simulated exercise using either a map or a sand-table. However, the Command Post Exercise is not yet another planning model for a simple "blocks world" problem, but a comprehensive decision support model for deliberation, generation, consolidation, selection and execution of a plan in a dynamically changing environment. It involves three main components:

- A simulated battlefield (as the problem domain);
- Commander (for the generation of a strategic plan), and
- Staff (for tactical implementation of individual objective given in the strategic plan).

The model of representing the command post exercise is illustrated as below:

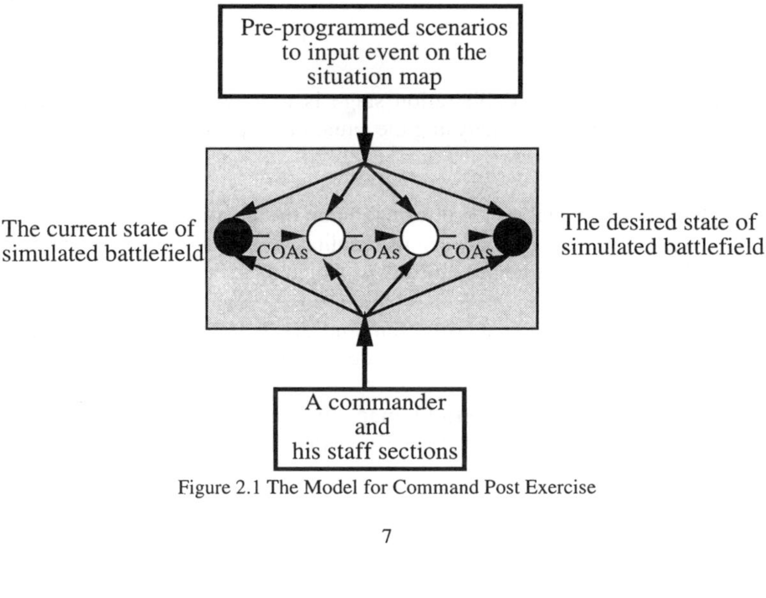

Figure 2.1 The Model for Command Post Exercise

The simulated battlefield attempts to include all of the relevant data such as weather, terrain, road, river, obstacles stet and the unit deployment of both sides. From the situation map, the commander and his staff are in the position to proceed with their study of information, analysing the desired goal before the deliberation of strategic plans. Usually the staff here is divided into four sections: administration section (S1), intelligence section (S2), operation section (S3) and logistic section (S4). In other more complex domains, additional sections such as fire support section would be required to co-ordinate the support from artillery, warship and tactical air force. The main task for these sections is to understand the current situation and identify the desired situation according to the mission (objective identified in the strategic plan) so that the course of actions (COAs) can be generated. The COAs are required to transform the current state into the goal state. After such deliberation of the strategic plan, the task for the commander is to merge and select the best COA as the operational plan, and put others as alternative plans.

However, what concerns us most here is not the military organisation but the mechanism for plan deliberation and generation, and the protocol where various COAs are consolidated, selected and executed. For example, in a ever changing battlefield, the operational plan often becomes unworkable without modification, and such modification or re-planning will in turn re-define the role to be undertaken by the Command and Control in the battlefield.

2.2 The Decision-Making Procedure

In this section, we will introduce the Standard Operating Procedure (SOP) as the basis for decision-making in the command post exercise, which consists of four stages: 1) deliberation; 2) planning; 3) war meeting; and 4) plan execution.

2.2.1 Deliberation

The main function of the deliberation stage is to study the current situation and identify the desired situation by analysing the situation map. The order of the designated mission is summarised as follows:

- To create and analyse the information on the situation map.
- To perform mapping between the qualitative goal of the mission and a list of achievable (quantitative) objectives, which must be accomplished in order to realise the goal.
- To study the current situation and its feasibility in reaching all the intermediate goals required in the desired formation.

The situation map is a battlefield map constantly updated with all relevant information concerning both sides (usually called the Blue and the Red) and the environment data that piece together the picture of the battlefield situation. The information include army organisation, weaponry, personnel deployment, logistic supply, equipment, fuel, ammunition, unit position, morale (loyalty and discipline), tactical doctrines and other intelligence reports. The environment data comprise weather report, terrain, road, river, mine field and other obstacles. For instance, let us apply the SOP into a chess domain, in which each position on the chess board could be described as one of the following states: blue (controlled by the blue side), red (controlled by the red side), conflict (controlled by both sides), and neutral (controlled by neither side). Accordingly each position on the chessboard could be defined further as either safe or dangerous. In other words, the situation map provides the problem domain, where the current situation could be displayed and the desired situation could also be indicated.

With the completion of the situation map, the commander is now in the position to identify a desired situation where political goal could be realised. However, the quantification of qualitative goal into achievable military objectives has never been perfect, which can only make the recognition process feasible on a probabilistic basis. In other words, the desired situation is normally presented as a desire "to capture an enemy unit" or "to occupy an important position or area". In the context of chess, to "win" (a qualitative goal) the game could be translated into "checkmate" (a quantitative objective) in the form of some attacking formation and the situation map will provide the basis where problem could be focused, i.e. all escape routes of the target (opponent's king), so that plans could be drawn up to pin down the target before the deliberation of any attacking formation.

With the desired situation (formation) in sight, the task for the commander and his staff is to assess the current situation and study the feasibility of planning for the formation. This assessment of the current situation is to clarify the following matters:

1) The available resources needed for reaching the desired situation;
2) The position of those resources; and
3) The study of hostile forces and their possible plans.

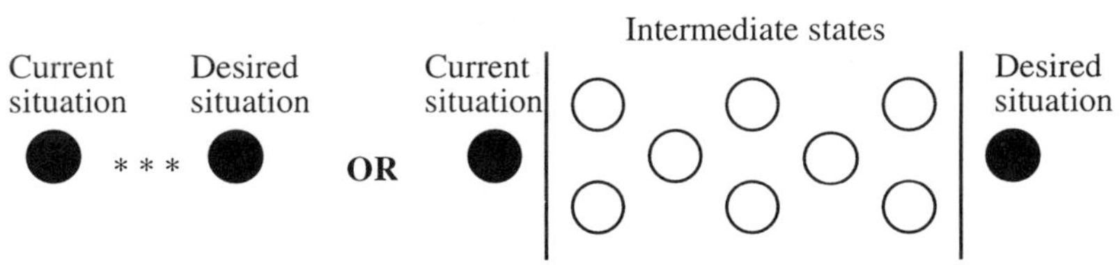

Figure 2.2 The Deliberation: from Qualitative Goal to Desired Situation

If desired formation is confirmed, a series of objectives can be identified as the intermediate goals between the current situation and the desired situation as shown in Figure 2.2. For instance, a checkmate formation in chess involves a sequence of captures and manoeuvres, with each of them as an intermediate goal in the overall formation. This mapping process relies heavily on the experience and expertise of the commander and his staff, or similar cases they have learned from books.

At this stage of deliberation, the quality, organisation, leadership, and material strength of the units are more important (necessary) conditions in the calculation, while the environment factors are considered only as vital conditions later in the tactical planning stage. What worries the commander now is the feasibility of the goal and its realisation in the form of military operation (strategy) other than the course of actions (tactic) needed to achieve the goal. In other words, he concentrates on **what** to do rather than how to **do** it.

Generally speaking, the strategy will be responsible for formulating the final desired situation and the possible intermediate objectives, while tactics known as the art of placing or moving combat forces involve working out the practical means or solution paths from one state to the others in line with the strategy. The structure of a formation is shown in the Figure 2.3 below:

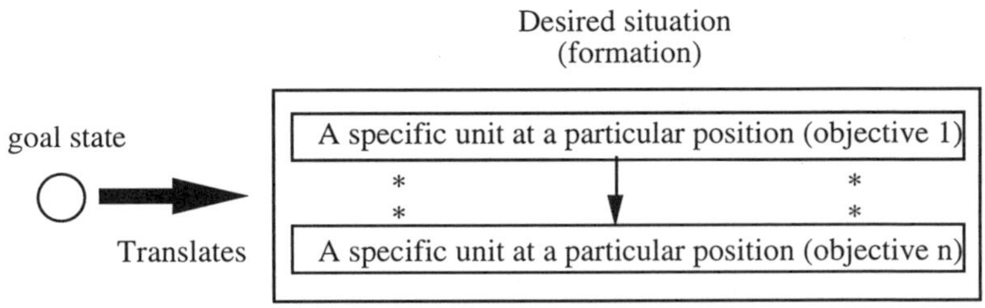

Figure 2.3 The Translation of a Goal into a Formation in the Strategic Plan

The strategists approach the problem at the highest level by formulating either the defensive or offensive formation to fulfil the ultimate goal, which is often decomposed into a number of sub-goals (intermediate states). The main goal can be realized if all or most of the sub-goals (in a probabilistic model) are achieved. The strategy deployed is determined by the current situation, and the strength or make-up of units under command. If his forces are superior in manpower, equipment and weaponry, the commander may then have the option of Moltke's "outer line operation" leading to encirclement. Otherwise, Jomini's "inner line operation" or Liddell Hart's "indirect approach" would probably be the only options. The former requires an overwhelming superiority in both manpower and resources to encircle or to break through enemy's defence, while the latter advocates the division and conquest by separating enemy's units to achieve local superiority, dislocating the enemy and reducing their means of resistance. Generally speaking, each formation may involve a number of objectives, and each objective prescribes a specific unit at a particular position or a task to accomplish.

The tacticians approach the problem from the lowest level of abstraction, formulating solution in the form of course of actions to move from one state to another, often without an overall picture (strategy) that includes the initial and desired goal states. Their decision is based on short-term advantage or under the guidance of some heuristics.

2.2.2 Planning

According to the desired situation identified at the deliberation stage, either strategically or tactically, the main task for planning is to produce fully connected solution paths between states. During the planning stage, the commander and his staff sections will use their own expertise and knowledge to develop solution paths to realise the objectives set out in the deliberation stage. The distinction between strategic and tactical planning here is essential, as the former provides the overview of the battlefield plan from start to finish, the latter would often only generate COA between two states.

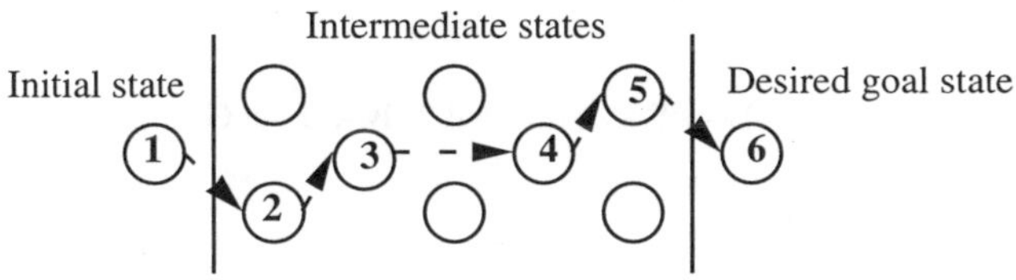

Figure 2.4 Strategic Plan with a Chain of Intermediate States

The strategic plan contains both the initial and goal states and defines the grouping or formation of states which might have solution paths formed at the planning stage, and it also sets out the interlocking co-operation between objectives. For instance, in a "pin and strike" formation , the COA for pinning should be in place before the COA for striking is put into action. In most cases, all the staff sections operate in a co-operative manner. Each views the situation on the situation map from their own perspective and considers the related problems accordingly. In order to reach some mature and compromised solution, ideas can be exchanged simultaneously between relevant sections, such as S1 with S4 and S2 with S3. The eventual outcome of a strategic plan should at least produce a path (plan) between the initial state and the desired goal state like that in Figure 2.4.

Figure 2.5 Tactical Plan Usually Involves No Intermediate State

As for the desired situation tactically identified by means of heuristics based on short-term consideration, it usually does not involve any intermediate state between the current state and desired state. The dash lines in Figure 2.4 and 2.5 indicate the order of execution in the strategic or tactical plan, by which pre-conditions and constraints are imposed on each plan (fulfilment of an objective). In planning, only two states are presented in the solution space as the means of working out the best possible ways of moving from state A to state B, where the environment factors on the situation map will now have effect. In this context, terrain, blocked road, damaged bridge or mine field will have to be taken into account in the course of finding a solution path. Here, if a formation in the strategic plan consists of two ordered objectives from current positions {A, B}:

- Objective 1 prescribes unit 1 to arrive at position E; and
- Objective 2 prescribes unit 2 to arrive at position G.

Then,

- Sub-goal 1 (Unit 1): **A** -> C -> D -> **E**; and
- Sub-goal 2 (Unit 2): **B** -> F -> **G** (Pre-condition: activated only after Sub-goal 1).

where the fully connected strategic plan is shown as follows if state G is indeed the ultimate goal state.

Sub-goal 1: **A** -> C -> D -> **E** -> Sub-goal 2: **B** -> F -> **G**.

2.2.3 War Meeting

The third stage in this decision-making procedure is a war meeting, where all proposed COAs are compared and discussed. Here, some forms of selection mechanisms would have to be installed to resolve conflict among different plans, or even between strategy or tactics considerations. The classic example is that of "The Inchon Landing" on 15th September 1950 during the Korea War [Rees 1964]. In the war meeting for Operation CHROMITE on 23 August 1950, and despite all the strong and violent objections from his subordinate commanders and Chiefs of Staff, General MacArthur said.....

> The very arguments you have made as to the impracticabilities involved will tend to ensure for me the element of surprise. For the enemy commander will reason that no one would be so brash as to make such an attempt. If experienced American amphibious specialists thought Inchon was almost out of the question, then so would the Communists.... I can almost hear the ticking of the second hand of destiny. We must act now or we wili die. Inchon would succeed, and it would save 100,000 lives. We shall land at Inchon and I shall crush them....

Sun Tzu, a most renowned Chinese military strategist, also said in Chapter 1 of The Art of War [Giles 1985; Lo 1991], that all warfare is based on surprise and deception: attack where the enemy is unprepared; and appear where the enemy is not expected. These are the strategist's key to victory. Inchon Landing was indeed not a normal reasoning deliberation from a conventional tactical viewpoint. The strategy of surprise and deception seems to have taken precedence over the risk and difficulty in its tactical implementation so much that it created a victory that appeared impossible and enabled the Americans to gain the upper hand at a critical stage in the Korea War.

During the war meeting, comments and suggestions are discussed around the table, with the commander exercising his authority to judge and approve each plan either autocratically, or democratically by majority voting. At the same time, they consolidate and merge all constituted parts (objectives) of a desired formation in a co-operative manner so that execution sequence is imposed on each of them. Finally, the most preferential solution path would be given priority as the formal operation plan, with other workable COAs as the stand-by. When the war meeting ends, the operation plan will be vividly demonstrated in the situation map which now turns into the "operation map".

2.2.4 Plan Execution

The plan execution is the final stage of the decision-making procedure, where a complete or almost fully connected solution path or plan is made operational. At this stage, the role of the command and control (C^2) is to ensure the execution of the selected plan, orchestrate all units concerned in the operation to reach the ultimate goal, and steer the battle through the uncharted environment and unforeseeable counter-operation from the opponent. In this way, local re-planning and modification of the operational plan is routine, as the official plan becomes impractical or impossible in a rapidly changing environment.

When a dead end is encountered, *dependency directed backtracking* [Currie and Tate 1989] does not always come into play. Since the earlier choice point in the desired formation or objective might have been dislocated or simply disappear from the situation map. Given the time critical nature in the battlefield, C^2 will first attempt to repair the current operation plan before activating one of the suitable stand-by plan, otherwise, a loop back to re-planting would sometimes become inevitable. This looping of activity will not cease until the order in the mission has been achieved (win) or become impossible (loss or stalemate).

In reality, every plan in the battlefield could never be absolute. Each plan is subject to various preconditions and constraints which themselves are constantly changing. Therefore, every plan is monitored from start to finish. Tactical plans of moving from one state to the other (COAs) are monitored by the strategic plan while strategic plans are themselves supervised by the political goal (mission). All these check and balance implies central control at the heart of the C^2 system; on the other hand, individual units are allowed to pursue their own plans as long as there is no violation of any preconditions or constraints, or change in the strategic plan. In this setting, local co-operation and negotiation could be supported with central command over-seeing and supervising the operation of its subordinates at arm's length, but able to intervene at each state interval, given option of changing strategy and consideration in the course of any plan execution.

2.3 The Summary

The brief description of the above standard operating procedure (SOP) covers the principle, role and function of various components in the command post exercise. It has, to a certain extent, provided us with the basic framework as a decision-making system for the dynamic environment:

- It should provide information, as well as advice at every stage of the SOP. This should include support for the decomposition of goal at the deliberation stage, generation of plans at the planning stage, selection and consolidation of plans at the war meeting stage, and command and control of the operational plan at the execution stage.

- Given that the massive information exist in the problem domain, probabilistic reasoning is possibly the only practical alternative in this highly dynamic environment. Therefore, advice has to be derived under a cloud of uncertainty, and the fuzzy matching between the qualitative goal onto quantitative objectives should be supported.

- The advice should be based on the experience and know-how of the experts/strategists (recognition paradigm), as well as COAs formulation by working through solution space (search paradigm). Hence, the top-down strategic plan from the commander could be complemented by a list of bottom-up tactical plans from various staff sections.

- The system should have a suitable control and consolidation mechanism for evaluating plans/COAs and resolving conflicts between strategy and tactical considerations.

- In reality, as time is regarded as a resource, advice should be given under certain time constraint. Otherwise, the first formulated plan or COA will be made operational, if there is no better plan formulated within the given time.

- The Command and Control should be equipped to modify and repair existing plans (either operational or stand-by plans) in order to cope with the uncertainty from both the opponent and environment.

To date, the complexity of the dynamic environment, as well as the sophistication needed in the decision-making process, has long confined this demanding system as the fantasy of the science. Nonetheless, advance in cognitive science and decision support system, coupled with the arrival of cost-effective parallel machines, has made this dream machine one step nearer to reality, and we will review the state-of-the-art in decision support technology in the next chapter before embarking on our model in later chapters.

CHAPTER THREE

THE OVERVIEW OF DECISION SUPPORT SYSTEMS

3.1 A Brief Historical Review

In the general perception, the decision support system (DSS) is conventionally known as a knowledge-based system (KBS) or intelligent knowledge-based system (IKBS), both of which are a family of computer-based tool designed for information retrieval in the course of decision-making. Actually, these "first generation" rule-based systems had very limited capacities and only dealt with matters in a relatively static environment, such as credit rating for loan application or means testing for supplementary benefits; they were unable to cope with complex, changeable and dynamic environments. However, for decades, developing alongside KBS or IKBS, there have been a number of probabilistic models under the general heading of machine learning: Neural Network, Genetic Algorithm, and other opportunistic learning systems. They did not come to prominence until the second half of the 1980s, where expert systems and knowledge information processing systems were in the spot light. For example, the knowledge information processing system in the Fifth Generation Computer Systems (Japan), the IKBS in the Alvey program (UK), and the Information Processing Systems & Software track of the ESPRIT program (EEC) are among the well known examples

The delayed emergence of probabilistic models is due mainly to the lack of understanding of their strength and weakness in the context of problem solving. Firstly, as the name may indicate, that any machine learning model needs to learn before it can recognise or predict. Secondly, its learning power relies on changing the weight or strength of connections between the input and output, either under supervision or using some kind of feedback to minimise the error. Thirdly, hit and miss are determined by threshold where hit is presumed when matching confident is greater than the threshold, or miss counts. Finally, many machine learning models are unable to generalise and abstract knowledge through training, and this confines their applications in pattern recognition mainly at low levels such as vision and image processing. Consequently, the perception in the 80s was that probabilistic models were only appropriate for low level learning while rule-based KBS or IKBS only applicable in the static environment.

However, recent advances in machine learning has begun to address the problem by which weights are introduced into rules to make applications of rule conditions on confirmation. Such techniques remove the rigid constraints of most logic languages and have paved the way for the design of evolving knowledge bases with capability to cope with uncertain and inconsistent information [Gillies et al 1992]. Although it is still at its early stage, a new development will no doubt emerge as a trend in the "second generation" systems. Its potential in coping with changes lies in the theory of fuzzy matching. Although some of these results, undoubtedly, shed new light in understanding of the design of decision support system, the architectural requirement of such complex system is unlikely to be supported by these techniques alone.

Given the functionalities of the military decision-making procedure outlined in command post exercise environment, we will discuss the state-of-the-art technology in Distributed Artificial Intelligence (DAI), particularly in planning and plan execution (command and control systems) in the following.

3.2 Distributed Artificial Intelligence

Generally speaking, Distributed Artificial Intelligence [Bond and Gasser 88; Avouris and Gasser 92] is the branch of AI concerning with how to co-ordinate behaviour among a collection of semi-autonomous agents for problem solving. It means that they can co-ordinate their knowledge, goals and plans to solve common problems collectively, or to make individually or globally rational decisions in the uncertain, multiple and conflicting perspectives. Although co-ordination has been described as the key research area of DAI, it is the approach to problem solving that really divides the field of DAI into cognitive and reactive methodologies [Demazeau and Muller 91, Gasser et al 87; Doran et al 92; Durfee et al 87b; Conte et al 91].

Cognitive systems are inward looking in the course of problem solving. They often have a model of the outside world (environment), or their interpretation of it held within the model. Solutions in the form of Course of Actions (COAs) or game tree are the prerequisites of this approach, and often require the support of complex architecture, which make them very costly as opposed to the reactive systems. Problem solving is by means of mapping the problem concerned onto the internal representation of the world held in their knowledge-base either by recognition or search. The strength of the cognitive approach lies in its ability to deliver solution or plan before execution, but most solutions are generated from its interpretation of the world held internally inside the model. When this interpretation become incompatible with the real world outside the model, the solution it generated becomes irrelevant.

Reactive systems, on the other hand, take the view that since complex planning in a dynamic environment is often a waste of time. It is perhaps more cost-effective to go for a simple reactive model based on stimulus-response. Reactive systems tend to be more outward looking in the course of problem solving; they often neither have any comprehensive representation of the outside world, nor do they take any past events (experience) into account from for drawing up a plan. Instead, they equip each agent with the necessary attributes and capability to deal with events as they unfold in the environment. Hence, reactive agents are unable to plan ahead and the solution they offer tend to be short-term without a global strategy, but the reactive approach is so effective in operating in a volatile environment [Brooks and Connell 86, Agre and Chapman 87, Steels 89, Wavish and Connah 90] that it has shifted the focus in planning methodology in recent years from cognitive to reactive approach, when problem domains seemingly moving from the "blocks world" to the real world of moving events [Ferber 89; Connah 91; Ferber and Drogoul 92].

Problem solving in a complex environment requires the decomposition of the problem into a list of achievable objectives so as to distribute the sub-tasks to a group of intelligent agent, or to invite for bid to solve the problem collectively. In DAI, the issue of decomposition is often addressed as task analysis or task partitioning, by which a complex task is broken down into a list of smaller sub-tasks; each of them requires less knowledge and fewer resources. As very little is reported on machine decomposition, most of the effort are devoted to the task distribution after the problem has been decomposed by the programmers or the designers.

In the Standard Operating Procedure (SOP), the deliberation stage requires the decomposition of the qualitative goal of the mission (to win) into a list of military achievable (quantitative) objectives. This decomposition process could be automated by mapping the "desire to win" into an attacking formation which consists of a number of objectives (sub-goals). The formulation of offensive formation is guided by some form of strategy (i.e the "outer line" strategy) and realised by a particular choice of tactics (i.e. the tactics of "pin and strike") for the operation. As for the issues of task distribution and resources allocation, many DAI techniques could be integrated into the SOP once the qualitative goal has been translated into a tactical formation with a list of objectives (sub-goals) ready to be distributed to all relevant units (agents). In here, the decision for task allocation could be based either on planned allocation (centralised organisation) or opportunistic market-like mechanism (decentralised organisation). The centralised allocation is based on commander assessment of the situation in terms of available resources and their locations, while the decentralised approach will broadcast the sub-tasks to all concerned for solution, followed by consolidating and merging all sub-plans from every units (agents) into one coherent and workable strategic plan that covers the completed formation.

In the course of planning, the issues of interaction, language, and communication among agents are as relevance in military planning as to DAI. Agents do need to interact in a co-operative fashion in order to solve the problem collectively, none more fundamental than the co-operative planning that exists between the strategists and tacticians; the attacking formulation is formulated and consolidated into a coherent strategic plan, which consists of a number of tactical plans (sub-plans). Within the framework of co-operative planning, the strategist is the proposer, the instigator and the consolidator of the operational and stand-by plans during the plan generation stage, whereas the tacticians are responsible for constructing plans for an individual sub-goal and are in charge of conducing negotiation and arrange assistance locally with other agents in the course of constructing their COAs. Ideas of sub-contracting, exchanging of meta-level information and message passing protocol of the DAI are all useful components in the design of a multi-agent military planning architecture.

At the war meeting stage, coherence, co-ordination and organisation are the main issues to be addressed. The primary difficult in a typical DAI system of establishing coherence and co-operation without centralised control does not exist here because there is always a centralised control in the battlefield. Starting from the conception of a strategy to a tactical formation, from consolidation of various tactical sub-plans into an overall strategic plan, from the execution of the operational plan to plan modification and pre-planning and at every stage, there is a visible centralised control, although local units (agents) are semi-autonomous and are able to function independently within constraints as long as no pre-condition has been breached. This centralised and hierarchical organisation at the global level (strategic level) is complimented by the market-like organisation at the tactical agents (local units) level to construct a solution path for individual sub-goal, and the SOP has provided us with an ideal platform to bring these two extreme organisational regimes within one framework. By the means of planning to integrate strategy (global level) with the tactical implementation (local level) will be addressed in the next section.

The coherence of the strategic plan is achieved when all sub-plans, which could co-exist spatially, temporally, locally or semantically within the same formation, are consolidated into one strategic plan. However, as the by-product of this reconciliation process, constraints and pre-conditions are attached and imposed on each sub-plans of the strategic plan, making co-ordination as the price to pay for system coherence.

However, in a battlefield system where time is always a critical factor in decision making, the need for re-planning is minimised to such an extent that in the Standard Operating Procedure, stand-by plans are treated as a necessity, in addition to the Command and Control (C^2) mechanism to monitor and repair the operational plan. In SOP, stand-by plans are redundant strategic plans designed as replacement to the operational plan, while the function of C^2 is to supervise and monitor the execution of the operational plan and to co-ordinate tactical re-planning of the operational plan as much as possible by repairing the plan and by relaxing the constraints either spatially, temporally or materially. However, operating in a dynamic environment, predictions and expectations generated from cognitive mode are far from adequate in coping with volatility of the real world. At the plan execution stage, reactive planning has demonstrated that it is more cost-effective to deal with the events locally rather than centrally. We will examine the issue of reactive planning in the context of the command and control in Section 3.4.

3.3 The Planning Methodology

Planning, as a means of aligning behaviour of agents toward the common goal with partition of task and allocation of resources, has been studied extensively in DAI for achieving or improving coherent collective behaviour. For the activities of several agents to be aligned by planning, interactions in the plans of different agents must be controlled. Traditionally, the control or co-ordination of plan interactions are organised either centrally by multi-agent planning [Steeb et al 81; Georgeff 83; Katz and Rosenshein 88,] or locally by distributed planning [Corkill 79; Hayes-Roth and Hayes-Roth 79; Hayes-Roth 85; Durfee and Lesser 87a]. In multi-agent planning, a single global agent is responsible to generate plans for multiple agents, by reasoning on how actions of different agents may interfere with one another. In distributed planning, a single plan is divided up for several agents to co-operatively generates their sub-plans for problem solving.

From the military's point of view, distributed planning is a result of interactions between the strategic and tactical agents, where the strategic agent produces the partially specified strategic plan (attacking formation) to be presented to the related tactical agents for the construction of COAs locally (multi-agent planning). On the other hand, the tactical planning is only feasible on a distributed basis, where COAs for different parts of the plan are generated and constructed by different agents. This hierarchical approach uses the idea of partial global planning to communicate with problem solvers to construct mutually coherent plans incrementally and resolve conflicts at each level, ultimately at the strategic level where all associated sub-plans are reconciled and merged into one global plan. In this context, the control and consolidation mechanism holds the key to this chaotic and multi-stream reasoning process.

A planning system is designed to devise or generate a set of course of actions (COAs) to achieve a given set of goals within the constraints of the environment. The plan here (often not fully connected plan) is the necessary condition for achieving the goal while the environment constraints are the sufficient conditions for generating the COAs (solution paths) to realise the goal. Generally speaking, most planning systems are originated from the state-based model, where changes from one stable state to another are caused by actions that form parts of a plan.

A typical problem domain in planning is that of the blocks world, where there are two blocks on a table and a list of operations to move them from one place to another. The plan could either be reasoned forward from the initial state or reasoned backward from the desired goal state. In other words, this would form the basis for our strategic or tactical planning in the military decision-making procedure. The strategic plan marks up the path from the goal state to the initial state by including the possible intermediate states and their formations. The tactical plans will be responsible for taking any objectives in a formation from the strategic plan and work out the related COAs under the constraints of the environment. In here, the distinction between the strategic and tactical planning is very hard to draw because the blocks world is so simple that almost all plans contain both the initial and goal states. On the other hand, the distance between them is often too close to decompose into sub-goals or feasible intermediate states.

As far as the solution space is concerned, a "closed world" is always assumed in the blocks world. But this is definitely not the case in the dynamic environment, where the solution space is unbounded and the preconditions of plans are determined by means of fuzzy or threshold matching. In recognising this handicap, Sacerdoti also discovered that certain information requested to complete the solution paths were always missing at a certain level; as a result, he had to leave them unspecified until they reached lower levels of abstraction. His ABSTRIPS planner [Sacerdoti 1974] proposed a "hierarchical planning" to view the problems or goals as a collection of intermediate states and sub-goals at the top level of abstraction. There is no COAs to connect these intermediate states (sub-goals) until at the lower levels of abstraction, where the details required for planning become available for the full solution paths to be completed by the agents in the domain. Sacerdoti's hierarchical planning enables implementation details of the plan to be ignored at the higher level and concentrates the mind of system on finding the intermediate states between the initial state and goal state.

A further relaxation in the order of actions in an evolving plan, known as "non-linear planning", was introduced by Sacerdoti in NOAH (Nets of Action Hierarchies) [Sacerdoti 1975a] to combine both hierarchical planning and non-linear planning [Sacerdoti 1975b] into one single framework for non-trivial problem solving. In here, the order of each COA may remain only partially specified until those ordering constraints and preconditions become available or satisfied at later stages in the planning cycle. Ordering constraints are only incorporated into a plan when the effects of one action are needed to satisfy a precondition. A set of "critics" have to be invented to determine the effects of the action that endangers the realisation of another action. Unfortunately, no attempt has been made clearly to define the role or function at each level of abstraction and the relationship between them. In fact, the idea of hierarchical planning is more a kin to Dijkstra's top-down structured programming or Wirth's step-wise refinement than to the planning of military operation, where strategy is studied as an art to conduct a war and tactical planning is demanded to generate COAs for the fulfilment of the military objectives (OBJs). Interestingly, Sacerdoti's ABSTRIPS planner has also uncovered and recognised the simplistic view of hierarchical planning that if no solution is feasible at the lower level of abstraction, a feedback mechanism in the form of failure report would be needed to trigger a re-planning at the higher level of abstraction.

Nevertheless, Sacerdoti's hierarchical planning has paved the way for strategic planning to operate in a dynamic environment. Often a strategic plan is only a text book plan without taking environment factors (constraints and preconditions) into account until reaching the lower level of implementation. In the military decision-making procedure, the strategic plan is usually a partially specified plan including only the current situation (initial state) and the attacking formations (objectives) of those intermediate states with invisible links that would only be established by the tactical agents in the context of situation map (environment factors). At this level of abstraction, what the strategist is interested in is to decompose the goal state into a formations of the intermediate sub-goals which might enable solution paths to be formed at the tactical level. A typical example is the filing of a non-scheduled flight plan. What concerns the pilot is the shortest possible paths between his base and the destination other than the weather and the airport landing slot at the initial stage. However, it is only when the information regarding weather and airport logistics become available at the later stage that the flight plan becomes operational. Dealing with complex problem domains, which involve many intermediate states between initial and goal state, as well as constraints attached on various part of the solution path, the hierarchical planning provides us with means to visualise plans at different levels of abstraction.

In the military decision-making procedure, the distinction between strategic and tactical planning is essential. The former provides a sequence of intermediate states and their formations from start to finish, and the latter aims to generate detailed COAs to achieve the objectives in the formations under the constraint of battlefield environment and the preconditions imposed by the strategic planner. This implies that there are two levels of abstraction that characterise the mechanism of "co-operative planning". The strategic planner issues the objectives as commands to the tactical agents for implementation (top-down), with the sub-plans from all associated agents being reconciled and consolidated into one global plan (bottom-up) at the later stage.

Even within the domain of tactical planning, some forms of co-operations do exist to enable a particular tactical agent to complete its path in the course of planning, such as a request for artillery support to protect an infantry unit to move from one state to another. Unlike the classic co-operative planning that was initiated by the strategist concerned, tactical co-operation is based on local negotiation and contractual arrangement between parties rather than command imposed from the strategic planner. When a command is handed over to agent X to move from state A to B, after assessing the environment factors on the situation map and the constraints imposed on the task, agent X may seek help and subcontract part of the task to other agents in order to complete its path from A to B. A feature that was absent from most early day systems until the appearance of O-Plan planning system [Currie and Tate 1989], which is currently under development at Edinburgh University. This system has begun to study the issue in the form of generating plans which achieve interacting goals, although it only focuses on plans where achievement of one of the conditions may interfere with the achievement of others, but not deal with the complexity of co-operation among a number of agents to jointly reach a goal at the tactical level.

The O-Plan, which is designed for the plan specification, generation and execution, has provided us with a very valuable framework in the use of "blackboard architecture" [Engelmore and Morgan 1988; Jagannathan, Dodhiawala and Baum 1989] as the situation map, as well as the co-ordination mechanism for task partitioning, which could be opportunistically consumed by a number of knowledge sources (KSs), a well-mapped model for the war meeting platform. However, the issue of control and consolidation for the selection and merging of COAs from various KSs has not been properly addressed in the O-Plan.

Another strength of the O-Plan lies in its search control techniques. In the O-Plan, the paths of the non-linear planning are completed mainly by means of search with the help of a planner's goal achievement procedure and domain specification to control and prune the search space. The system heuristically prunes the search space and uses domain knowledge to guide the search through the remaining space. However, on discovering an unfruitful path, a chronological backtracking would go to the most recent choice point and explore an alternative path, a search control strategy that implies a static environment where the intermediate/ultimate goal states remain stationary. However, in the battlefield or other dynamic environment such as the foreign exchange markets, the target is not often stationary, although plans are formulated with the target on a particular position. This is the role for command and control to ensure that the conditions attached with each plan remains valid in the process of plan execution, an issue that has not been comprehensively addressed in the O-Plan.

3.4 The Command and Control (Plan Execution) Systems

Generally speaking, command means to give an order and control means to assure that the order is executed in a prescribed manner towards the goal. Collectively, they centre on how to generate an order; how to guarantee the order be delivered safely, timely and accurately; and how to remedy it if the unexpected happens.

In 1979, the US Department of Defence sponsored a three-day symposium on command and control which concluded that "there is no adequate foundation for a theory of C^2 and hence no principles for overall system design and evaluation" [Wohl 1981]. Although a series of international conferences on Command, Control, Communications and Management Information Systems has have been held since then, none of them have seriously addressed the issue of plan execution but mainly coverage of equipment, organisations and scene analysis (situation map). A typical example is that of SHORE (Stimulus; Hypothesis; Options; Response) paradigm [Wohl 1981] in tactical air defence systems, which outlines the functions of C^2 system as follows:

1) Stimulus: data acquisition from sensors or intelligence;
2) Stimulus: sensor data interpretation and data fusion;
3) Hypothesis: situations or threat assessment;

4) Options: decision plans or goal generation for desired outcomes or resource allocation;

5) Response: implementation of plans and monitoring of response/actions to ascertain success through sensors or intelligence [process returns to 1)].

On these functions, great efforts have been made at each level, specially in Stimulus and Hypothesis (low levels) for "data fusion" and "situation assessment", by means of AI technologies, mainly based on "blackboard architecture" for problem solving. For instance, the framework of MXA (Multiple Expert Architecture) [Rice 1984; Lakin and Miles 1987; Tailor 1988] is for the requirement of signal understanding and its application project known as ARE (Admiralty Research Establishment) [Lakin, Miles, and Byrne 1986] for naval command and control purpose; the framework of ADX (Air Defence threat assessment Expert system) [Bell 1984] and its later version BLOBS (BLackboard OBjects) [Middleton 1987; Zanconato 1988] use an object-oriented language designed to support both continuous reasoning expert systems and simulation application. Yet little progress has been made at higher levels of functionality, such as "Options" and "Response", in plan generation and execution.

As stated earlier, the function of command and control is to ensure the execution of the operational plan. However, in a dynamic environment when everything moves, the eventuality of a plan that is no longer applicable would have to be always expected. In the process of plan execution, there are a number of areas where operational plan could run into problems. Firstly, one of the objectives that forms part of the desired formation may have disappeared on the side of the opponent. Secondly, a more serious problem might be that the target for the desired formation has simply moved to another location. As a result, the operational plan would become meaningless. The former case could be rectified by re-routing or replacing the sub-plan concerned with a stand-by plan, while the latter requires re-planning to focus on new targeted position, or identify an alternative target as the focus for new plan deliberation, both of which imply a restart of the complete planning cycle.

In the light of rapidly expansion in DAI applications, much recent work in problem solving has moved away from complex planning to shallow planning [Rosenschein 1982; Chapman and Agre 1987] by means of reactive planning [Ambros-Ingerson and Steel 1988]. In recognising the weakness in traditional planning systems to cope with dynamic environment, reactive planning equips agents with a number of attributes to react promptly to environment changes. For instance, a crash-avoidance command prevents the robot from running into an obstacles [Kaelbling 1987]. In essence, the major difficulty with planning in the dynamic environment has always been the uncertainty to plan ahead without knowing the changes anticipated in the environment. Hence, Interleaving Planning and Execution (IPE) has been advocated to interleaving planning and plan execution at intermediate stage interval [Ambros-Ingerson and Steel 1988].

Although these innovations help to enhance the performance of planning in a dynamic environment, reactive planning alone in the absence of strategic plan implies passive tactical moves, and interleaving planning and execution without comprehensive plan generation would make it impossible to evaluate the quality of each plan before execution. As a matter of fact, reactive planning and IPE are designed for plan execution to cope with uncertainty in dynamic environment, which should have been seen as the techniques to compliment complex planning, but not as the replacement of them. In the next chapter, we shall present an architectural platform where comprehensive plan generation (hierarchical, multi-agent and distributed plannings) and plan execution (reactive planning and IPE) are combined in a single frame work (standard operational procedure).

3.5 The Summary

Based on the above study, the major issue of our proposed decision support system to be discussed falls into three fronts:

- The co-operative planning (at the plan generation stage);
- The process of control and consolidation (at the war meeting stage); and
- The plan modification and reactive planning (at the plan execution stage).

Firstly, there should be two kinds of co-operative planning. One exists between the strategic plan and the tactical plan, and the other is embedded in the tactical plan. For the former, the strategic plan recognises a sequence of states from the current state to the desired state and the tactical plan searches the best path to achieve each objectives in the formation. For the latter, the order and constraints of forming a workable path for a formation is determined jointly between the related tactical agents concerned.

Secondly, the control and consolidation process may also happen at two places. One at the global level for the selection of operational plans, and the other at the bottom level for merging appropriate COAs to realize plans.

Thirdly, reactive routines together with some interleaving tactical re-planning and execution enhance the survival rate of an operational plan, and the inclusion of stand-by plans reduces the probability of strategic re-planning during run-time. These activities are overseen and supervised by the Command and Control (C^2) in order to achieve the predetermined goals.

CHAPTER FOUR

THE MULTI-AGENT DECISION SUPPORT SYSTEM

4.1 The Metaphor

To help clearly illustrate the process of decision-making, a metaphor is used here to explain the inherent links and subordinate relationships in the organisation structure. Let us imagine that a decision-maker and his staff are racing against time for a feasible plan (a course of actions) in a crisis. In the operational room, a large blackboard hangs on the wall to record and update all of the relevant information with the problems concerned.

At the conference, the chairman is explaining the issues concerned on the blackboard and inviting suggestions from his staff. Amongst them, the strategists will examine the situation to identify a desired situation, by means of recognition, based on personal experience or cases recorded in books. On the other hand, tacticians will examine the situation and try to search for the best following state based on short-term rather than long-term considerations. Once the desired situation, if any, has been identified, the strategists will present and project it from the prospective of the current situation, and ask the tacticians to study the feasibility of the plan and generate appropriate COAs.

Finally, only one plan will be chosen from the meeting as the operational plan and other plans will be kept as stand-by alternatives. The finalised operational plan is issued to the plan executor as instruction for implementation. Steering the plan through a volatile environment, the executor will examine the plan in the light of changes in the environment from the planning stage, adjust and modify it accordingly in the direction towards the desired goal state.

As a whole, the plan execution is by far the most vital part of problem solving in a dynamic environment, where operational plan is often only a static plan reasoned from an internal representation of the environment. Some forms of adjustment is inevitable, depending on the severity of the mismatch between the internal model and the real world outside the system. However tactically, the more capable the plan executor with skill and know-how to fix and repair the plan reactively, the more likely that operational plan could be adjusted and modified appropriately to survive in a dynamic environment. If however all the measures fall to save the operational plan, then stand-by plans will be activated to replace the operational plan in the first instance before restarting the planning cycle all over again. This process could repeat from time to time until the problem is solved or impossible to be solved.

In addition to the incompatibility between the internal representation of the cognitive model and the outside world, there is an element of time lack between the construction of a plan and the execution of that plan, and the longer the time gap, the higher the chances of discrepancy developed between them caused by changes in the environment. Hence, the plan installed for execution might have been taken over by the unforeseen event beforehand. As a result, urgent action may be required temporarily to suspend the operational plan in order to deal with the task of higher priority. Figure 4.1 sums up this problem solving procedure on a multi-agent platform where each COA of the operational plan is examined on a move-by-move basis so as to take into account of in the light of proposals from other perspectives. A decision is then taken to select the most appropriate action at the time, which is to proceed with planned action, to gain immediate advantage, or to react in steering the situation away from disaster.

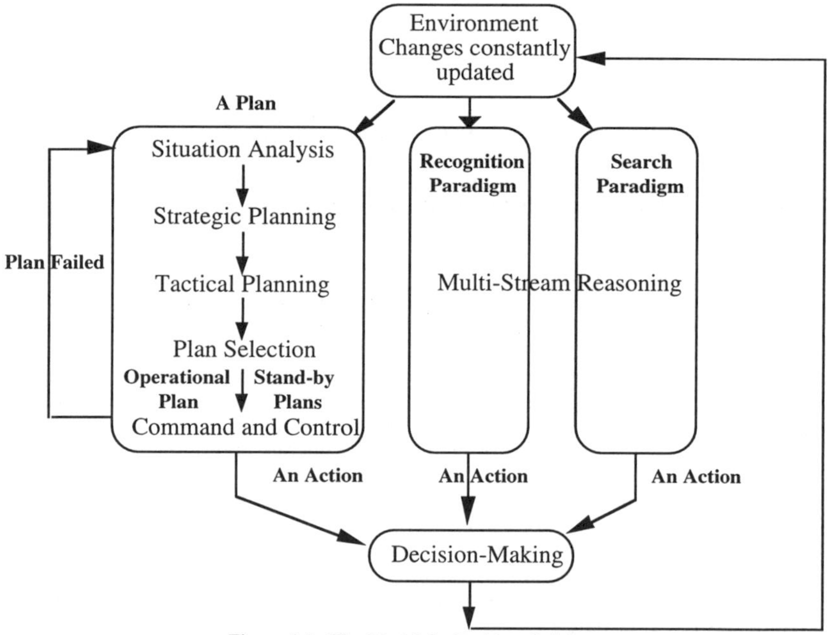

Figure 4.1. The Model for Problem Solving

4.2 The Problem-Solving Methodology

Putting this metaphor in the context of SOP, the situation analysis is to form the basis on which experts will find possible solutions from different points of view. Amongst them, the pure recognition of the text-book solution is the one most likely to be selected if available. The planning solution uses the recognition to look for possible desired formation and search paradigm to transform the current state into one of the desired state. In due course, when plan becomes operational, the command and control will monitor and steer it through the environment, and in turn, put forward its planned action in completion with other proposals in the decision-making stage to identify and select the best possible course of action. Finally, exhaustive and heuristic searches are sources of useful tactical moves, especially in the absence of any long-term strategic plan, to manoeuvres into advantageous position or out of the danger zone.

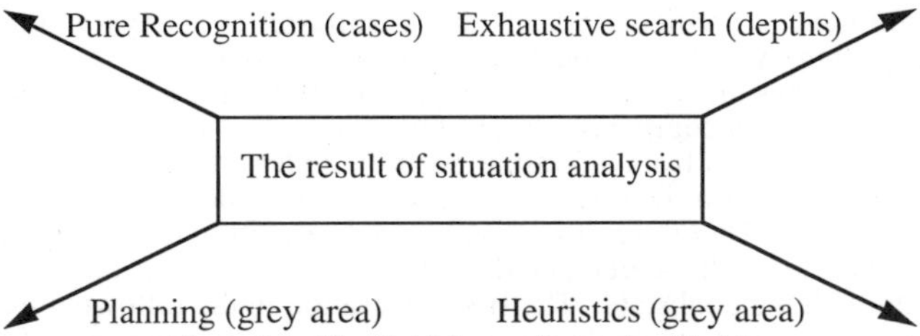

Figure 4.2. The Multi-Stream Reasoning Model

In principle, there should be no limit about the number of reasoning threads in the model. However, the four reasoning paths above cover most application in real-life problems. The quality of the pure recognition depends on the amount of knowledge or cases in the Cognitive model; the quality of the exhaustive search relies on the depth of search in the problem domain; and the quality of the heuristic search is determined by its rules knowledge engineered to cover the grey area. The grey (uncertain) area means the scope of the problem-solving states which can not be dealt with by neither pure recognition nor exhaustive search alone.

4.2.1 The Multi-Stream Reasoning

Deliberation is undertaken usually by a number of problem solvers as shown in Figure 4.1, either through recognition or search. Recognition will be first attempted to map both current state and the desired goal state with cases in the knowledge base to produce a fully connected solution path that satisfy the ultimate goal. If a match is secured, then a classic text-book solution becomes a reality; otherwise planning for possible desired situation will be the norm. In planning, more than one "what-if" scenarios may be put forwarded by the strategist for the tacticians to study their feasibility of forming solution path from the current state to the desired state. In other words, planning involves mapping both current and desired states by recognition, and generates a partially connected plan for tactical agents to link up these intermediate states. However, the fundamental difference between planning and pure recognition paradigm is in the solution paths they generate; the text-book solution is a fully connected path, and hence, searching is no required, while the strategic plan is a often a partial plan joining the initial and goal states by intermediate states, where connections are established by means of searching.

However, as far as the search paradigm is concerned, both exhaustive search or heuristic search tends to be forward reasoned; starting from the current positions looking ahead for the best possible next move without an ultimate goal in sight. The knowledge-poor exhaustive search has to rely on examining all paths in the cause of finding a solution, while the more knowledgeable heuristic search agent will explore the most promising paths based on rules from the experts.

4.2.2 Planning for Problem Solving

In a closed or isolated world, all input vectors are contained in the knowledge base and the environment is predictable such that a solution is always guaranteed by the **recognition** paradigm, which is in the case of the pure recognition. However, in the real world, this is not always the case. Therefore, people often have a back-up plan to **search** for alternatives in case **recognition** should fail to produce a solution. Once search is requested, it normally starts from a familiar position under constraints. This implies that the search is either based on the result of recognition or guided under the supervision of recognition (heuristic). Therefore, it is wise to use recognition to identify goal states (or objectives) so as to direct the search paradigm to find the most feasible path that connect the current state with the goal state. The first illustration in the following diagram shows the case of heuristic search, while the second illustration shows the case of goal directed search.

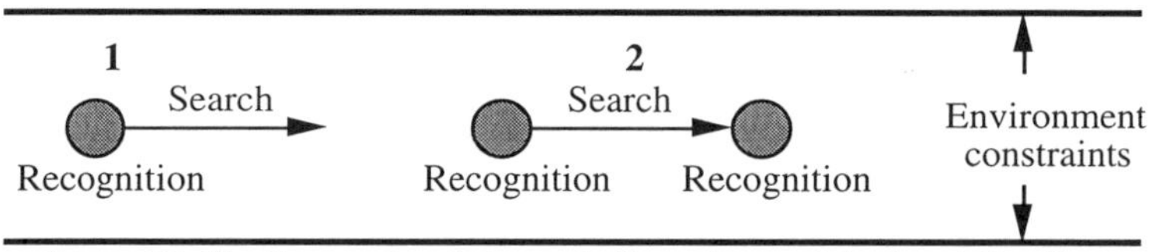

Figure 4.3. The Co-operations between the Recognition and the Search Paradigm

Within the framework of the Standard Operating Procedure, the goal-oriented search has been used extensively in the form of co-operative planning between the strategic and the tactical agents: the **recognition** of desired state is followed by decomposing it into a list of quantitative sub-goals, which in turn, could lead the relevant tactical agents to **search** for a set of appropriate course of actions (COAs) that realise the strategic goal.

> **Given:** the current state and the desired goal;
> **Produce:** the final desired situation with a list of all of the possible intermediate states by recognition paradigm. This is complimented by the support of the search paradigm to study the feasibility of the partial plan.

4.2.2.1 The Situation Analysis

Situation analysis is requested by all the relevant agents at the beginning of the problem-solving cycle to understand the current situation. In here, the blackboard is the global database constantly updated with events unfolding in the battlefield, and at the same time, it also functions as a distribution centre to dispatch relevant information to all agents concerned. However, most information available on the blackboard need to be interpreted as part of the problem solving process. These analyses or interpretations of the environment generally fall into two categories: objective and subjective analysis. The objective analysis describes and interprets the physical environment which is common to all the agents while the subjective analysis interprets the environment in a specific way useful only to some of them. In the case of chess, the four different colours used on the chess board is a fine example of the objective analysis, where **blue** (controlled by blue side), **red** (controlled by red side), **yellow** (conflict area, controlled by both sides) and **white** (neutral area, controlled by neither side) are displayed as indication of the state of current situation. While the subjective analysis would label each state as being **risky, neutral**, **safe** or **rewarding** from either blue or red prospective, setting up the scene for strategists to identify desired formation from current situation. Hence, it is more cost-effective to analyse these information centrally and display the results of the objective analysis globally on the blackboard, and in so doing turning the pure fact reporting blackboard to a much more informative situation map.

Other examples of objective analysis can be found in CASSANDRA-II [Craig 1989], where spaces at different heights are analysed and indicated on the blackboard for aiding to solve the air traffic control problem. Similarly, in the problem of "solving jigsaw puzzles" [Nii 1986], the position on the edges of each template are highlighted in comparison to other positions in the process for placing the puzzles. On the other hand, the subjective analysis is used in these examples to representing issues concerned by an individual or a group of individual agents in the given task domain. For instance, an aircraft could be placed in the space provided that the air space at certain height is free (in CASSANDRA-II), or a puzzle could be placed in a particular position provided that it fits-in with all the other adjacent pieces on the board (in "solving jigsaw puzzles").

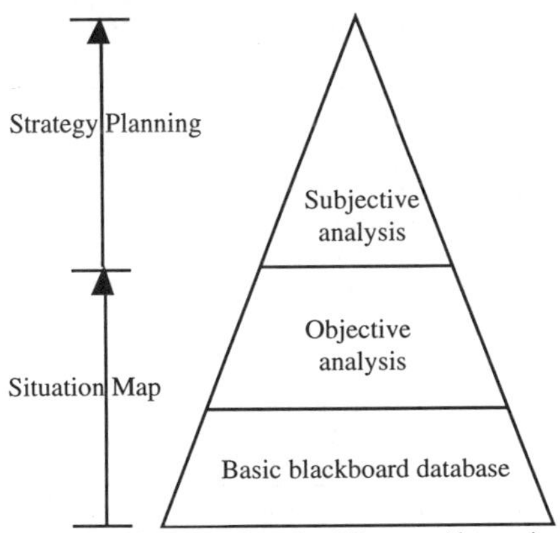

Figure 4.4. The Three Levels of Feature Abstraction

Conceptually, these provision and interpretation of information could be visualised through a model with three-level of abstraction (Figure 4.4):

1) the blackboard database displays and updates events unfolding in the environment;
2) the objective analysis (battlefield analysis) interprets these information, marks and indicates the states of interest with the relevant factors in the blackboard database;
3) the subjective analysis is applied from an individual prospective to visualise the desired situation and deliberate plan in the light of the results from the other two levels.

4.2.2.2 The Strategic Planning

Data on the blackboard and analysis indicated on the situation map often offer clues to the solution of the problem concerned. These clues are like the islands in the solution space, which could be treated as the intermediate states awaiting to be connected as possible tracks leading to the desired solution. Functionally speaking, the subjective analysis stage marks the beginning of the plan deliberation stage in SOP. By studying the material resources and manpower strength of both sides in the subjective analysis, a strategy could be mapped out, which in turn, determines which tactics to use in the given circumstances. In here, a potential strategic plan developed from particular tactics could be generated by matching part of the current situation (i.e. material resources) with the formation held in the knowledge base for a possible desired situation that fulfils the ultimate goal. Finally, each formation available in the strategic plan could be decomposed into a set of sequential objectives.

Strategic Plan (recognition, knowledge-rich system):

The Condition Part: Patterns are stored as the combinations of the specific resources in the problem domain. Hit is achieved when those resources required are available in the given current situation.

The Action Part: When match will identify and offer one or more formations which consist of a list of objectives, such as placing specific resources at appropriate locations in a pre-determined orders to fulfil the ultimate goal, the objectives may be ordered.

Prerequisite: A library of patterns as database for matching the current and the possible goal positions in the problem domain.

The strategic plan, when generated, provides the "quantitative objectives" in a tactical formation that allow the search paradigm to find the most promising path from a known position to the related position (objective). These quantitative objectives in a formation should be seen clearly as "a specific unit at a particular place" which allows the tactical agent to search for a path (Figure 4.5).

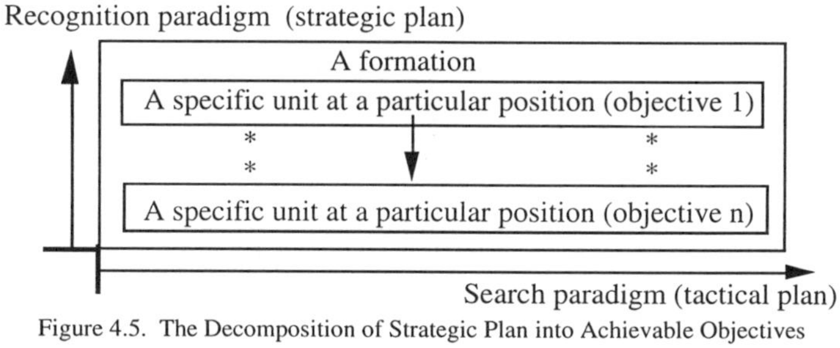

Figure 4.5. The Decomposition of Strategic Plan into Achievable Objectives

The order of execution for each objective is controlled and determined by the strategic plan and hence, each tactical plan is activated only when the control is handed over to it in a pre-determined order during plan execution stage, provided that all attached conditions are met and embedded constraints have been satisfied. Generally speaking, the co-ordination of the plan is organised at the strategic planning level to ensure coherence in the plan so that the framework of constraints and expectation about the behaviour of tactical agents will work concertedly to reach the ultimate goal. In this setting, the organisation of the plan is imposed onto the tactical agents to develop solution paths and merge them in the manner required and defined by the strategic plan.

The co-ordination of the plan without conflicting paths simply involves attaching order of execution for every sub-plan to be activated accordingly during plan execution since there is no "conflict" existing between any tactical paths. For instance, if we assume that there are only two tactical paths within the plan, Figure 4.6 indicates the order of execution for Path 1 before Path 2.

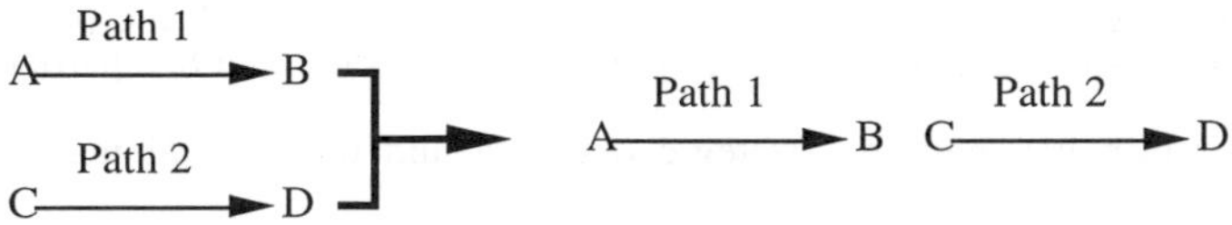

Figure 4.6. The Co-operative Plan without Conflicting Paths

However, for co-operative plan with conflicting paths (Figure 4.7), additional constraints would have to be placed on those inter-dependent paths to ensure the proper functioning of the plan. For instance, if we assume that there are two conflicting tactical paths in the plan, in which Path 1 before Path 2 at the strategic plan level, but State X should not proceed until State C passed beyond State B at the path (sub-plan) level, then the sequence of execution is shown as follows:

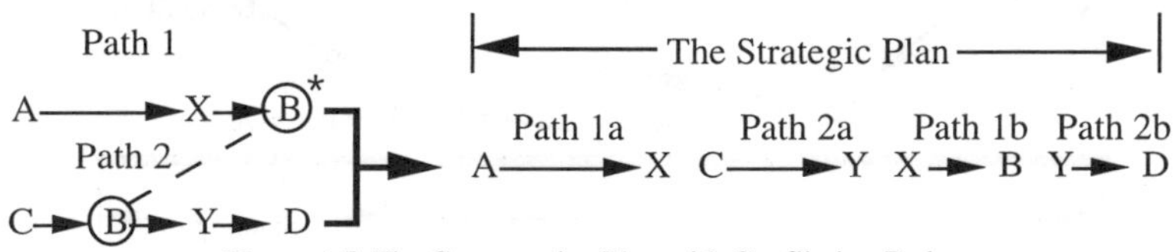

Figure 4.7 The Co-operative Plan with Conflicting Paths

A constraint (*) here is placed on State B in Path 1 not to activate the transformation from State X to State B until Path 2 have passed State B the aim is to stop the Path 1 before reaching its destination (State B) and allow Path 2 to pass through the conflicting area (State B) before transferring the control to Path 1 to proceed with (X -> B). This will be discussed more thoroughly in Chapter 6 with the help of a case simulation.

4.2.2.3 The Tactical Planning

Given the strategic plan, the tactical agents are responsible for:

1 Taking the objectives in the possible formation of the strategic plan as its sub-goals; finding the most promising path for each sub-goal that connects its current position to each individual desired state associated with an objective;
2 Merging all tactical paths according to the formation and order specified in the strategic plan, if all of the paths for the objectives would possible;
3 Proposing all feasible solution paths to the war meeting.

In other words, the tactical planning could be summarised in the following:

Tactical Planning (search, knowledge-poor system):
The Condition Part: serves to study and satisfy all relevant constrains (temporal, resource, and domain constraints) and to examine all associated pre-conditions for a given objective in a formation of the strategic plan.
The Action Part: attempts to find the most feasible paths between the current state and the intermediate states (objectives), or goal state in a given formation.
Prerequisite: Each tactical agent should be equipped with the practical means and know-how to realise the plan of moving "a specific unit to a particular place".

The co-operation between the strategic planning and the tactical planning can be illustrated in Figure 4.8.

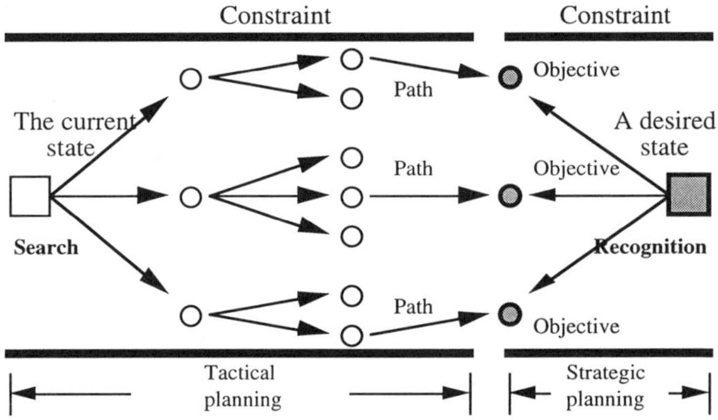

Figure 4.8 The Co-operative planning between the Strategic Agent and the Tactical Agent

4.2.2.4 The Plan Selection

Once each strategic plan has been merged and consolidated into workable plan, the quality of the plans can be measured spatially, temporally, or in terms of resources required as to which is the best plan available. Based on these information, one of the following mechanisms could be installed to select the operational plan.

- **Autocratic Control Protocol**: Decision is made on the preference of the chairman.
- **Democratic Control Protocol**: Decision is made by majority voting system.
- **Credit Scoring Control Protocol**: Decision is made on the merit of the expert who put forward the proposal.

As each plan carries some risks and uncertainty on one hand and rewards and gains on the other, one of the simplest criteria is to attach the material gain on each plan balanced with the length of the path needed to reach its goal, bearing in mind that "the shorter path, the better solution." Other more sophisticated selection schemes involve the use of risk analysis by taking into account the time, uncertainty and risk/reward factors for the calculation of optimum criteria.

4.2.2.5 The Command and Control (C^2)

Given the operational plan, the command and control is responsible for plan execution. With the exception of the operational plan getting through the environment without a hitch, most plan executions require some kinds of modification in order to avoid defeat. These actions could take one of the following forms:

- Modification of the current plan;
- Selection of the best stand-by plan; or
- Re-planning or start of the process all over again.

Plan Modification

Plan modification occurs when the assumption of the operational plan fails to hold, perhaps due to unforeseen blockages along the solution path, or changes in the environment which leads to discrepancy between the reality and the plan. As a result, part or all tactical paths of the current plan may become impossible that repair or rectification of the solution path could happen in one of the following ways: 1) detour and 2) buffer.

1) **Detour:**
In our methodology, detour means to find other workable routes in order to reach any points of the original path through by-passing and avoid the blockage. In most cases, this only involves one of the tactical paths, leaving other paths intact. It implies minimum effort to remedy the operational plan as shown in the following (Figure 4.9). As the path from State A to B is made impossible by a blockage, a detour path is formulated to by-pass the blockage and return to the nearest intermediate state.

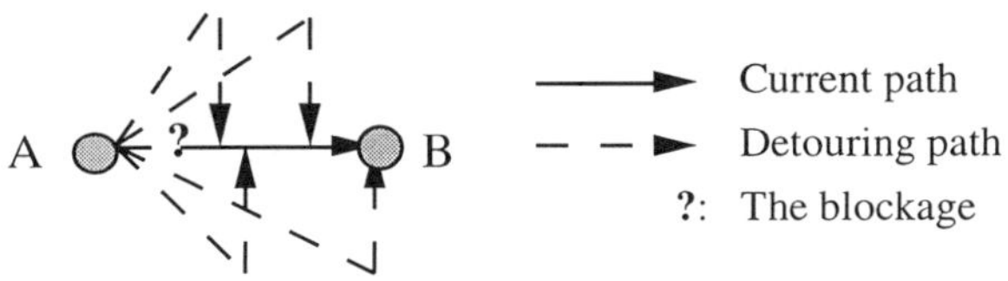

Figure 4.9. The Detours of the Current Path

2) **Buffer:**
On the other hand, buffer offers another way to remedy the situation by delaying the execution of the current active path and opting for another path in the remainder of the current plan until the previously blocking path has become possible again. This implies local negotiation between agents temporally to transfer control from the currently active tactical path to another path(s) in the operational plan. Figure 4.10 shows the buffering activity between two non-conflicting paths, where the buffer is the segment of C to X in Path 2, and State X is a position before the end of Path 2.

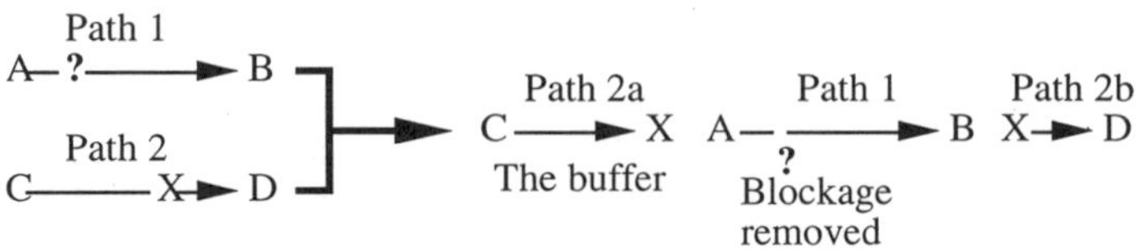

Figure 4.10. The Buffering of Tactical Plan with Unconflicting Paths

However, for a plan with conflicting paths, an additional care is required to satisfy the constraint. In the example shown below (Figure 4.11), the buffer segment is from State C to W in Path 2, while the COA from State A to B in Path 1 is suspended until the blockage has disappeared in its path. A constraint (*) placed on State B in Path 2 does not proceed until Path 1 have passed State B on its way to its destination, which means the buffer segment will stop just short of State B on Path 2 before transferring the control back to Path 1, hoping that the blockage has disappeared to allow Path 1 to proceed with plan.

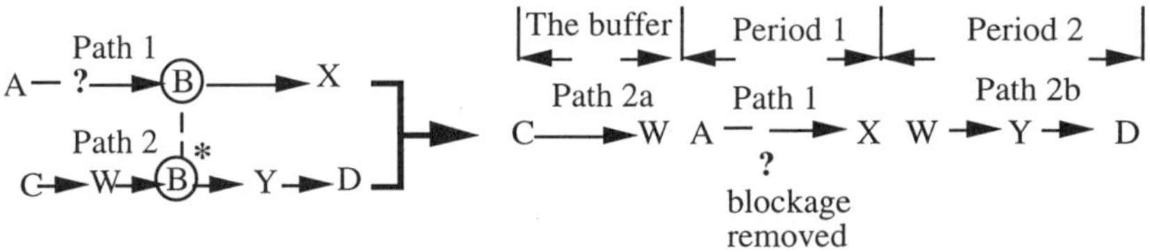

Figure 4.11. The Buffering of Tactical Plan with Conflicting Paths

Buffer, when possible, represents the most cost-effective remedy for the realisation of the operational plan, without adding any extra state along the solution path. However, it does rely on the power of negotiation that enable the tactical agents to organise the transfer of control locally, without the need to involve C^2 in the co-ordination of this rectification.

Stand-By Plan

When the minor plan modification fails to deal with the problem of blocked path or unsafe environment, the next alternative for the Command and Control is to select the best suitable stand-by plan as the replacement of the current operational plan. However, the feasibility of each stand-by plan, which was formulated to target on different formation, needs to be checked against the consequence of changing current situation, mainly due to partially implemented operational plan and event changes in the environment. Firstly, the availability of all units associated with the new formations need to be checked. Secondly, some tactical paths within the stand-by plan need to be modified to make the stand-by plan operational for the sake of the present positions of all units concerned. Here, only those stand-by plans with identical objectives and constraints would be first considered. In other words, selection of stand-by plans involves situation analysis (both objective analysis and subjective analysis) to verify the feasibility of the plan (formation) to fulfil the remaining part of the strategic plan.

1) **Stand-by plan with similar objectives and compatible material resources:**
If the stand-by plan is only a variant formation from a similar strategic plan, which shares a large number of objectives and based on compatible resources, the rectification of the stand-by plan involves nothing more than modifying one or some of the existing tactical paths with the consideration of their present positions and keeping their objectives or sub-goal states mainly intact.

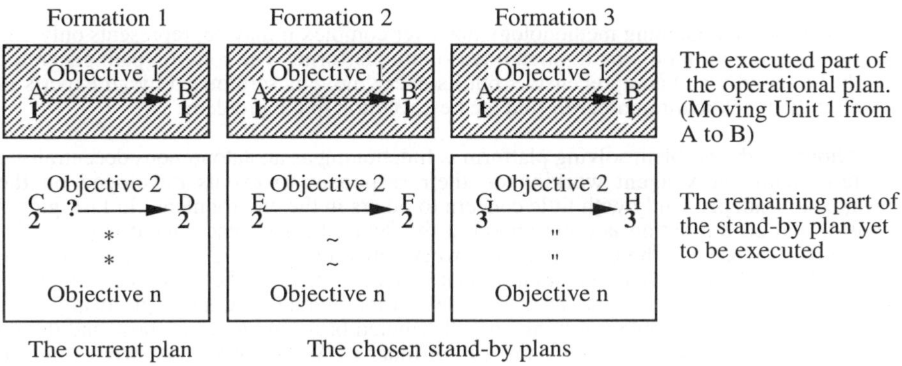

Figure 4.12. Two Kinds of Stand-By Plans in Relation to the Current Plan

In Figure 4.12, the stand-by plan (Formation 2) shares a common tactical path with the current operational plan of moving Unit 1 from State A to B, but has a different sub-goal state (or objective) of moving Unit 2 from State E to F, instead of from State C to D in Formation 1, and hence, replacement of current plan with one of the stand-by plan (Formation 2) involves planning a new path from State C to State F, and if this is possible the stand-by plan for Formation 2 can be made operational (Figure 4.13).

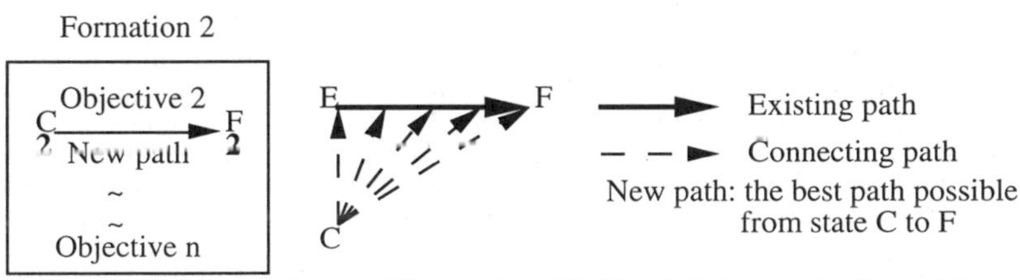

Figure 4.13. The Rectification of Existing Stand-By Plans in Relation to the Current Plan

2) **Stand-by plan with similar objectives but incompatible material resources:**
For stand-by plans with similar objectives but incompatible resources, they often involve the substitution of objectives in the current plan with the objectives from one of the stand-by plans. For instance, the rectification of the stand-by plan Formation 3 would involve substituting the "Objective 2 (moving Unit 2 from State C to D) to Objective n in Formation 1" with its own "Objective 2 (moving Unit 3 from State G to H) to Objective n".

Finally, if the target in the strategic plan has changed its position, or been made impossible by whatever cause, the re-planning from the beginning would be inevitable and the Command and Control would be forced to return the control to the system master for activating the planning cycle all over again.

4.3 The Architectural Platform: The Multi-Agent Model

The proposed planning methodology however complex it may be, represents only one section of the option on a multi-stream reasoning platform. The solution path generated might be lengthy and comprehensive, but its every move is scrutinised by all experts in front of the blackboard in order to find the best solution to the problem.

Globally, the problem solving platform is functioning as an autonomous decentralised system, with every agent working on their responses to events developed on the blackboard independently with little concern to others in the environment. In fact, global control and co-ordination is quite unreal at this level, because each agent is driven by stimulus-response and there is no basis to work collectively toward a single global goal. At this level, the activity in the environment is akin to those in the honey bee colony or Human society, in which each agent operates on its own agenda, although locally, it is possible to organise problem solving on a distributed basis and to decompose and divide up the tasks to be shared among the sub-ordinates. We believe most work done in Distributed Problem Solving (DPS) address the issue at the this level.

It is similar to the operation of equity markets around the world, every player in the market is driven by fear and greed, and responds to market accordingly. It is very difficult to identify a visible co-ordination operating amongst players. If there is any plan or attempt to control or influence the market, it is only possible to organise it at the local level: attempt to create a fault market by organising third party share buying or supporting scheme, spreading rumour about brokers' down grading, or imminent take-over bid. In other words, planning starts at the local level, while other players in the market will only respond accordingly based on their own instinct, or cognitive model held internally inside agents to reason and predict about the market.

Unlike most of the "first generation" KBS or IKBS, where the solution is generated by the knowledge acquired from an expert or a single group of experts, the multi-stream reasoning platform is supported by a decentralised multi-agent architecture, where tasks are displayed on the blackboard, identified and consumed by individual agents on an opportunistic basis. However, once inside the agent, the architectural mapping between the models and platforms could come in a number of ways to support the operation of problem solving at the local level: SISD (Single Instruction Single Data streams) machine for the exhaustive search agent, SIMD (Single Instruction Multiple Data streams) machine for the pure recognition agent and heuristics agent, and a combination of both for the planning agent.

As far as the database is concerned, the data are stratified into global and local levels. The global database (the blackboard) is a shared memory and accessed mainly by reference for the purpose of updating, with the flexibility of transferring data from the central database to the local database (situation map) within each agent by means of call by value. This configuration enables each agent to operate independently at the local level and restricts the global communication only at the process level. Inside the agent, a self-timing scheme is used for synchronising. Generally speaking, the global data communication is from the blackboard (global shared memory) to the situation map (distributed local memory) of each agent, and the proposals from each agent are channelled back to the system master for decision making.

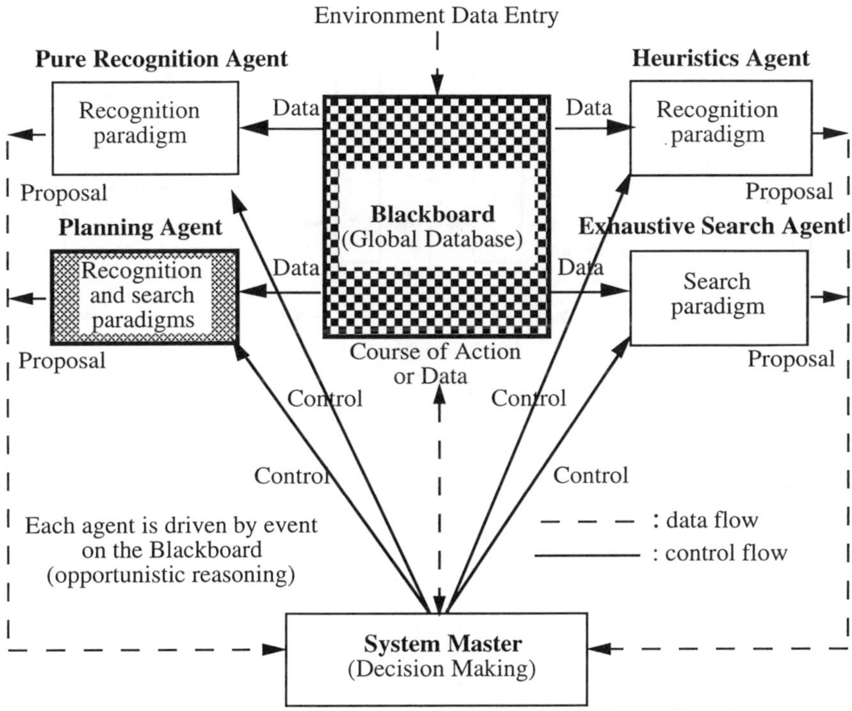

Figure 4.14 The Multi-Agent Architectural Platform for Multi-steam Reasoning

4.3.1 The Pure Recognition Agent

The pure recognition agent reasoned by induction and attempts to pattern matching the current and desired situations with the cases built up in the library. Perfect match is rare, and hence, fuzzy matching is often used, which implies the use of a probabilistic engine alongside the knowledge-base to enhance the chances of a match. If the matching of both current and desired situation is possible, a text-book solution is generated or otherwise partial matching on both current and goal states above the threshold will be acceptable as a hit, and in turn generate a much lower quality solution.

The process of recognition could be speeded up with the deployment of a SIMD type array processor, where both current and desired state could be used as search keys broadcasting to the cases in the knowledge-base for pattern matching.

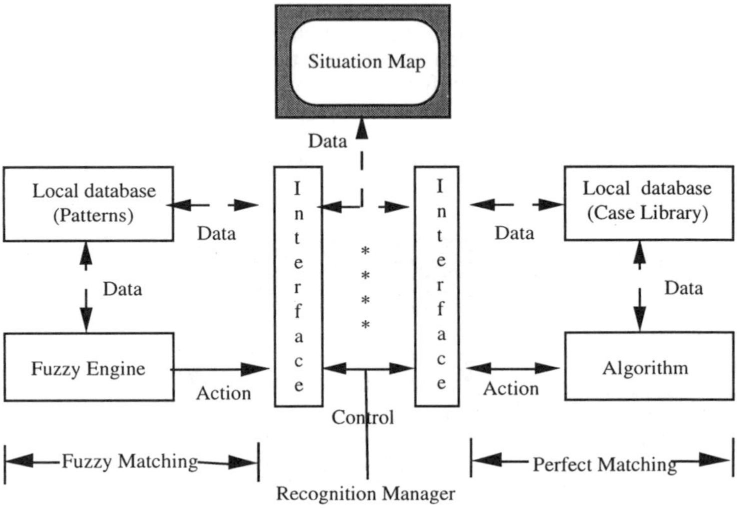

Figure 4.15. The Architectural Organisation of the Pure Recognition Agent

4.3.2 The Heuristics Agent

The heuristics agent shares a great deal architecturally with the recognition agent, except that it is only looking for a match for the current situation with a sense of direction guided by a set of heuristics. The agent bases on the belief that it is statistically advantageous to follow the rules knowledge engineered from the experts. The performance of this agent is critically depending on the amount of high quality rules installed on its knowledge-base and therefore, the inclusion of an array processor inside the reasoning engine would, no doubt, enhance the throughput of a system with a huge knowledge-base.

4.3.3 The Exhaustive Search Agent

As we have stated earlier, the quality of the exhaustive search is depending on how far it could search. Since every node on the tree is unique, there could be quite a complex task to go for parallelism. Hence, sequential control-flow architecture is the conventional machine to go for yet there is no disguise to the fact that a MIMD (Multiple Instruction Multiple Data streams) type parallel control-flow machine could make a big impact if nodes could be searched in parallel. Traditionally, exhaustive search rolls on the bandwagon of the "A type" chess algorithm, by which the performance of the system ultimately lies in the power of the machine. However, a control flow architecture would probably be the most likely organisation to be used, either on an uni-processor or multi-processors.

4.3.4 The Planning Agent

The working of the Standard Operating Procedure is inherently centralise such that the whole planning cycle from plan deliberation to plan execution works under the shadow of the commander. This implies a control-flow mechanism at the global level to oversee the task of decomposition and distribution among the agents, and exercise whatever selection protocol adopted to finalise the best course of action. With this control mechanism, the human organisation hierarchy is revealed. The planning manager is always in control at the strategic plan level and once the control is passed down to the tactical level, total autonomy is respected. Each agent is free to work out whatever path or COA they see fit. However, every solution proposed by each tactical agent must be reconciled, merged and integrated into the formation, before being forwarded for consideration.

This organisational requirement reveals the need for at least two kinds of abstractions for the problem solving. At the top level, strategic agent would activate a matching process (recognition approach) to identify a desired situation, which could be decomposed into a list of intermediate states or achievable objectives (OBJs) before issuing them to the tactical agents as instruction to work out their COAs.

Architecturally, the planning agent involves a strategic agent supported by a group of tactical agents for the realisation of an identified strategic plan. The strategic agent could either function inductively with a collection of case library or deductively with a set of rules as shown in Figure 4.16. While the tactical agents are supported by their own local knowledge-base and algorithms to map out the connections between every intermediate states.

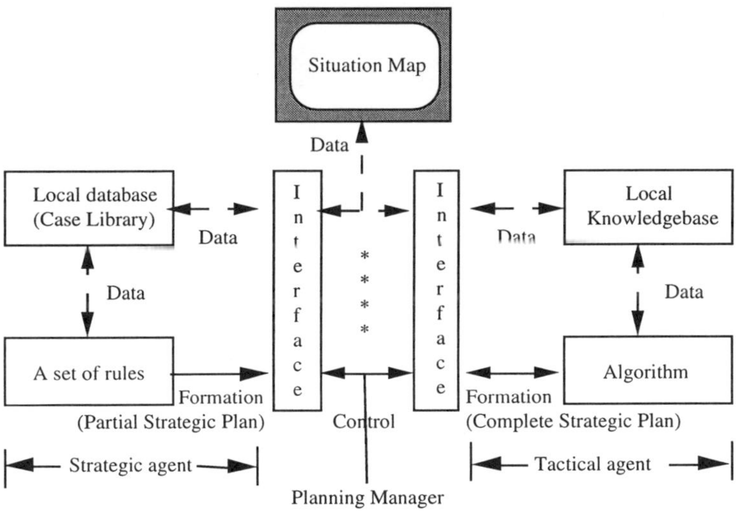

Figure 4.16 The Architectural Organisation of the Planning Agent

4.4 The Summary

In this chapter, we have introduced the problem solving methodology and its related architectural platform. The combination of the recognition and search paradigm within the framework of the Standard Operating Procedure is not only bringing about the best of both worlds in problem solving, but also putting forward a concept of co-operative planning between the strategic and tactical planning, which jointly generates solutions for a common goal. Furthermore, Command and Control has addressed the issue of plan execution in a dynamic environment by means of reactive planning, plan modification or the stand-by plans.

As far as the battlefield management system is concerned, we have addressed not only the issues of stimulus and hypothesis (low level structures in SHORE paradigm), but also the issues of options and response (high level structures in SHORE paradigm), which are the kernel of our investigation. In the next two chapters, we intend to test our methodology and platform in a chess environment to examine their abilities in problem solving.

Finally, and the most importantly, in comparison with the O-plan, our two-level co-operative planning in conjunction with the deployment of Command and Control (C^2) for plan execution has given the concept of "backtracking" a new meaning: the "backtracking" in a dynamic environment means "detour" or "path modification" in the cause of plan realisation.

CHAPTER FIVE

THE TESTBED: CHINESE CHESS

5.1 The Background

The problem solving methodology presented in the previous chapters is a model that is capable of combining the recognition and search paradigms under the guidance of certain control strategies. However, its capability in solving complex problem in an unbounded solution space need to be tested, and the issue we like to focus here is planning. The Chinese chess with its simplified battlefield has been chosen as the testbed to examine planning at both the strategic level and at the tactical level. The impact of plan modification, use of stand-by plans and reactive planning could also be assessed in the context of plan realisation.

The Chess is a zero-sum two-person game [Von Neumann and Morgenstern 1944] with finite and unambiguous input vector. This means that every move of the opponent could be predictable if a complete game tree were available. However, even within the closed world of chess playing, the multiply of moves in the complete game tree between both players is so huge that attempt to construct such a search tree will inevitably lead to "combinatorial explosion". However, in the absence of a complete game tree, the "principal continuation" could only be established either by exhaustive search or heuristics search to locate the most rewarding path or move. It is in this context that chess has been a favourite testbed for the study of AI since 1950 when Shannon was investigating the potential of the electronic computers to "think" [Shannon 1950a]. To his amazement, he found it possible to use computer to work out all potential next-moves in chess, where each alternative is weighted by possible risk and reward. Alan Turing [Turing 1950; Turing 1953] also shared the observation. The selection of moves could be based on the gains and losses in terms of material and positional values, and/or any other parameters which we wish to include in the calculation for deciding next move.

> *The thinking process is considered by some psychologists to be essentially characterized by the following steps: various possible solutions of a problem are tried out mentally or symbolically without actually being carried out physically; the best solution is selected by a mental evaluation of the results of these trials; and the solution found in this way is then acted upon. It will be seen that this is almost an exact description of how a chess-playing computer operates, provided we substitute "within the machine" for "mentally"* [Shannon 1950b]

Looking at just one ply ahead, the machine is able to examining all the alternatives under that node and work out the best possible move among them. Nevertheless, this one-ply approach does suffer from the "horizon effect" [Berliner 1973] of being unable to look beyond the one-ply tree. However, there is no reason not to extend the numbers of plys the machine can look through. The further it searches, the more chances of its picking up a better path for the next move and ultimately if the machine were able to walk down the search tree from the opening to checkmate (end-game), with every path reaching its terminated condition, the solution space of this chess game would be bounded, and its domain would have been a "closed world" problem, where winning the game should be almost guaranteed. Nevertheless, in a typical chess game, there could be in average 32 alternatives per move and about 50 to 60 moves between the two players in a game, representing a search space of a total combination of between 32^{50} to 32^{60} possible nodes. If this were possible on a super computer, using recognition paradigm to match the input vector onto a path in the game tree, then it would be quite possible to generate a winning solution. This is known as the "A Type" approach as proposed by Shannon [Shannon 1950a].

Some pruned versions of this endless game tree have been investigated by a number of people conducting exhaustive (full width) searches based on a number of moves it could look ahead (a fixed depth), followed by a "quiescence search". A typical quiescence search would be: captures and checks at ply 1, captures-only after ply 1. KAISSA from the Institute of Control Science, Moscow [Adelson-Velskiy et al 1970], TECH II from MIT and the Chess 4.5 from Northwestern University [Slate and Atkin 1977] were typical examples of this approach. Although the "A type" approach is only a subset of the complete game tree, which usually looks only at several moves ahead but it is still unbelievably large for a normal computer to deal with. On the other hand, others were investigating a more selective search based on rules and heuristics, known as the "B type" approach [Shannon 1950a].

The objective of the "B type" algorithms aims at a even smaller sub-tree by applying rules and heuristics to minimise the number of paths that suits a normal machine in the hope to achieve the success rate of the "A Type" approach. For instance, at the very early stage, Bernstein [Bernstein et al 1958] adopted the limitation of the search tree to the "best 7" at every node; Greenblatt [Greenblatt et al 1967] used well-selected quiescence rules aiming at tactical solidity. Other examples can also be found in [Harris 1974; Berliner 1979; Harris 1977; Palay 1983]. However, being selective sometimes could be a handicap of overlooking some subtle moves during the cut-off as compare to the full width search of the "A type".

A less well-known goal-oriented approach, known as the "C type" was investigated by a number of people but with little success and could only play mediocre chess [Newell et al 1958]. This approach advocates that moves should be driven by goal or formation identified beforehand [Newell et al 1958; Church et al 1977; Wilkins 1980]. The main difficulty in this approach is how to recognise a goal and how to decompose goal to generate a plan to achieve its end. Nonetheless, advance in problem solving technology has enabled us to re-examine the issue from the prospective of co-operative planning, where the goal is identified by the strategic agent while the tactical agents work out the move-by-move solution path to transform current situation into a desired winning situation.

To demonstrate the strength and examine the weakness of the proposed problem solving methodology, a number of end-game formations will be used here. Firstly, the end-game formations are identified by the machine with the help of embedded case library in the strategic agent. This involves a number of pieces to be deployed at the position set out in the case library to checkmate. Secondly, preconditions and constraints of the formation are checked by the strategic agent. Thirdly, all tactical paths that are feasible from their current positions to the desired positions could later be merged into a number of related strategic plans. Fourthly, plans are selected at the decision-making (control and consolidation module) stage, where only one of them will be the operational plan and the rest as stand by plans. Finally, the execution of the plan is undertaken by the Command and Control module (C^2) to steer the plan through the uncertain world in which the opponent's plan is unknown. In the event of disruption, some forms of reactive planning such as detour, re-routing, or modification of plan will be initiated in order to seek an alternative path to the same destination or to cope with the unexpected development in the environment.

5.2 The Domain

Like the Western chess, the Chinese chess [Figure 5.1] is a two-person war game, where the conflict is in full swing under a combat environment supported by simulated military forces from both sides (the blue and the red) on a simplified battlefield (the chess board). The chessboard is a 9 x 10 grid, forming 90 possible positions (intersections) and a river in the middle to divide the board into two identical territories, each occupied by a different forces at the beginning of the game.

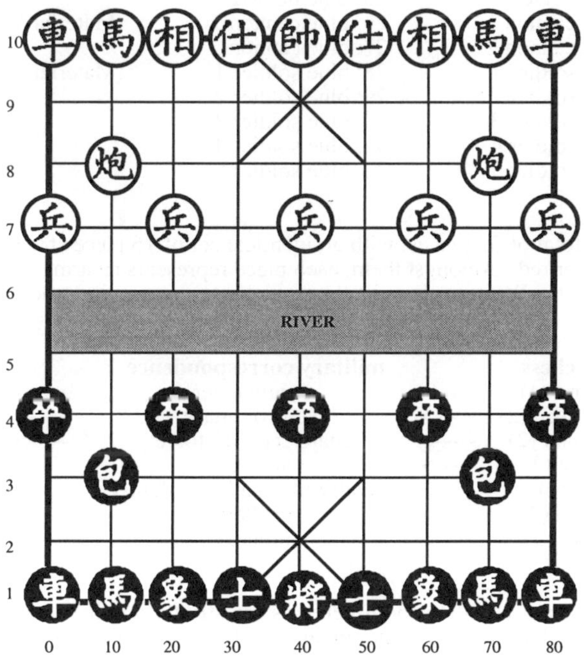

Figure 5.1. The Chinese Chess Board

Furthermore, within each territory, there is the fortress (general headquarter or castle) which is formed by four square boxes marked with a large cross linking each opposite corner, where general and its staff (mandarins) are confined to. For the purpose of illustration, we will give each point on the board an unique ID number. Such labelling system starts from the bottom to the top and from the left to the right. In other words, the bottom-left corner is Number 1 and the top-right corner is Number 90. In the similar fashion, the other ID numbers could be easily recognised by adding up the rank number (1, 2, 3, 4, 5, 6, 7, 8, 9, and 10) with the file number (0, 10, 20, 30, 40, 50, 60, 70, and 80) at each cross point on the chess board. In this study, we will also use an unique number to denote each piece, which together indicates the movement of each piece on the chess board.

1: red general	17: blue general	(Material Value = 16,000)
2: red mandarin 1	18: blue mandarin 1	(Material Value 120)
3: red mandarin 2	19: blue mandarin 2	
4: red elephant 1	20: blue elephant 1	(Material Value = 120)
5: red elephant 2	21: blue elephant 2	
6: red chariot 1	22: blue chariot 1	(Material Value = 600)
7: red chariot 2	23: blue chariot 2	
8: red horse 1	24: blue horse 1	(Material Value = 270)
9: red horse 2	25: blue horse 2	
10: red cannon 1	26: blue cannon 1	(Material Value = 285)
11: red cannon 2	27: blue cannon 2	
12: red soldier 1	28: blue soldier 1	(Material Value = 20)
13: red soldier 2	29: blue soldier 2	
14: red soldier 3	30: blue soldier 3	
15: red soldier 4	31: blue soldier 4	
16: red soldier 5	32: blue soldier 5	

There are a total of 32 pieces, with an identical set of 16 pieces for both side marked with either blue or red. Amongst them, each piece represents an army unit, resembles the its counterpart in the Western chess in almost a one-to-one correspondence.

Chinese chess		**military correspondence**		**Western chess**
• general (1)	----->	commander	----->	king;
• mandarin (2)	----->	staff or guard	----->	queen;
• elephant (2)	----->	guard/security force	----->	bishop;
• chariot (2)	----->	armour	----->	rook;
• horse (2)	----->	cavalry/mechanised infantry	----->	knight;
• cannon (2)	----->	artillery	----->	**none**;
• soldier (5)	----->	infantry	----->	pawn.

As the focuses of attention, both generals are strictly confined within their fortress and are not allowed to face each other in an open file. This rule enables the general to be used as part and parcel of certain offensive formations, especially near the end game, for pinning down the mobility of the opponent general. But unlike the queen in the Western chess, the mandarin is playing a more defending role for protecting of the general within the fortress, complemented by the elephants covering the area outside of fortress but within its own side of the river. Therefore in here, mandarins and elephants are both defensive pieces working together for the protection and security of the general. On the other hand, the offensive pieces in Chinese chess, are those with unrestricted mobility to strike deep into opponent territory; the chariots, the horses, the cannons, and the soldiers all come under this category.

The Chinese chess is a game of movement and capture. Players take turns to move one of his own pieces but not allowed to abandon a move. The game is over when the general from either side is captured, or a draw is agreed. The legal moves of all of pieces are summarised as follows:

- The general moves one point at a time, either horizontally or vertically, but never diagonally. He may not be out of the fortress and has 9 legal positions within it.

- The mandarin moves one point at a time but only diagonally. It has only 5 legal positions within the fortress, i.e. position [31, 33, 42, 51, 53] or the positions [38, 40, 49, 58, 60].

- The elephant moves two points diagonally at a time, and may not skip over any pieces along its path to complete its move. Moreover, it may not cross over the river to operate in enemy territory, and they have only 7 legal positions [3, 21, 25, 43, 61, 65, 83] or [8, 26, 30, 48, 66, 70, 88].

- The chariot may move across any number of points either vertically or horizontally to any where on the chessboard, so long as it does not skip over any pieces in its path.

- The horse may move two points either vertically or horizontally before making a 90° turn in any direction to complete a "L" shape path, so long as it does not skip over an occupied point.

- The cannon may move across any number of points either vertically or horizontally any where on the chessboard and may not skip over any piece, except in the case of capture. It needs a screen to hit the target but may skip over only one piece for this purpose.

- The soldier may move one point forward at a time, but once crossing the river, it may move one point forward or one point sideways, and hence each soldier has 47 legal position. However, it may never move backwards even if it reaches the bottom line of other's territory.

5.3 Some General Strategies

The development of strategy in Chinese chess may generally classify into opening, middle and end games. In here, various distinct tactics have been developed at different stage of the game, which to a great extent, reflect the thinking and objective behind each strategy. In this section, we would discuss the strategies at each stage.

5.3.1 The Opening

There are a few variations at the opening. For the past centuries, a number of well-known openings have been developed, widely used and reported in the literature. Some of the most popular openings are:

- Cannon opening;
- Horse opening;
- Soldier opening;
- Elephant opening.

Cannon openings are among the most popular offensive openings to seize initiative by occupying the central file as shown in [Figure 5.2 - 5.7]. The strategy here is to create positional advantage in paving the way for a "outer line strategy" at the later stages.

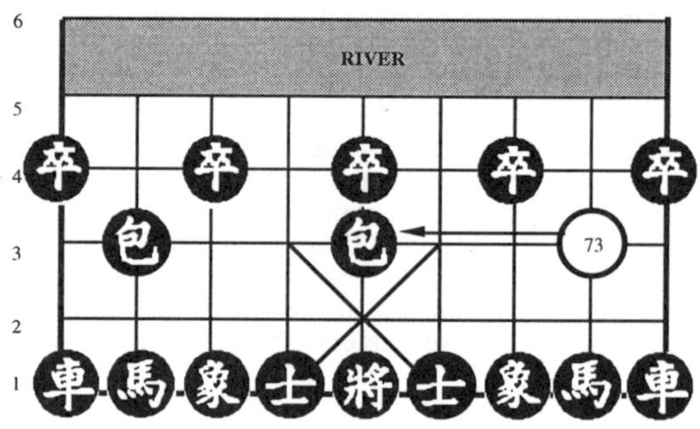

Figure 5.2. The Central Cannon
(A cannon is placed to occupy the central file)

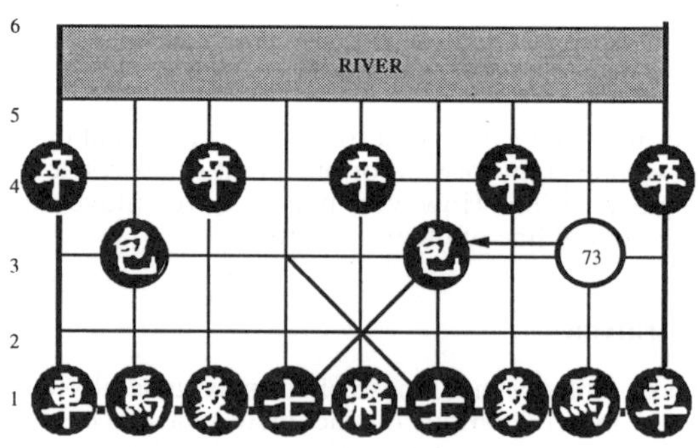

Figure 5.3. The Guard's Corner Cannon
(A cannon is placed at the nearer fortress's corner)

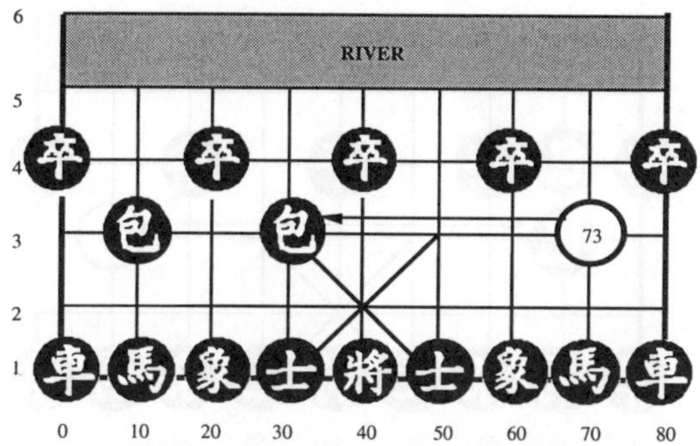

Figure 5.4. The Crossing Fortress's Cannon
(A cannon is placed at the far corner of the fortress)

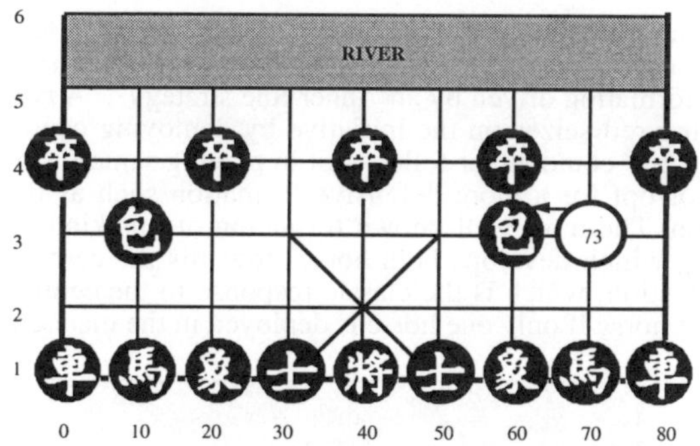

Figure 5.5. The Conceal Cannon
(A cannon is placed behind a soldier on file 20 or 60)

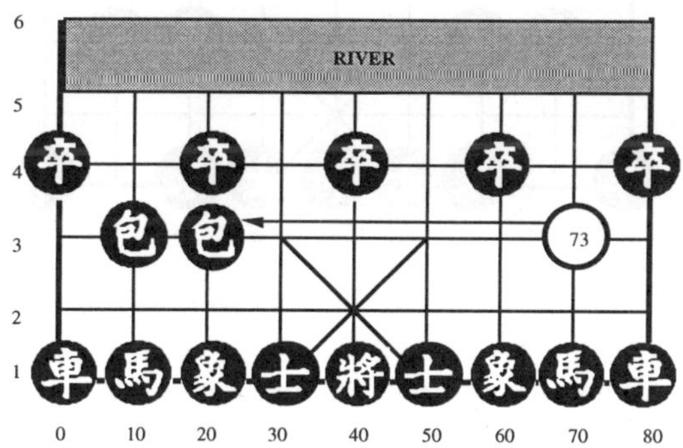

Figure 5.6. The Crossing Fortress's Conceal Cannon
(A cannon is placed along the cannon behind a soldier on file 20 or 60)

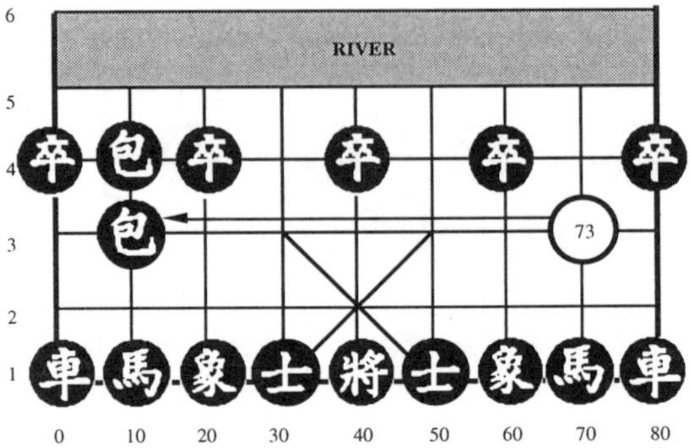

Figure 5.7. The Off-Sided Double Cannons
(Two cannons are aligned on file 10 or 70)

Horse Openings, due to its mobility, the horses are less effective as offensive pieces at the opening, and hence, the horse opening is generally regarded as part and parcel of a defensive opening formation driven by an "inner line strategy". A typical situation when the opponent playing red seizes on the initiative by deploying central cannon opening, and the blue in response could either follow suit in playing same form of cannon opening to regain control, or opt for a more defensive formation such as the horse opening to contain the situation. The most well-known formation of this kind is the double central horses [Figure 5.8], which develops both horses towards the centre, giving the central soldier double protection, which is the classic response to the central cannon openings. Known as the single horse if only one horse is deployed in the manoeuvre.

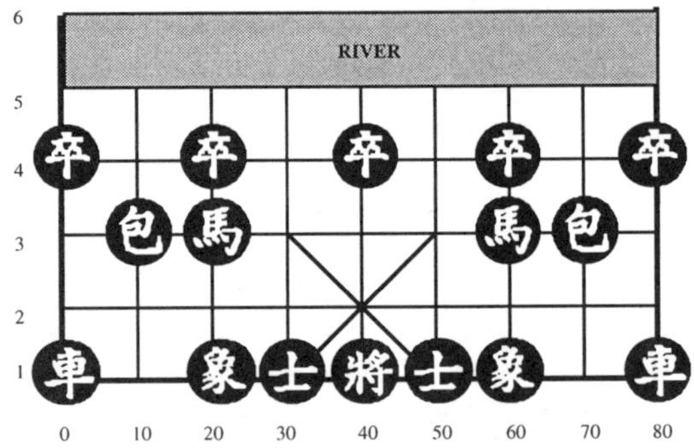

Figure 5.8. The Double Central Horses
(Both horses are placed at position [23] and [63])

Soldier Openings, follows a some what "indirect approach" in terms of strategy, by moving the soldier at position [24] and [64] forward, and in so doing, keeping the option open to develop its horse, or cannon (Conceal Cannon) in the following move. It is often referred to as the angel's guidance [Figure 5.9], and usually played by red to delay the formulation of tactics until blue has made its opening.

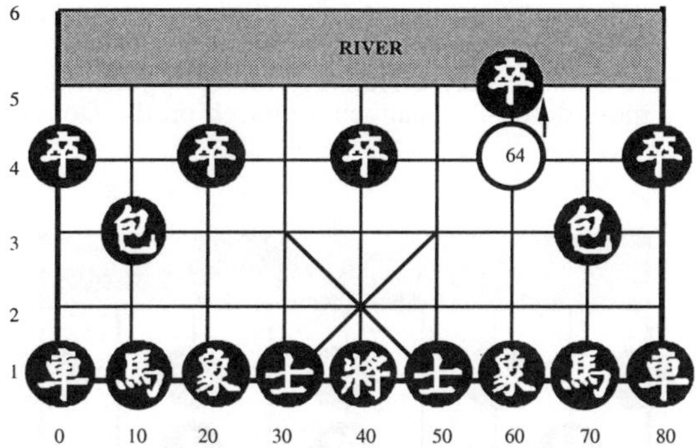

Figure 5.9. The Angel's Guidance
(The soldier at position [24] or [64] is moved forward)

Elephant Opening, this is yet another typical defensive opening, usually played by the blue side, where one of the elephant is placed at the central file to protect the general against central cannon attacking, known as the flying elephant [Figure 5.10]. This is one of the classic reactive routines that we will be installed during plan execution to be triggered by checkmate.

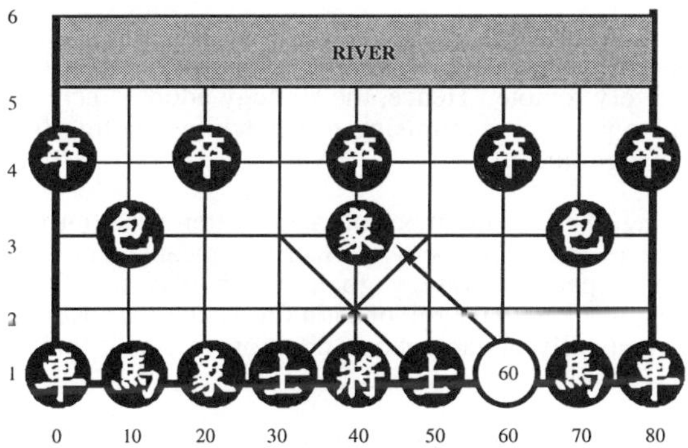

Figure 5.10. The Flying Elephant
(An elephant is placed to protect the central file)

The general strategy adopted for the opening is determined mainly by which colour one is playing. Whoever starts first could always adopt an offensive strategy, such as the central cannon opening to control the central file, paving the way for the deployment of other pieces in developing into an attacking formation at later stage. For instance, the horse on the same side may move forward to strengthen the central soldier defence. By doing so, the nearby chariot (rook) could move out promptly from its position into forming an alliance with the cannon and horse as shown in [Figure 5.11]. On the other hand, such an offensive alliance may effectively block opponent's routes and force its counter-moves into a more defensive manoeuvre based on the Double Horses or Flying Elephant opening.

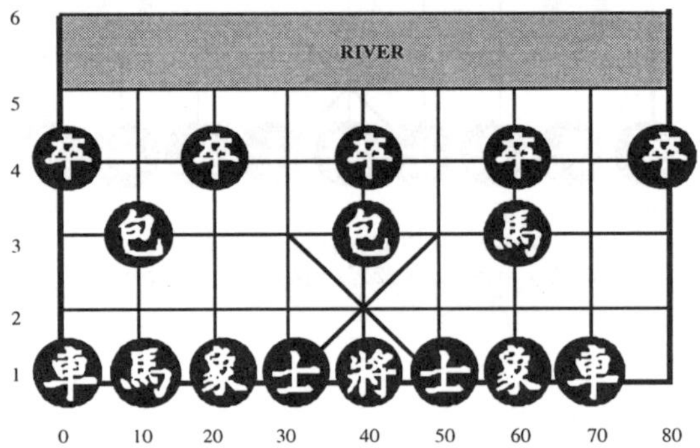

Figure 5.11. An Opening Offensive Alliance
(The cannon, horse and chariot are developed for a formation)

5.3.2 The Middle

As we move into the middle game, the variations on the chessboard are now becoming so diverse that matching them with the pre-condition of the text book examples is beginning to look very remote. Hence, the strategy adopted here is to play tactically, looking for immediate gains or minimising losses while awaiting for a plan to emerge either by search or recognition.

Generally speaking, there is a number of tactics often used during the middle game: 1) sacrifice, 2) exchange and 3) manoeuvre. Sacrifice means to give up a piece or pieces in order to achieve a specific strategy goal, which may justify the current losses. Exchange is to trade a piece with the opponent's for a superior position. Manoeuvre is to move a piece to a tactically advantageous position to break through the opponent's defence.

Sacrifice: As shown in Figure 5.12, the blue horse at position [48] is threatened by the red chariot at position [18]. The blue horse could move away and give up its offensive superiority of being a step away from checkmate, but the blue cannon at position [33] could attack the red mandarin at position [40] to improve its positional superiority at the cost of sacrificing the horse [Figure 5.13].

the blue cannon moves from [33] to [40], the red chariot moves from [18] to [48],
the blue cannon moves from [40] to [10], the red chariot moves from [90] to [88],
the blue cannon moves from [10] to [80].

The reasoning process of this case is that the blue horse at position [48] has a number of escape routes, we would assess the pros and cons of some of these routes:

Route 1: (considered as a bad tactical move by the blue side)
the blue horse moves from [48] to [27], the red chariot moves from [18] to [28];
the blue cannon moves from [33] to [23], the red soldier moves from [25] to [24];
the blue cannon retreats from [23] to [22], the red soldier moves from [24] to [23];
the red player could capture either the blue horse at [27] or the blue cannon at [22].

Route 2: (considered as a bad tactical move by the blue side)
the blue horse moves from [48] to [67], the red chariot moves from [18] to [68];
the blue cannon moves from [33] to [37], the red horse moves from [80] to [59];
the blue chariot moves from [52] to [57], the red chariot moves from [90] to [70];
If exchange did take place, the blue player would lose three pieces in return for two, and in the process giving up its positional superiority.

Route 3: (considered as a good tactical move by the blue side)
the blue cannon moves from [33] to [40], the red chariot moves from [18] to [48];
the blue cannon moves from [40] to [10], the red chariot moves from [48] to [78];
the blue chariot could moves from [52] to [12] in order to form a favourable formation.

Route 4: (considered as a good tactical move by the blue side)
the blue cannon moves from [33] to [40], the red chariot moves from [18] to [48],
the blue cannon moves from [40] to [10], the red chariot moves from [48] to [18],
the blue chariot could moves from [81] to [71], threatening red horse at [80].

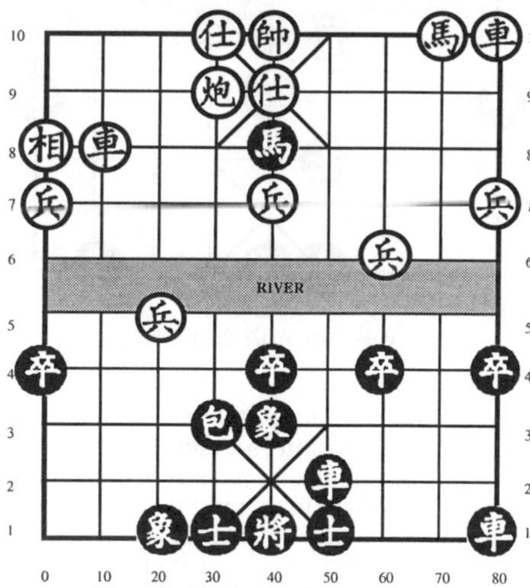

Figure 5.12. Before the Sacrifice

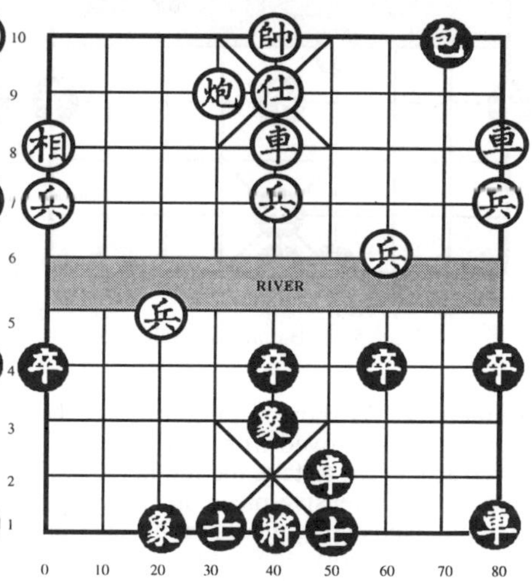

Figure 5.13. After the Sacrifice

Exchange: As shown in Figure 5.14, the red general is checkmated by the blue cannon at position [47]. Since it is the red's turn to move, the red general has a number of options to avoid defeat. One of them is to move a red mandarin either from [40] or [60] to position [49], but this would seriously weaken one wing of his defence and give the central blue cannon at [47] a superior position to capture red chariot at [77] and dominate the left wing of the board with the double cannons as summarised in Route 1.

Route 1: (considered as a bad tactical move by the red side)
the red mandarin moves from [60] to [49], the blue cannon captures red chariot at [77];
the red chariot captures blue chariot at [17], ***********************************.
the red losing the defence of its left wing.

Other alternative route is examined in the following:
Route 2: (considered as a good tactical move by the red side)
the red cannon moves from [48] to [44], the blue mandarin moves from [42] to [33];
the red cannon moves from [58] to [78], the blue cannon captures red chariot at [77];
the red chariot captures blue chariot at [17], the blue cannon captures red cannon at [78];
the red horse in turn capture cannon at [78], and the advantage of the blue cannon is removed [Figure 5.15].

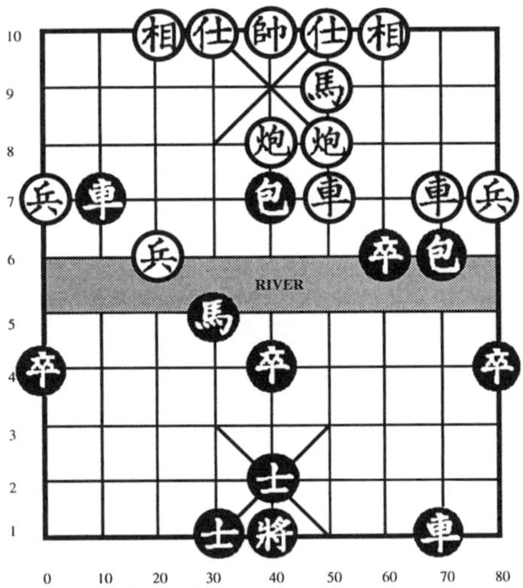

Figure 5.14. Before the Exchanges

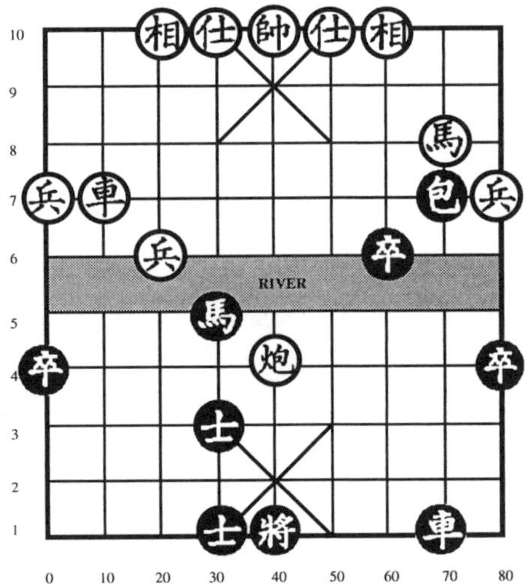

Figure 5.15. After the Exchanges

Manoeuvre: As shown in Figure 5.16, the game could enter into a stalemate situation if the red cannon moved from [66] to capture blue horse at position [6], and the blue rook moved from [25] to take the red horse at [26]. In this development, what remains on the board is one offensive piece on each side of the game, which often end up in stalemate. To avoid exchanging pieces in this case and focus on occupying the central and left wing of the blue territory, the red player could position itself into a possible winning position as shown in Figure 5.17.

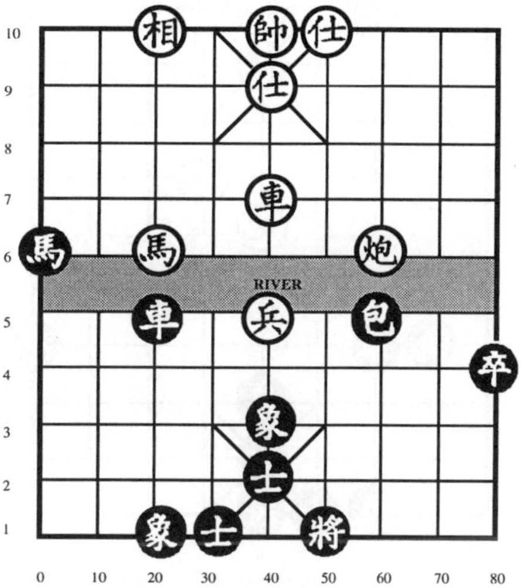

Figure 5.16. Before the Manoeuvre

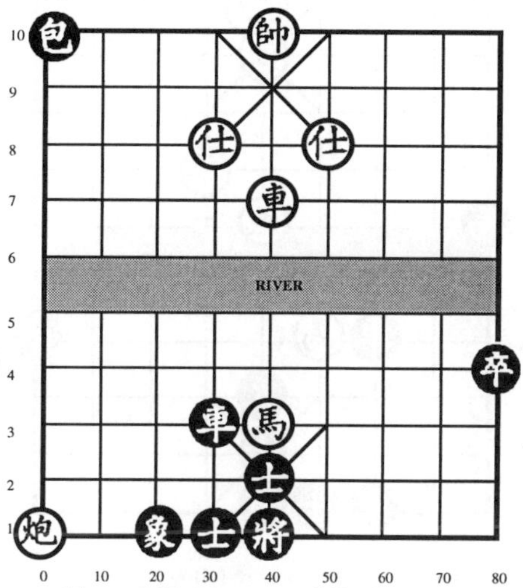

Figure 5.17. Manoeuvre following Route 1

Route 1: (considered as a good tactical move by the red side)

the red soldier moves from [45] to [35],	the blue chariot captures the soldier at [35];
the red cannon captures blue horse at [6],	the blue chariot returns from [35] to [25];
the red mandarin moves from [49] to [58],	the blue cannon moves to checkmate at [70];
the red mandarin moves from [60] to [49],	the blue cannon captures elephant at [30];
the red cannon moves from [6] to [1],	the blue cannon moves from [30] to [10];
the red mandarin moves from [49] to [38],	the blue chariot moves from [25] to [23];
the red horse moves from [26] to [34],	the blue chariot moves from [23] to [33];
the red horse moves from [34] to [55],	the blue general moves from [51] to [41];
the red horse captures blue elephant at [43],	*********************************.

the red horse could move from [43] to [62] to checkmate.

Route 2: (considered as a good tactical move by the red side)

the red soldier moves from [45] to [35],	the blue chariot moves from [25] to [24];
the red chariot moves to checkmate at [57],	the blue general moves from [51] to [41];
the red horse moves from [26] to [34],	*********************************;

the red cannon moves from [66] to [46], making the situation uncomfortable for blue.

Route 3: (considered as a good tactical move by the red side)

the red soldier moves from [45] to [35],	the blue chariot moves from [25] to [24];
the red chariot moves from [47] to [7],	the blue horse moves from [6] to [14];
the red chariot returns from [7] to [57],	the blue general moves from [51] to [41];
the red horse moves from [26] to [45],	*********************************;

the red cannon moves from [66] to [46], and now red is in control of the central file.

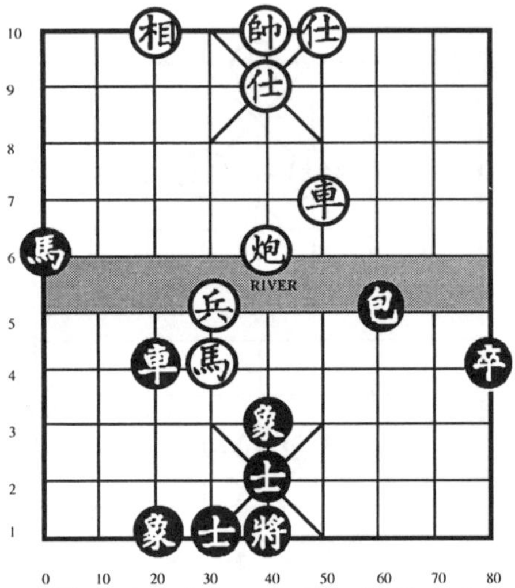

Figure 5.18. Manoeuvre following Route 2

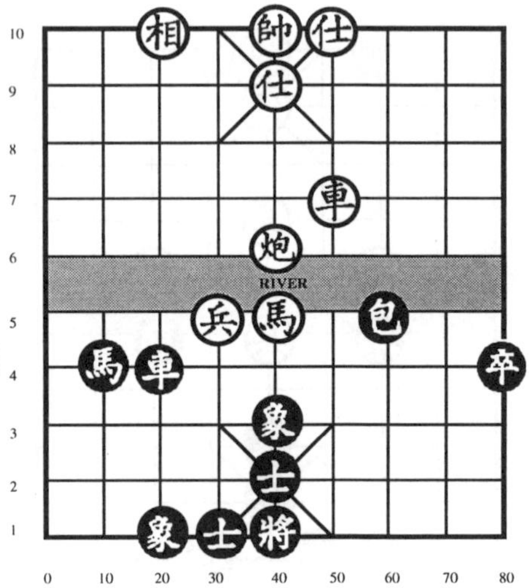

Figure 5.19. Manoeuvre following Route 3

It is often hard to play middle games when there is no strategic plan in sight. Nonetheless, short-term benefit and threat are main concerns for both sides. The concepts of sacrifice, exchange and manoeuvre are very useful in dealing with short-term considerations, not only suitable to middle game, but also applicable at different stages of the game.

5.3.3 The Ending

Unlike the opening and the middle game, there are normally very few pieces remain on board at the end game stage, and therefore, it is much more easier to formulate plan lending to checkmate. However, there are a number of heuristics that could be taken into consideration in the development of tactical formation:

1. Two chariots are difficult to defeat:
   1) a horse, a cannon, two mandarins, and two elephants;
   2) a chariot, a cannon, and two mandarins.

2. A chariot and a horse are difficult to defeat a chariot and two mandarins.

3. A chariot and a cannon are difficult to defeat:
   1) a chariot and two mandarins;
   2) a chariot and a soldier;
   3) a chariot and two elephants.

4. A chariot and a soldier are difficult to defeat:
   1) two soldiers , two mandarins, and two elephants;

2) two cannons and two elephants;
3) two cannons and a soldier;
4) a chariot and a soldier.

5. Two cannons are difficult to defeat:
1) two elephants;
2) a cannon.

6. A horse and a soldier are difficult to defeat:
1) two mandarins and an elephant;
2) a cannon and two elephants.

7. Two soldiers are difficult to defeat:
1) a cannon and a mandarin;
2) two mandarins;
3) two elephants;
4) a mandarin, a soldier, and an elephant.

8. A chariot is difficult to defeat:
1) two horses;
2) two cannons;
3) two cannons and a soldier;
4) two soldiers and a cannon;
5) two soldiers and a horse;
6) two mandarins and a cannon;
7) two elephants and a cannon;
8) a horse, an elephant, and a soldier;
9) three soldiers;
10) two soldiers and two mandarins;
11) two soldiers and two elephants;
12) two mandarins and two elephants.

9. A horse is easy to stalemate:
1) a cannon and two mandarins;
2) two elephants;
3) a cannon;
4) a soldier.

10. A cannon is easy to stalemate:
1) two mandarins;
2) a mandarin;
3) the single general.

Using these heuristics in material assessment before developing any formation would in some way reduce the possibility in deploying a wrong formation. The plan in the end game is usually formulated as a checkmate formation , which often involves a number of pieces to be moved from their current positions to their desired goal positions, provided that a path from their current position to the goal positions is available. Furthermore, a number of books [Donnelly 1974; Lai 1987; Lai 1990; Lai 1991a; Lai 1991b; Lai 1992] should be of interest to those who like to find out more about Chinese chess.

5.4 The Design and Implementation

The reasoning process of the proposed problem solving methodology as applying to the Chinese chess is usually triggered by a move (changes of event in the environment). Initially, it will attempt to find a pre-installed plan from the case library (knowledge base) in the Pure Recognition Agent, which connect the present state on the board to a desired state. However, perfect match is often only possible at the opening stage, where the initial situation is the beginning of the game, and any desired state could be developed from a pre-programmed solution path fetched from the library provided that the path has not been blocked by the opponent during opening skirmish. For instance, the Cannon Opening.

Matching of both current and desired situations beyond the opening stage have been quite difficult even with fuzzy matching. Therefore, it is more practical to focus on a few relevant pieces in the current situation that the system has intended to develop as the basis for pattern matching. This approach is adopted by the Heuristic Agent to ignore all but a few selected pieces on the board. The use of heuristics increases the likelihood of obtaining solution from the case library after the first few opening moves. The syntax used here for moving a pieces is "**move(Piece-ID, From, To, Value)**", and the fundamental difference between these two types of pattern matching is the value attached to them; solution generated from perfect matching of both current and goal states is 6000 points, while solution obtained with heuristics by matching just a subset of the current situation is usually less valuable.

In contrast to the Pure Recognition and Heuristics Agents, the Exhaustive Search Agent relying on the blackboard and situation map to analyse and understanding the current situation. It generates move by calculating the current risk and reward in terms of positional and material advantages for any tactically motivated move.

As far as planning is concerned, it is activated when a feasible formation (goal, or desired situation) is identified according to the current situation (in which all relevant pieces are presented and could be moved from their current positions to their individual designated positions, required by the strategic formation). Although the plan is a series of COAs to be implemented according to the sequence and order imposed by the embedded strategic agent, it is to be put forward for consideration on a move-by-move basis in competition with the proposed moves from other agents. In here, a value of 6000 points is attached to an overall checkmate plan, which is inclined to decrease for any additional state in the solution path. In other words, the longer the path, the greater the uncertainty, and the smaller value would be attached to each move concerned.

In the opening game, the first few moves could often be made by "pure recognition" with the help of a case library and thereafter by the heuristic agent and exhaustive search agents based on short-term tactical consideration. However, as the game enters a decisive phase of the middle and end-game, attack formation will begin to emerge so that the goal-oriented plans will be more likely to compete for consideration. In this context, the multi-agent architectural platform will swing into action to decide and select the best move by means of their attached values on a move-by-move basis. This reasoning and decision-making process is summarised as follows:

1 To conduct an analysis on the current situation.

2a To proceed with perfect pattern matching from the case library.
If a perfect match is found
then its associated move is generated i.e. **move (Piece-ID, From, To, Value)** from the library as a move to be considered in the war meeting (control/consolidation).

2b To proceed with heuristics matching only on relevant pieces in the case library.
If all required pieces in the formation are available on the chess board
then its associated move is generated i.e. **move (Piece-ID, From, To, Value)**.

2c To proceed with strategic planning by identifying the target and attack formation.
If target is identified (feasible) and formation can be formulated
then generate strategic plans (partial plan) based on current and desired positions.
repeat
1) select pieces associated with the strategic plan once at a time;
2) issue the desired positions for the chess piece connected with the tactical agents to search for a path (COA);
until all paths concerned have been investigated and merged into a co-operative plan.
If plan is selected the complete plan will be forwarded by C^2 to the war meeting for consideration on a move-by-move basis:
move (Piece-ID, From, To, Value) *
plan [(Piece-ID, [From, State 1, ..., Goal_state])].

2d To proceed with tactical search based on the situation analysis, positional table, and the material value of related piece as the basis to calculate the positional and capturing advantage: **move (Piece-ID, From, To, Value)**.

3 All proposals from 2a, 2b, 2c and 2d are put forward for consideration in the war meeting, and the proposal with the highest value will be selected as the operational move.

4 Print out the advice and other necessary messages.

5.4.1 The Exhaustive Search Agent

As stated in the algorithm above, the exhaustive search agent checks and analyses the situation for every pieces on the chess board so that it can warn of any threat of imminent capture or checkmate undetectable by other agents. On the other hand, it also provides the bottom-line solution in the absence of any solution from other agents. In the case of chess, each tactical agent under the exhaustive search agent supports only one type of pieces. Their knowledge or expertise covers the "legal move generation", the assessment of material losses/gains and any possible positional risk/reward for every potential positions on the chess board. Theoretically speaking, more parameters could be included for value assessment, and the depth of search could be certainly extended to whatever levels as required. However, in our implementation, only one ply search is applied here within the exhaustive search agent.

Table 5.1. The Positional Values of Red Chariot
(Their current positional value is -2)

	0	10	20	30	40	50	60	70	80
10	車	10	6	14	12	14	6	10	車
9	8	4	8	16	8	16	8	4	8
8	4	8	6	14	12	14	8	8	8
7	6	10	8	14	14	14	8	10	6
6	12	16	14	20	20	20	14	16	12
					RIVER				
5	12	14	12	18	18	18	12	14	12
4	12	18	16	22	22	22	16	18	12
3	12	12	12	18	18	18	12	12	12
2	16	20	18	24	26	24	18	20	16
1	14	14	12	18	16	18	12	14	14

Given the current position, the assessment value is calculated on the basis of both material and positional changes due to the proposed move confirmed by the legal move generator. The positional values of every offensive piece are computed by means of a positional table similar to the one above, and a complete collection of positional table for all offensive pieces is presented in Appendix D. Furthermore, in our implementation, the tactical agents are also used to support the process of situation analysis to generate "colour" for the planning agent by means of legal move generators.

5.4.2 The Pure Recognition Agent

In the chess domain, the knowledge base of the pure recognition agent is a collection of cases from books and experts; each case is structured as an action part of a proposed move conditioned on the current situation. The state of the chess board required covers the entire chess board with all surviving pieces. The proposal accompanying a predetermined value is to move pieces from their current positions to the desired positions.

At the beginning of the game, securing a match for both current and desired situations is never a problem, and therefore, a list of COAs covering initial state (shown in figure 5.20) to the desired state (as shown in figure 5.21) is generated, but with the condition that the situation on the board should be checked before the activation of each move in the COAs. Details of this solution path can be found in Appendix A covering Case 1, then Case 4 to Case 19. Arriving at the desired situation, the red side would gain "240" in material (an elephant and a mandarin) and "54" in positional value as opposed to "40" by its opponent. However, more importantly, it will be within easy reach of winning.

As a text-book solution, each proposed move is given the highest possible score (value) of "6000" as shown in figure 5.20 of moving the red cannon 1 (ID:10) from position "18" to position "48". However, this value will be reduced in the case of fuzzy matching subject to the degree of matches achieved. Theoretically, the knowledge base could grow through "knowledge acquisition" by adding whole range of cases covering from opening to end-game. Nonetheless, only 23 cases are installed here in the knowledge base to support the "pure recognition".

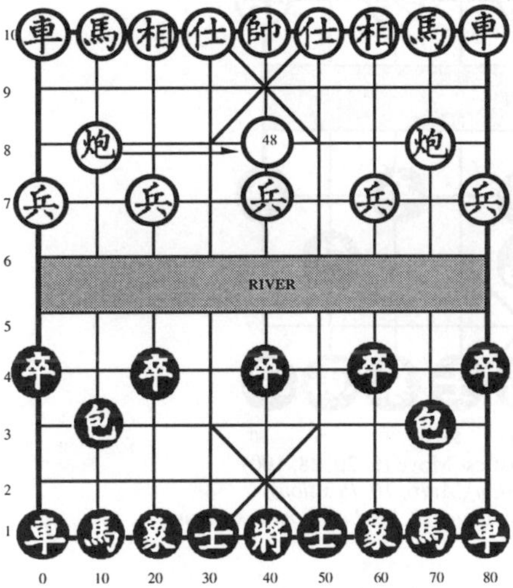

Figure 5.20. The Current Situation:
The Proposed Move (10, 18, 48, 6000)

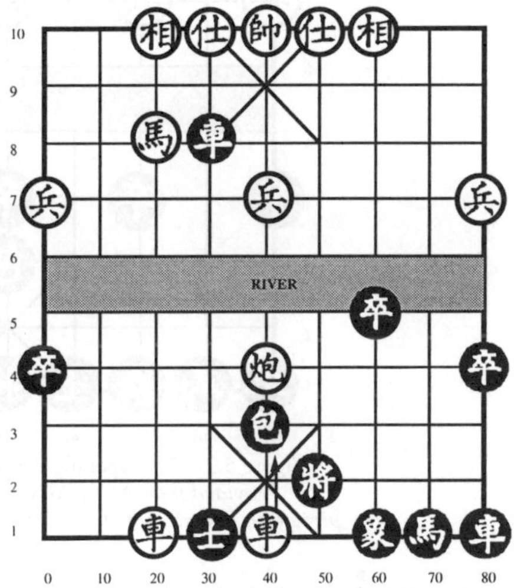

Figure 5.21. One of the Desired Situation:
The Proposed Move (7, 41, 43, 6000)

5.4.3 The Heuristics Agent

The condition for generation of pre-programmed solutions is the very high degree of matches required, which is very difficult to secure after the initial few moves. A relaxation of this constraint could greatly improve the chances of a hit by applying the condition only to a selective pieces at specific positions or areas, instead of all surviving pieces on the entire chess board. The heuristics agent has a knowledge base with a collection of criteria or pre-conditions that need to be satisfied for the generation of a solution. However, as different strategies are used at different stage of the game, we will present only two sets of heuristics here for this investigation; one for the opening and the other to cover just general rule of thumb.

1) The opening heuristics

Following the central cannon opening, the opening heuristics tends to focus on just two or three pieces to form a basic opening formation, and normally involves a cannon, a horse and a chariot on the same wing of the chess board as shown in Figure 5.22, where the cannon is used to develop attack along the central file, the horse is for the protection of the screen (central soldier) and the chariot is for strengthening the offensive formation. In our implementation, there are eight opening heuristics which are listed in Appendix B.

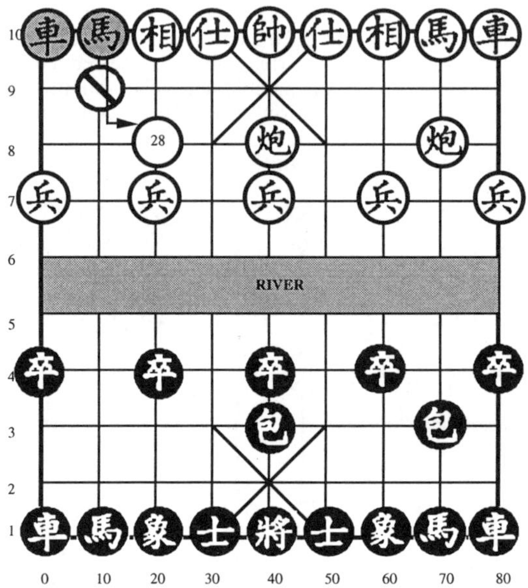

Figure 5.22. The Opening Heuristics: Move (8, 20, 28, 100)
Provided that At (8, 20, Position), At (6, 10, Position),
No_piece (19, Board), Safe (28, Colour), Legal (8, 28, Legal_moves): true;

2) The general heuristics
In addition to the opening heuristics, there are a number of general rule of thumb aim at establishing local superiority based on the basic opening patterns and opponent's counter-moves. In here, we have installed a total of 26 heuristics, covering mainly the opening stage (See Appendix C) in five areas:

- Tactical move
- Right attack
- Left attack
- Central attack
- Double cannons

However, additional cases could be included to cover both the middle and the ending stage. Furthermore, like other agents, all proposals from the heuristic agent carries a value for selection purposes, but with generally a much lower assessment value compared with the text-book solution.

Tactical move usually develops in absence of any other obvious line of heuristics to follow. Some familiar and useful moves in the opening stage are chosen for this purpose. The basic principles are to increase mobility and occupy advantageous positions. For instance, moving the red horses forward to either position 68 or 28 are the typical manoeuvring for horses either at the opening or later stage of game. Other tactical moves involve manoeuvring the red chariots out of their starting positions, or moving the soldiers on file 20 or 60 one step forward to increase mobility for the for red horses to reach the river bank. An example is displayed in Figure 5.23.

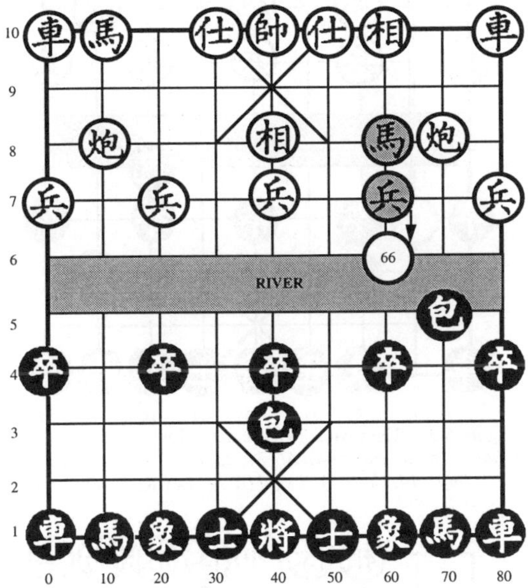

Figure 5.23. Tactical move: Move (15, 67, 66, 15)
Provided that At (15, 67, Position), Alive (9, Position), Safe (66, Colour), Legal (15, 66, Legal_moves): true;

Right Attack Heuristics attempt to apply pressure from the right side of the chess board by moving a chariot to one of the following positions: 12, 14, 15, and 16. Each of these position serve a purpose for possible gain in either positional or material value:

- the purpose of occupying position 12 is to pin down opponent's horse and chariot;
- the purpose of occupying position 14 is to threaten the blue soldier at position 24 and block its horse at position 23;
- The purpose of occupying position 15 or 16 is for the control the river banks.

However, the pre-condition for these rules is the presence of red chariot at 20, blue horse and soldier at position 23 and 24 respectively, and the confirmation that any one of the four positions is safe and available. An example is displayed in Figure 5.24 and others are in Appendix C.

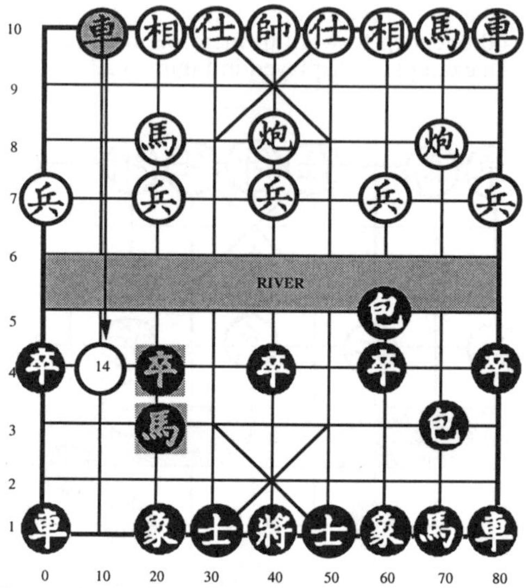

Figure 5.24. Right Attack Heuristics: Move (6, 20, 14, 100)
Provided that At (6, 20, Position), At (24, 23, Position), At (29, 24, Position), Safe (14, Colour), Legal (6, 14, Legal_moves): true;

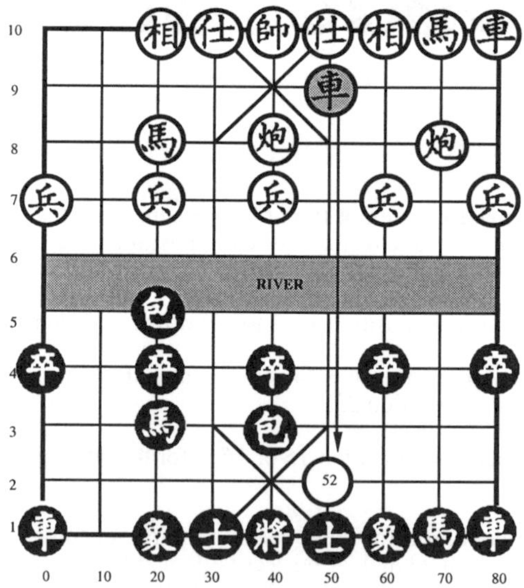

Figure 5.25. Left Attack Heuristics: Move (6, 59, 52, 100)
Provided that At (6, 59, Position), Safe (52, Colour), Legal (6, 52, Legal_moves): true;

Left Attack Heuristics attempt to apply pressure on the left side of the chess board by moving a chariot to either position 52 or position 54.

- The purpose of occupying position 52 is to threaten the opponent's general.
- The purpose of occupying position 54 is to capture the opponent's soldiers at position 44 and 64 and pave the way for subsequent attacks.

An example is shown as Figure 5.25 and others are in Appendix C.

Central Attack Heuristics follow the central cannon opening of targeting at the central file, by either deploying the central cannon to capture the opponent's soldier, or strengthening it with moving a horse to position 36 or 56. The condition to trigger this heuristic is the presence of the red horse at position 28 and the blue soldier at position 44, with the confirmation that it is safe for the red horse to be moved to position 36 as shown in Figure 5.26.

The capture of the blue soldier at position 44 paves the way for the deployment of the Double Cannons formation. Since the ultimate target along central file is the opponent's general, one of the pre-condition for such formation is the presence of blue general at position 40 and both red cannons at the appropriate positions as indicated in the Figure 5.27, with the condition of the rules stated below the diagram.

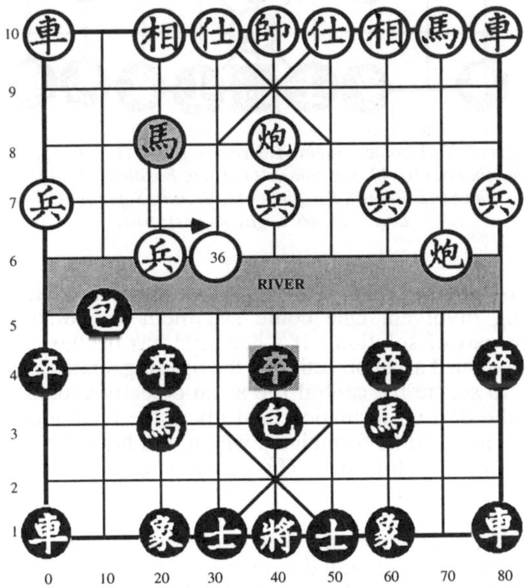

Figure 5.26. Central Attack Heuristics: Move (8, 28, 36, 100)
Provided that At (8, 28, Position), At (30, 44, Position), Safe (36, Colour), Legal (8, 36, Legal_moves): true;

Double Cannons Heuristics align two cannons along the central file, with no other piece between the opponent's general and the first cannon. When in positions, the double cannons would have between them the central file under their finger tips as displayed in following diagram, other variations of Double Cannon heuristics can be found in Appendix C.

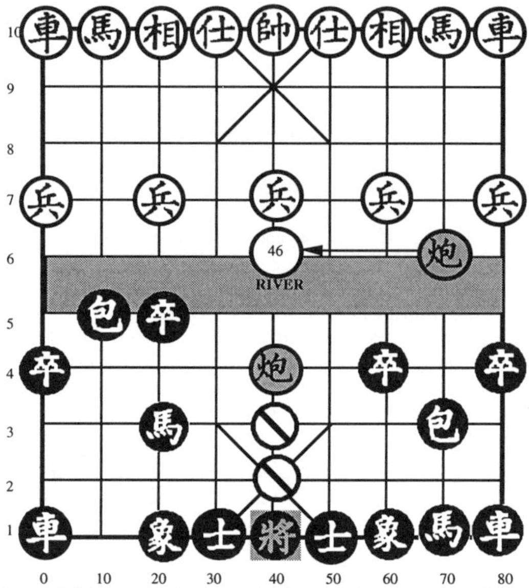

Figure 5.27. Double Cannon Heuristics: Move (11, 76, 46, 700)
Provided that At (10, 44, Position), At (11, 76, Position), At (17, 41, Position), No_piece (42, Board), No_piece (43, Board), Safe (46, Colour), Legal (11, 46, Legal_moves): true;

Heuristics are basically just rules generalised by experts as advice to be followed with very little reasoning involved. One could see them as isolated but advantageous fragments that form part of solution. If a heuristic has become an essential part of a strategy, it could be pursued as an objective of the opening strategy and be developed as a plan. For instance, to secure the central file as an objective could be decomposed into double cannons as the desired formation, and given the beginning of the game as the current situation, a plan could be formulated which will have the end effect of joining a number of heuristic fragments together. This could be achieved in four plys as shown on page184:

1) Cannon opening as shown Figure 5.20 (Case 1 of Appendix A);
2) Capture the central soldier with the central cannon (Central Attack Heuristics);
3) To move another cannon to the river bank (Heuristic 1 of double cannons); and
4) To move it again behind the central cannon later (as shown in Figure 5.27).

5.4.4 The Planning Agent

Lying between the two ends of the problem solving spectrum are the planning and heuristics agents covering the grey area, where pure recognition and the exhaustive search have failed to produce a solution. In the grey area, the heuristic agent only attempts to focus on selective part of the current situation, other than on desired situation. The planning agent is thus designed to bridge the gap between the stringent matching requirement of the pure recognition and the lack of focus suffered by the heuristics agent. It combines the insistence of the pure recognition to match on both the current and desired situations, and eases off the matching requirement to only the relevant piece involved in the formation. However, in order to cope with the volatility of the dynamic environment, and compensate for the matching inaccuracy, the COAs formulated during the planning stage is constantly examined by the Command and Control during plan execution to ensure that the operational plan is feasible and compatible with events unfolding in the environment.

5.4.4.1 The Situation Analysis

In reference to the data organisation of our multi-agent model, the global database (the blackboard) for the Chinese chess takes the form of a chess board, with the entire domain showing the where-about of every piece of the game. The situation analysis takes the form of colour attributed to the 90 positions on the chess board as an indication of the status on those positions. Based on this objective analysis, in-depth subjective analyses could be projected from either the blue or red prospective indicating risky, neutral, safe or rewarding positions. With the involvement of all agents in the system, "the security of each individual location" and "the status of each distinct piece" on the chess board could be generated. The organisation of situation analysis involves three levels of abstraction, and can be visualised through the following model:

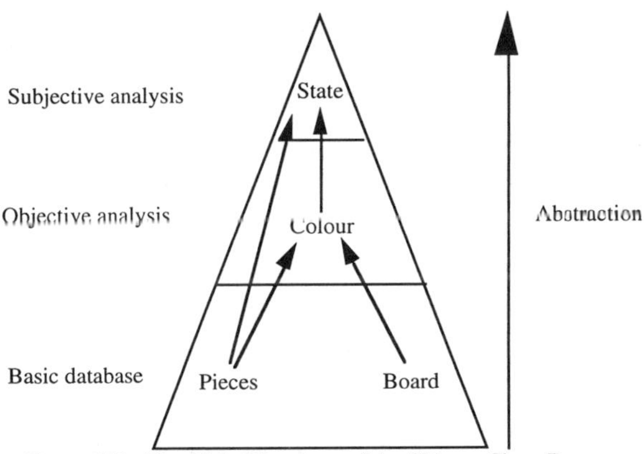

Figure 5.28. The Global Database of the Chinese Chess Program

The Basic Blackboard Database (Pieces on the Chess Board)
In the basic database, positions of chess pieces are represented by the **pieces** predicate with **32** arguments, while the chess board situation is represented by the **board** predicate

with **90** arguments. The 32 arguments used in the **pieces** predicate are in fact the piece ID number range from the red general (ID: 1) to the blue soldier (ID: 32) shown as follows:

pieces (50, 40, 60, 30, 70, 10, 90, 20, 80, 18, 78, 7, 27, 47, 67, 87,
41, 31, 51, 21, 61, 1, 81, 11, 71, 13, 73, 4, 24, 44, 64, 84)

where piece "1" (red general) is at position "50"; piece "2" (red mandarin 1) is at position "40"; and piece "3" (red mandarin 2) is at position "60", ...etc. The value of zero here means that the related piece is no longer on the board. To keep tracking the movement of every piece on the board, the function **update-piece** is used here to update the information on the board.

On the other hand, the **90** arguments on the **board** predicate below are used to represent the status of each position on the chess board. The value of its argument is the ID of a specific piece which is occupying at that position. Similar to the pieces predicate, the value of zero indicates the related position is unoccupied.

board(22, 0, 0, 28, 0, 0, 12, 0, 0, 6,
24, 0, 26, 0, 0, 0, 0, 10, 0, 8,
20, 0, 0, 29, 0, 0, 13, 0, 0, 4,
18, 0, 0, 0, 0, 0, 0, 0, 0, 2,
17, 0, 0, 30, 0, 0, 14, 0, 0, 1,
19, 0, 0, 0, 0, 0, 0, 0, 0, 3,
21, 0, 0, 31, 0, 0, 15, 0, 0, 5,
25, 0, 27, 0, 0, 0, 0, 11, 0, 9,
23, 0, 0, 32, 0, 0, 16, 0, 0, 7)

Here, position "1" is occupied by piece " 22" (blue chariot 1); position "2" is unoccupied; so is position "3"; position "4" is occupied by piece " 28" (blue soldier 1), etc. The board is immediately updated by the function **update-board** after any changes on the board.

The Objective Analysis (The Colour on the Situation Map)
The situation analysis is supported in the chess domain by the **colour** predicate. A colour is shown on all the 90 positions as an indication of its status in one of the following four colours:

white (neutral, a position where both sides can not attack);
blue (a position where blue pieces could occupy);
red (a position where red pieces could occupy); and
yellow (a position where both sides could occupy).

Understandably, it has the same set of 90 arguments as the **board** predicate, however, the value of each argument is not an integer but a tuple of "Colour" and "Attacker" as shown in the following:

colour((Colour, Attacker), ...)

In this predicate, the "Colour" could be one of **white**, **blue**, **red**, or **yellow**. Each colour has a related "Attacker" which is identified with a piece ID and its material-value. Attacker could be an empty list if the colour were white, a list if the colour were blue or red, or two lists if the colour were yellow. This **colour** predicate is supported by the function **get-colour** in conjunction with the **board** predicate to generate the interpretation of the situation on the chess board. In our implementation, the assessment from the tactical agent is in a form of a particular piece associated with its material strength.

The Subjective Analysis (The State)
Finally, given the pieces on the chess board and the attached colours, the subjective analysis from the **red** or the **blue** prospective assess the current situation of every piece on the chess board, by using the predicate **state** with **32** arguments to study the status and the potential value associated with its next possible move.

state((State, Value), ...)

In this predicate, the "State" has one of the following status: **risky**, **neutral**, **safe**, or **rewarding** projected from either **red** or **blue** prospective. As far as the **red** player is concerned, the risky position means that a red piece is at a blue position or at a yellow position with little protection; the neutral position means that a red piece is at a white position; the safe position means that a red piece is at a red position or a yellow position with sufficient protection; and the rewarding position means that a blue piece is at a red position or a yellow position with little protection. The reverse is true for the **blue** player. In here, the attached "Value" is the possible gain or loss in material value if the evaluated moves actually take place.

The **state** predicate is supported by a **get-state** function to compare the offensive and defensive strength concerning a specific piece on the board. Therefore, the associated value for a neutral and safe state is simply zero, while the value of rewarding or risky state is the maximum possible gains (rewarding) or the minimum losses (risky) in the event of capture or exchange pieces. This process of subjective analysis may be summarised as:

Risk: (from the red player's prospective)
if there were a red_horse_1 at a "yellow" position, where,
the blue attackers were [(blue_soldier_2, 20), (blue_horse_1, 270)], and
the red attacker were [(red_cannon_1, 285)],
then the state would be **risky** with losses of **270** (the material value of horse),
risk the blue could capture the red_horse_1 with its blue_soldier_2,
or losing both red horse and cannon in exchange for blue_soldier_2,
(value: -270 + 20 - 285 = -535).

Reward: (from the red player's prospective)
if there were a blue_horse_1 at a "yellow" position, where,
the blue attackers were [(blue_chariot_1, 600)],
the red attackers were [(red_horse_1, 270), (red_cannon_1, 285)],
then the state would be **rewarding** with gains of **270** (the value of horse).
reward the red could capture the blue_horse_1 with its red_horse_1,
or taking both blue horse and chariot in exchange for red_horse_1,
(value: 270 - 270 + 600 = 600).

5.4.4.2 The Strategic Planning

Within the planning agent, the embedded strategic agent is responsible for formulating a plan to fulfil the goal of the game. It constantly checks the balance of strength between both sides as the basis for strategic decision, if the attacking side has at lease two major offensive pieces (i.e. horse, cannon or chariot), the Moltke's "outer line strategy" leading to encirclement with the "pin and strike" tactic should be considered, provided that the number of attacking positions match up with the number of attacking pieces. The pinning here is an attempt to constrain the mobility of the target, while the striking is an final and fatal assault to capture the target. The decomposition of the " outer line strategy" into a "pin and strike" tactical formation is summarised as follows:

1) To identify the possible offensive pieces; {Precondition}
2) To identify the target; {Striking position}
3) To identify the attacking area; {Pinning + Striking positions}
4) To identify a formation; and {Co-operative plan}
5) To identify all the possible variations of that formation. {Paths Consolidation}

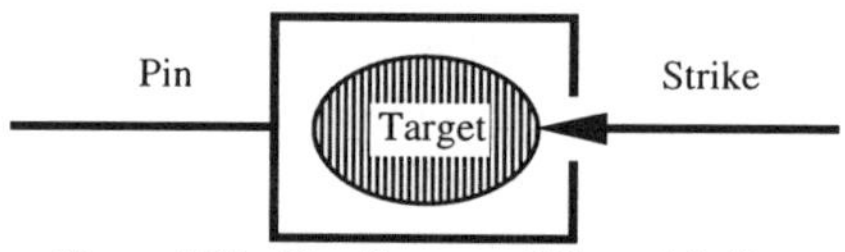

Figure 5.29. The Concept of Pin and Strike

The pre-condition for strategic planning is the confirmation of material resources available for the formation, and by identifying the target and all its next legal moves, an attacking area could be defined. Tactically, the positions where checkmate could be launched at the current target position is known as the striking positions; and the positions where pieces could occupy so as to hold up the movement of the target are known as the pinning positions. Hence, given their current positions of all attacking pieces and the pinning and striking positions, where these pieces could be manoeuvred into (desired situation), a variation of formations could be formulated when the sub-plans of pinning are merged with the sub-plan of striking.

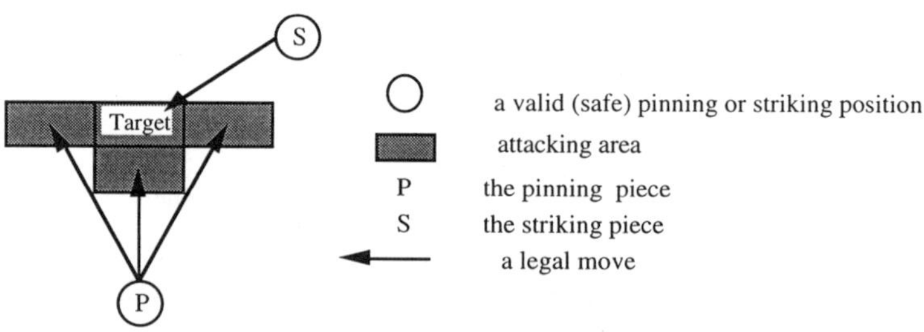

Figure 5.30. The Formation of the Pinning and Striking Positions

In Figure 5.30, a valid pinning or striking position is a "safe" position where an offensive piece can launch its assault into the attacking area, and a strategic plan is formulated when pinning and striking sub-plans could co-exists and be merged into one desired formation. In our implementation, there are three "pin and strike" formations installed in the knowledge base:

1) The Double Cannons Formation;
2) The Horse Screen Formation; and
3) The General Attacking Formation.

Double-Cannon Formation as indicated earlier in the heuristic agent that double cannons could be formulated as a desired situation in the planning agent. This involves two cannons in alignment in a single file or single rank targeting the general. The first cannon is used as a screen for the second one. Any attempt to place a piece between the target and the first cannon could easily be taken out by the second cannon using the first cannon as the screen. Figure 5.31 shows an end-game situation where double cannons are launched as part of the "pin and strike" formation.

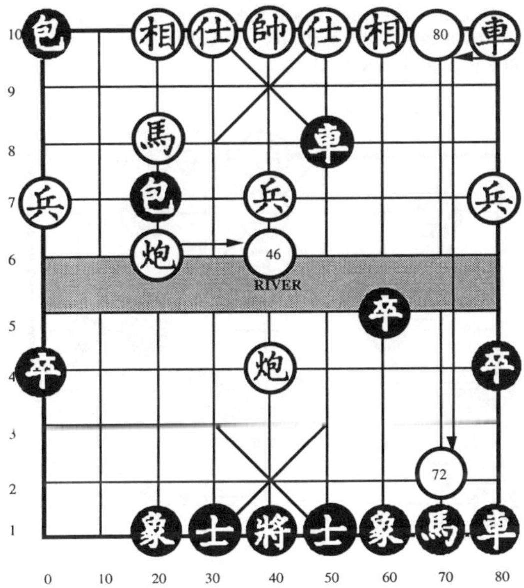

Figure 5.31. The Double-Cannon Formation

In this methodology, the embedded strategic agent will attempt to identify the target and all its legal moves underpinned by an appropriate strategy. In the above example, the general at position 41 is targeted as the striking position and its only legal move at position 42 will become the pinning position, and collectively, an attacking formation

[(9, 72), (11, 46)] could be brought together as shown in Figure 5.31, with its reasoning process highlighted in the simulation printout.

------------ Computer enters Planning Reasoning (Planning Agent) ------------
*** Strategic Agent ***
Offensive pieces:[8,9,10,11] {8:red horse1; 9:red chariot2; 10:red cannon1; 11: red cannon2}
Looking for possible targets.......
Target is opponent general...... {Checkmate}
The targeting positions: [41, 42] {As shown in Figure 5.31}
Formation: Double-Cannon Formation........ {Special pin and strike}
The possible offensive formations: [[(9, 72), (10, 46)]]
Number of formations : 1 {One attack formations}

Horse Screen Formation involves the use of a horse both for pinning down the movement of the target (general) and for serving as the screen for the cannon to checkmate. One special feature of the Horse Screen formation is the potential of the horse to cover two attacking positions at once, as shown in Figure 5.32. The dotted lines trace the paths of the two red pieces from their respective current positions to their desired positions, while the solid lines mark the paths of the two blue horses tracing from their current positions to attacking positions. In other words, both sides in the set-up in Figure 5.32 have plans to check each other.

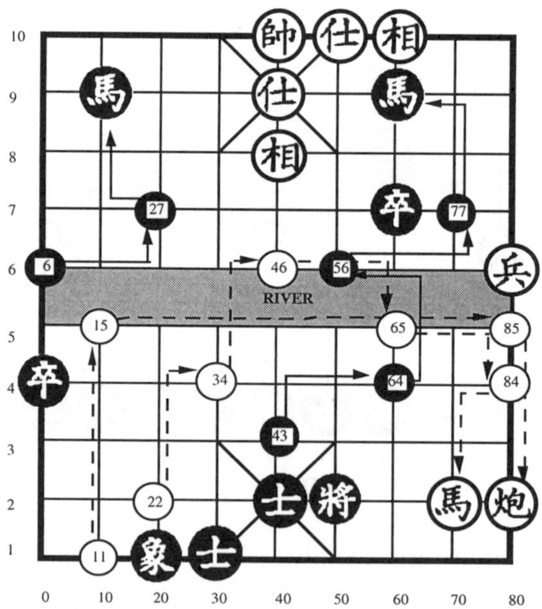

Figure 5.32. The Horse Screen Formation

------------ Computer enters Planning Reasoning (Planning Agent) ------------
*** Strategic Agent ***
Offensive pieces: [8, 10] {8: red horse 1; 10: red cannon 1}
Looking for possible targets.......
Target is opponent general...... {Checkmate}
The targeting positions: [52, 53, 51] {As shown in Figure 5.32}
Formation: Horse_screen formation .... {Special formation}
The possible offensive formations: [[(8, 72), (10, 82)]]
Number of formations : 1 {One attack formations}

General Attacking Formation is triggered when neither Double-Cannon nor Horse Screen Formation is able to produce a plan. In this case, there is no suggestion of which piece should be used in the formation rather than to identify the target and the attacking area before finding offensive pieces to cover those positions as shown in Figure 5.32. Given the attacking positions [40, 50], the opponent (blue player) will instruct each blue horse to study the feasibility of attacking these positions, as indicated in the messages from the simulation. Obviously, there are a number of overlapping between the pinning and striking positions, which have to be ultimately consolidated into a single formation. In this case, four attacking formations are possible.

------------ Opponent enters Situation Analysis ------------
------------ Opponent enters Planning Reasoning (Planning Agent) ------------
*** Strategic Agent ***
Offensive pieces: [24, 25] {24: blue horse 1; 25: blue horse 2}
Looking for possible targets.......
Target is opponent general...... {Checkmate}
The targeting positions:[40, 50] {As shown in Figure 5.32}
Formation: General attacking formation .... {Normal pin and strike}

Offensive piece: 24,
The valid attacking positions:
[(24, 19, 1, [40], [50]), (24, 28, 1, [40], [50]),
(24, 29, 1, [50], [40]), (24, 69, 1, [50], [40])]
{ Attacking position: [(Piece ID, Desired position, The number of targeting positions, [The targeting positions], [Outstanding positions])] }
Offensive piece: 25,
The valid attacking positions:
[(25, 19, 1, [40], [50]), (25, 28, 1, [40], [50]),
(25, 29, 1, [50], [40]), (25, 69, 1, [50], [40])]

The possible offensive formations:
[[(25, 19), (24, 69)], [(25, 28), (24, 69)],
[(24, 28), (25, 69)], [(24, 19), (25, 69)]]
{Offensive formation: [[(Piece ID, Pinning position), (Piece ID, Striking position)]] }

Number of formations: 4 {Four attack formations}

Finally, with the attack formation formulated, the strategic agent will issue the pinning and striking positions to all tactical agents concerned to search for an appropriate path that joint their current positions to each desired position under the constraint of the environment.

5.4.4.3 The Tactical Planning

Working concurrently and independently, the embedded tactical agents connected with the formation will start from their present positions, searching forward one state at a time until they have reached the desired positions. In here, the movement of each piece is governed by its legal moves generated from the knowledge-base, and the intermediate states on its path are determined by the environment. In other words, only safe positions on the board can be considered as the intermediate states. The goal of each sub-plan is to find the shortest and safest path that connects its current position to the desired position specified in the attacking formation, as illustrated in the following algorithm:

1. Conducting subjective analysis to establish safe positions on the board,
2. Making the current position of an offensive piece as the root of the search tree,
3. **while** the current position is not the desired position **do**
    begin
      Generating all legal moves in the safe area as the children of the current tree,
    end
4 **If** the current position = the desired position
    then the path from the root to the position is the solution path,
    else there is no path available.

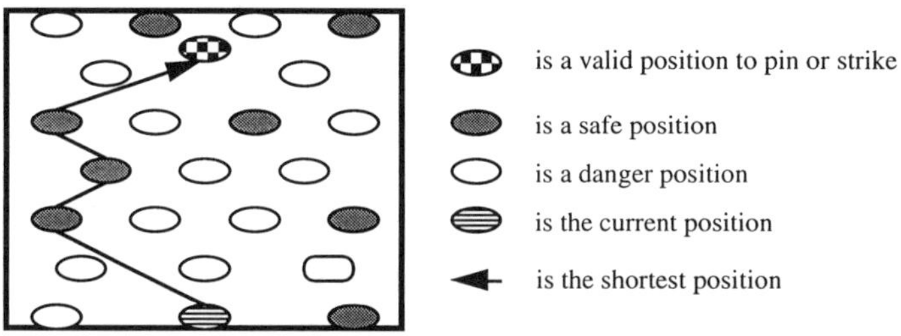

Figure 5.33. Tactical Path Constructed with Constrained Search

As determined by the strategic plan, all paths here which belong to the same formation are included in one plan. The order of execution is the pinning path(s) before the striking path. However, the formation would be abandoned if any of its related path has been proved to be impossible. Therefore, at the end of tactical planning, the number of fully connected formations ready for selection is either equal or smaller than the partial strategic plans issued before tactical planning, given the fact that only the shortest path would be recommended for consideration. Using the Horse Screen Formation as shown in Figure 5.32, the result of issuing the possible offensive formations: [[(8, 72), (10, 82)]] for tactical planning is shown in the following.

*** Tactical Agent ***

The possible offensive plans:
  [[(8, [22, 34, 46, 65, 84, 72]), (10, [11, 15, 85, 82])]]
Number of plans: 1 {One possible strategic plan}

At the end of the planning stage, only one plan is feasible, which moves the red horse (ID: 8) from position 22 to the pinning position at 72, and the red cannon (ID: 10) from position 11 to the striking position at 82, as summarised in the strategic plan.

Strategic plan: pinning with (8, [22, 34, 46, 65, 84, 72]),
striking with (10, [11, 15, 85, 82]), and
the sequence of control is first pin and last strike.

On the other hand, the blue player with four possible offensive formations has returned with four strategic plans, however, only one will be selected as the operational plan.

```
*** Tactical agent ***

The possible offensive plans:
    [[ (25, [43, 35, 27, 19] ), (24, [6, 25, 44, 65, 57, 69] )],   {8 moves to checkmate}
     [(25, [43, 35, 16, 28 ), (24, [6, 25, 44, 65, 57, 69] )],     {8 moves to checkmate}
     [(24, [6, 25, 44, 36, 28] ), (25, [43, 64, 56, 77, 69] )],    {8 moves to checkmate}
     [(24, [6, 27, 19] ), (25, [43, 64, 56, 77, 69] )] ]           {6 moves to checkmate}
Number of plans: 4                                          {Four possible strategic plans}

------------ Opponent enters Decision-Making (Plan Selection) ------------
Evaluating ......
The best Plan :
    [ (24, [6, 27, 19] ), (25, [43, 64, 56, 77, 69] )]             {6 moves to checkmate}

The stand-by plans:
    [ [(25, [43, 35, 27, 19] ), (24, [6, 25, 44, 65, 57, 69] )],   {8 moves to checkmate}
      [(25, [43, 35, 16, 28] ), (24, [6, 25, 44, 65, 57, 69] )],   {8 moves to checkmate}
      [(24, [6, 25, 44, 36, 28] ), (25, [43, 64, 56, 77, 69] )]]   {8 moves to checkmate}

Strategic plan: pinning with (24, [6, 27, 19] ),
                striking with (25, [43, 64, 56, 77, 69] ), and
                the sequence of control is first pin and last strike.
```

5.4.4.4 The Plan Selection

In planning, the strategic plan is a chain of moves designed to reach the desired situation with a maximum reward of 6000 points. However, in the context of uncertainty rising from opponent's counter-move, the degree of uncertainty is multiplied by the length of the solution path, and therefore, the value rewarded is decreased by a factor of two for any additional state in the solution path. In other words, a plan with 3 moves (2 additional states) to checkmate should have an assessment value of 1500 points ($6000 / (2^2) = 1500$) taking into account of time and uncertainty involved in realising the plan. In here, the operational plan is selected on the basis of its length as shown in the previous example of selecting the plan with six moves as the operational plan, which is the shortest and safest solution path.

5.4.4.5 The Command and Control (C^2)

In charge of steering the operational plan through the dynamic environment, the Command and Control is also responsible for verifying all the conditions and constraints attached on the operational plan before activating a move accordingly. The verification procedure involves asking the following questions:

1) Does the target (general) remain in the plan? {Re-planning}
2) Does the desired position in current path remain safe and possible? {Stand-by plan}
3) Is the next intermediate state in current path safe and possible? {Detour/buffer}

In the domain of Chinese chess, the uncertainty is arising from the opponent's counter moves. If this causes one of the three questions above to return with a negative answer, then C^2 would swing into action by activating an appropriate remedy to rectify the problem accordingly.

1) An intermediate state within the current path has been blocked:
   In this situation, detour or buffering could be brought in to rectify the situation. With detour, the original formation of the strategic plan remained intact, and C^2 would only involves in "repairing" the current path by searching for alternative way to get around the blockage. The tactical agent(s) will now draw a new path from its current position to its desired destination. The same selection criteria applies in deciding on the new path and the plan with shortest path will be chosen. Alternatively, the operational sub-plan could be buffered, with control temporally transfer to active other sub-plan in the same formation.

2) The desired position in the current solution path has become impossible:
   This situation resorts to stand-by plans with similar objectives but possibly incompatible resources. Failure to equip with such an alternative would certainly means re-planning from the start all over again.

3) The target (general) has moved from the original targeting position.
   All the previous plans would be invalid if the target no longer at its original position. This is, by far, the worst situation where C^2 could find itself sending a failure report to the planning manager, asking for a new plan with a different targeting position.

The Horse Screen Formation in Figure 5.32 involves a detour to repair its plan, although an unsuccessful buffering was attempted at the first instance. Following its strategic plan of [(8, [22, 34, 46, 65, 84, 72]), (10, [11, 15, 85, 82])], the computer playing red makes its first move of **H (horse), 22 -> 34** (Figure 5.34). The opponent (blue) responds with moving **h(horse), 6 -> 27** in according to its plan: [(24, [6, 27, 19]), (25, [43, 64, 56, 77, 69])], thus blocking the computer plan to move the red horse 1 from position 34 -> 46 and forcing its command and control to re-examine its operational plan (as in Figure 5.35).

The detour involves moving red horse 1 (ID: 8) from its current position at 34 to the desired position at 72 without passing through position 46. This has resulted in a revised plan of [(8, [34, 13, 32, 44, 63, 84, 72]), (10, [11, 15, 85, 82])] as shown in Figure 5.36. The cost of this modification is the revised plan has been lengthened by one extra state.

Move: 1 Computer moves: H (horse), 22 -> 34
Red: [[(8, [34,46,65,84,72]), (10, [11,15,85,82])]
Blue: none

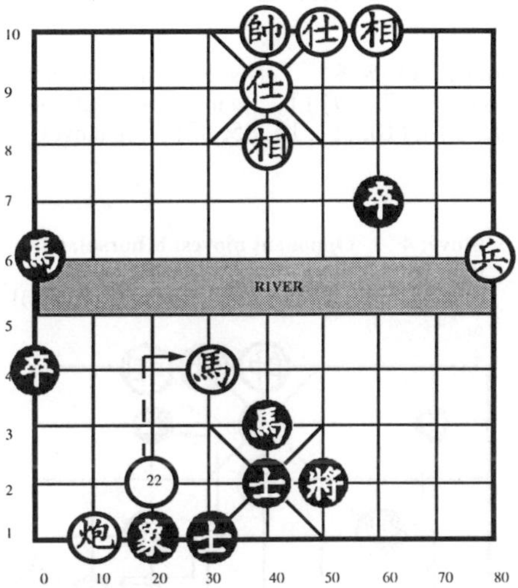

Figure 5.34. Red Horse moves 22 -> 34

Move: 2 Opponent moves: h(horse), 6 -> 27
Blue: [(24, [27,19]), (25, [43,64,56,77,69])]
Red: [[(8, [34,46,65,84,72]), (10, [11,15,85,82])]

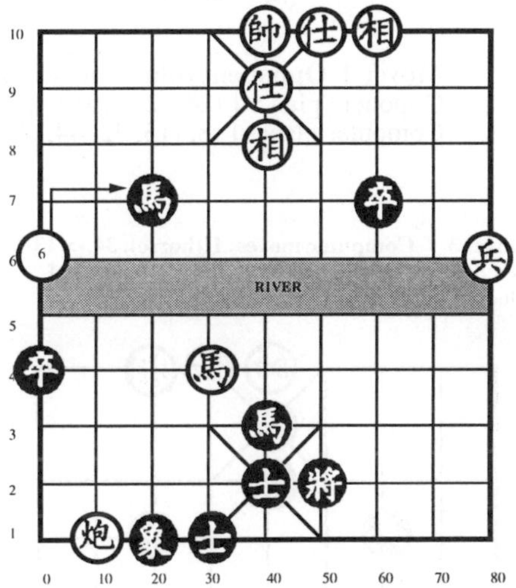

Figure 5.35. Blue Horse moves 6 -> 27

------------ Computer enters C2 Stage for Plan Execution ------------
The current plan can not be executed ...... {(8, [34, 46, 65, 84, 72])}
Control temporarily pass to sub-plan: (10, [11, 15, 85, 82]) {but buffering is impossible}
The best alternative amongst the stand-by plans: [ ] {Including stand-by formations}

Looking for alternatives to the current plan.... {Including modifying current formation}
{Using [(8, 72), (10, 82] as the goal positions, and [(8, 34), (10, 11)] as the current positions}

The best alternative to the current plan: {Detour}
[(8, [34, 13, 32, 44, 63, 84, 72]), (10, [11, 15, 85, 82])] {9 moves to checkmate}

The best plan: [(8, [34, 13, 32, 44, 63, 84, 72]), (10, [11, 15, 85, 82])]
The stand-by plan: [ ]

Strategic plan: pinning with (8, [34, 13, 32, 44, 63, 84, 72]),
striking with (10, [11, 15, 85, 82]), and
the sequence of control is first pin and last strike. {As in Figure 5.36}

However, this in turn has denied blue horse 1 (ID:24) from moving into position 19, and force it to modify its operational plan. Again buffering is first attempted, and prove to be possible under the circumstances.

------------ Opponent enters C2 Stage for Plan Execution ------------
The current plan can not be executed ...... {(24, [27, 19])}
Control temporarily pass to other sub-plan: (25, [43, 64, 76, 57, 69]) {Buffering}
{After the move, the control return back to the operational sub-plan: (24, [27, 19])}

Move: 4 Opponent (blue) moves: h(horse), 43 -> 64 {As shown in Figure 5.37}
Opponent plan : [(24, [27, 19]), (25, [64, 76, 57, 69])] {4 moves to checkmate}
Computer plan: [(8, [13, 32, 44, 63, 84, 72]), (10, [11, 15, 85, 82])] {8 moves .. }

Move: 3 Computer moves: H(horse), 34 -> 13
Red: [(8,[13,32,44,63,84,72]),(10,[11,15,85,82])]
Blue: [(24, [27,19]), (25, [43,64,56,77,69])]

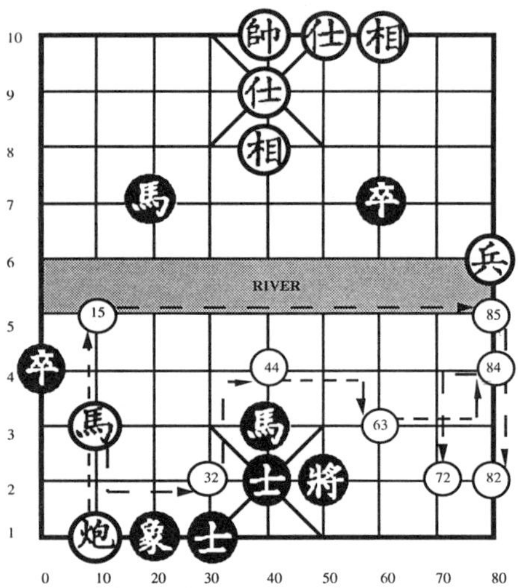

Figure 5.36. [(8: 22 -> 34), (24: 6 -> 27), (8: 34 -> 13)]

Move: 4 Opponent moves: h(horse), 43 -> 64
Blue: [(24, [27,19]), (25, [64,76,57,69])]
Red:[(8,[13,32,44,63,84,72]),(10,[11,15,85,82])]

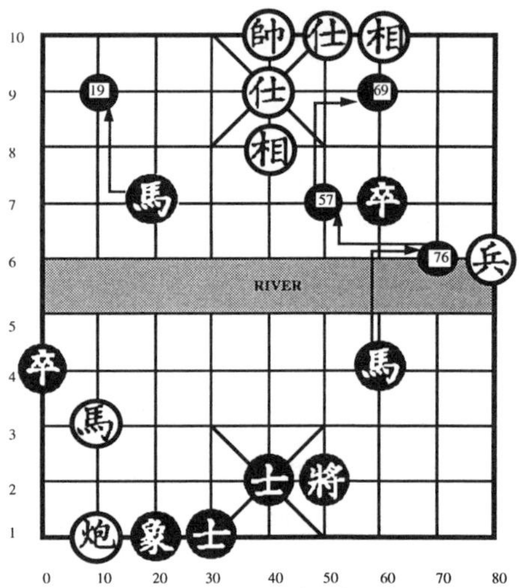

Figure 5.37. [(8: 34 -> 13), (25: 43 -> 64)]

If buffering were not possible, then stand-by plans would be examined as a possible replacement for the current plan. In here, there are three stand-by plans available for the blue player. Amongst them, [(25, [43, 35, 47, 28]), (24, [27, 46, 65, 57, 69])] has been found to be the most suitable one to substitute for the failed plan. However, the formation of this stand-by plan [(25, 28), (24, 69)] is some what difference from the current plan of [(24, 19), (25, 69)], and given that the current position of the blue horse 1 (ID: 24) is at 27 instead of position 6, as indicated in the original stand-by plan (24, [6, 25, 44, 65, 57, 69]), modification would have to be organised using [(25, 43), (24, 27)] as the current positions and [(25, 28), (24, 69)] as the desired goal positions to modify the stand-by plan into a new operational plan [(25, [43, 35, 47, 28]), (24, [27, 46, 65, 57, 69])]. This can be achieved within the command and control framework without the need to re-plan all over again.

------------ Opponent enters C2 Stage for Plan Modification ------------

The current plan can not be executed...... {(24, [27, 19])}

The best alternative amongst the stand-by plans : {Including stand-by formations}
[(25, [43, 35, 47, 28]), (24, [27, 46, 65, 57, 69])] {7 moves to checkmate}
{Using [(25, 28), (24, 69)] as the goal positions, and [(25, 43), (24, 27)] as the current positions}

Looking for alternatives to the current plan.... {Including modifying current formation}
{Using [(24, 19), (25, 69)] as the goal positions, and [(25, 43), (24, 27)] as the current positions}

The best alternative to the current plan: [ ]

The best plan: [(25, [43, 35, 47, 28]), (24, [27, 46, 65, 57, 69])] {7 moves checkmate}
The stand-by plan: [ ]

Strategic plan: pinning with (25, [43, 35, 47, 28]),
striking with (24, [27, 46, 65, 57, 69]), and
the sequence of control is first pin and last strike.

------------ Opponent enters C2 Stage for Plan Execution ------------

Move: 4 Opponent (blue) moves: h(horse), 43 -> 35 {As shown in Figure 5.38}
Opponent plan : [(25, [35, 47, 28]), (24, [27, 46, 65, 57, 69])] {6 moves ... }
Computer plan: [(8, [13, 32, 44, 63, 84, 72]), (10, [11, 15, 85, 82])] {8 moves ...}

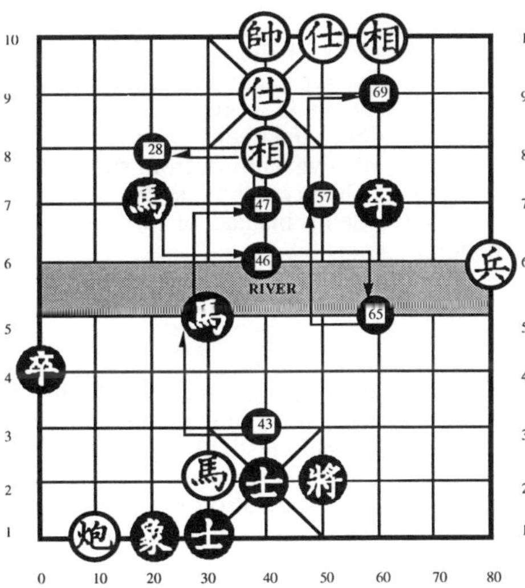

Figure 5.38. New Operational Plan for the Blue Player

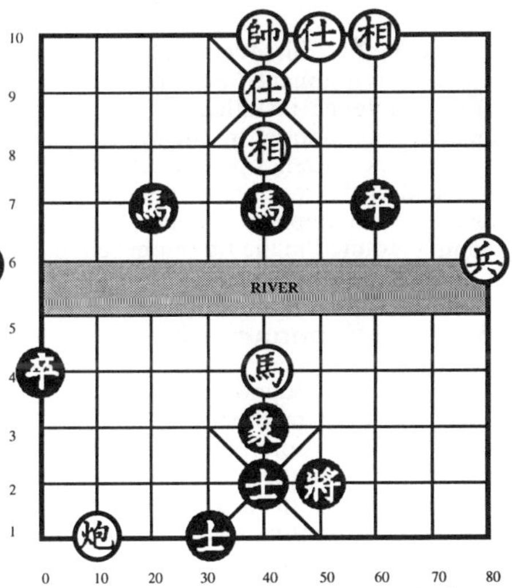

Figure 5.39. Reactive Plan for Elephant Defence

Once the revised plan has been made operational, the outcome of the game would be determined by the length of the opposing plans if they were allowed to run their course without interruption. In this case, blue player with a six move plan will emerge as the winner. However, as we follow through the development of the game, the blue general will be checkmated at move 7, an event unforeseen during plan construction stage and threatening the smooth execution of the current plan.

Move: 5 Computer (red) moves: H(horse), 13 -> 32 {As shown in Figure 5.38}
Computer plan: [(8, [32, 44, 63, 84, 72]), (10, [11, 15, 85, 82])] {7 moves .....}
Opponent plan : [(25, [35, 47, 28]), (24, [27, 46, 65, 57, 69])] {6 moves ... }

Move: 6 Opponent (blue) moves: h(horse), 35 -> 47
Opponent plan : [(25, [47, 28]), (24, [27, 46, 65, 57, 69])] {5 moves to checkmate}
Computer plan: [(8, [32, 44, 63, 84, 72]), (10, [11, 15, 85, 82])] {7 moves .....}

Move: 7 Computer (red) moves: H(horse), 32 -> 44
Computer plan: [(8, [44, 63, 84, 72]), (10, [11, 15, 85, 82])] {6 moves ... }
Opponent plan : [(25, [47, 28]), (24, [27, 46, 65, 57, 69])] {5 moves to checkmate}

------------ Opponent general is threatened ------------
------------ Opponent enters defensive mode ------------ {As shown in Figure 5.39}

Move: 8 Opponent (blue) moves: e(elephant), 21 -> 43 {Elephant defence}
Opponent plan : [(25, [47, 28]), (24, [27, 46, 65, 57, 69])] {5 moves to checkmate}
Computer plan: [(8, [44, 63, 84, 72]), (10, [11, 15, 85, 82])] {6 moves to checkmate}

Incidentally, this event helps to highlight the weakness of the cognitive model in dynamic environments and underline the strength of reactive planning in the form of elephant defence installed to protect the general as shown in Figure 5.39. This is triggered and imposed by the system master autocratically in the event of emergency to supersede the current operational plan. The operational plan will return from suspension at the end of the reactive action and proceed as before. Quality wise, the overall effect caused by the elephant defence is merely a one move delay instead of the costly re-planning required in the traditional cognitive model.

5.5 The Summary

The decision support mechanism for the Chinese chess program is based on the problem-solving methodology and architectural platform presented in the previous chapter, with the sole purpose of providing us with a suitable testbed to examine and evaluate the strength and weakness of our problem solving methodology. A six-case study will be set-up in the following chapter to look at the operation of co-operative planning, examining each remedy in the command and control in repairing the operational plan, and finally to assess the impact of a multi-stream reasoning when all four agents; namely pure recognition, search, heuristics and planning agents, are brought together on the multi-agent platform to provide the best possible advice in winning the chess game.

CHAPTER SIX

THE CASE STUDIES

Given the multi-agent decision support platform, could the proposed problem-solving methodology be able to cope with the complexity of the chess domain? Would it be capable of playing chess by planning towards its goal? How would the multi-streams reasoning agents enhance and compliment the planning agent in decision making? These are the issues we have set out to investigate with the help of a six-case study. However, in order to understand the functions of each agent outlined in 2a, 2b, 2c and 2d of the algorithm in the previous chapter, we would look at the planning agent in isolation and examine it in details in the first five cases of end-games, before integrating it with three other agents in the final case study, to assess the impact in guiding the chess playing at different stages of the game, which demonstrates a chess game from start to end.

The set-up of the first case is a simple end-game based on a "pin and strike" checkmate formation, which includes the merger of two sub-plans in a co-operative manner. The second case is set up in a more complex situation, where each side has a co-operative plan to checkmate. This case is designed to demonstrate how C^2 steer each co-operative plan through the game without awareness of their opponent's plan. The third case attempts to introduce certain flexibility to allow the temporary suspension of a sub-plan and transfer the control to activate other pending sub-plans on a move-by-move basis. The fourth case involves two sub-plans sharing one intermediate state in their paths of the same co-operative plan and highlights how constraints could be imposed to realise the strategic plan. The fifth case attempts to push the planning agent to its limit by undermining its "pin and strike" tactics by allowing the target to depart from its position. In contrast with all previous cases, where plans are formulated under the assumption that the target remained stationary throughout the execution of the operational plan. In this case, the "general" has been given a reactive plan to move whenever its mobility has been reduced, this in turn will trigger a re-planning process. In this situation, the re-routing or plan modification of the C^2 become irrelevant, and the system would have no alternative but to start plan deliberation all over again. The final case as the climax of our investigation will examine the impact and improvement when all the four agents are operating together in decision making to play the game from start to finish.

The simulation here is written in PARLOG (PARallel proLOG) language [Clark and Gregory 1986; Gregory 1987]. There are twenty one cases of cannon opening included in the knowledge base for the pure recognition agent, supported by another thirty four cases of patterns for the heuristic agent. Only one-ply search is used here for breadth-first search agent with evaluation based on the material and positional values. As far as the planning agent is concerned, only the "pin and strike" tactics are used in this implementation. Hence, this chess program is by no means a robust product designed for tournament, but simply a system for testing idea, and for verifying our claim that it is possible and feasible to provide decision support in a dynamic environment, such as playing chess by goal-oriented approach that is now a reality.

6.1 The Case Study One

This is a very simple end-game that involves only a few pieces in which the machine could generate a reasonably short plan in details to illustrate the reasoning process within the planning agent. In this case study, as shown in Figure 6.1, the end-game formation involves two red horses that are driven and advised by the decision support system (computer) to checkmate the blue (opponent) general by means of the "pin and strike" tactics. One horse is for pinning the target (blue general) down from moving to position 52, while the other horse for striking the general at position 51, assuming their own general remains in control of the centre file to stop its counterpart from moving into position 41.

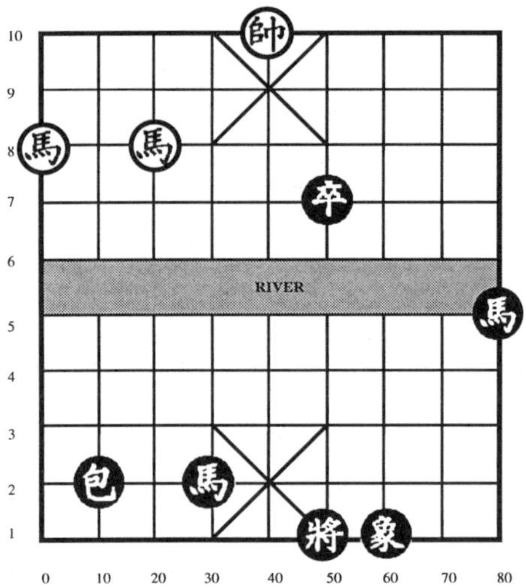

Figure 6.1. The Current Situation

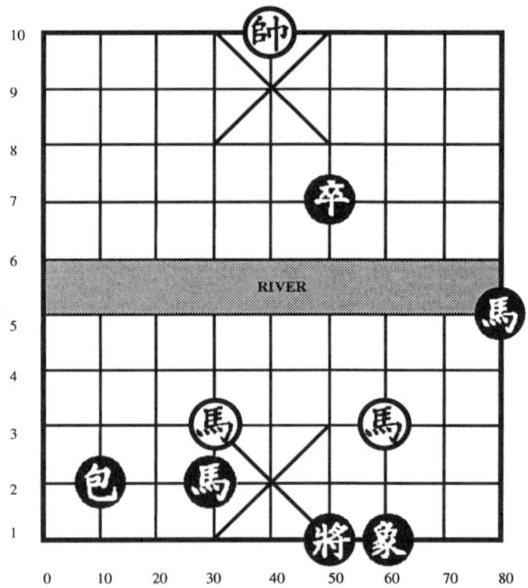

Figure 6.2. The Desired Offensive Formation

To locate the target (which is the blue general in this case), the strategic agent will identify the attacking pieces and the checkmate formation before instructing the tactical agents to study the feasibility of moving all relevant pieces from their current positions to their individual designated position. The pre-condition for any plan is that all required pieces must be presented on the chess board. In other words, the strategic plan is an indication of all relevant pieces in a formation on the chess board, which achieve the goal (i.e. checkmate). The tactical agents would then search through the game tree and report back to the planning manager (in the decision-making stage) that all the paths are available. Initially, each piece in the attacking/defensive formation is separately considered as a plan to move from its current position P_s to the desired position P_d, with command issued to a tactical agent to find the path between P_s and P_d. The co-operative plan is formed by merging all sub-plans from each piece collectively putting the formation in place as shown in Figure 6.2 .

Following the algorithm outlined in Chapter 5, the situation analysis has identified two possible attacking positions [51, 52] with the blue general as the target in a "pin and strike" formation, the two objectives are

1) to deny the blue general [piece ID: 17] the freedom to move into position 52; and
2) to checkmate the general at position 51.

Given the current positions of the two horses shown in Figure 6.1, there are many pin-and-strike positions [31, 32, 33, or 63] where the two horses could take. Each individual house may have a number of paths between their current positions and one of the possible desired positions [51, 52]. This has resulted in eight possible formations, however, only three formations are feasible with fully connected COAs (paths), when the pinning and striking sub-plans are merged into one viable co-operative plan (strategic plan).

```
------------ Computer enters Situation Analysis ------------
------------ Computer enters Planning Reasoning (Planning Agent) ------------
*** Strategic Agent ***
Offensive pieces: [8,9]                          {8: red horse 1; 9: red horse 2}
Looking for possible targets.......
Target is opponent general......                 {Checkmate}
The targeting positions:[51,52]                  {As shown in Figure 6.2}
Formation: General attacking formation.......    {Normal pin and strike}

Offensive piece: 8,                  Offensive piece: 9,
The valid attacking positions:       The valid attacking positions:
 [ (8, 31,1,[52],[51]),               [ (9, 31,1,[52],[51]),
   (8, 32,1,[51],[52]),                 (9, 32,1,[51],[52]),
   (8, 33,1,[52],[51]),                 (9, 33,1,[52],[51]),
   (8, 63,1,[51],[52]) ]                (9, 63,1,[51],[52]) ]
{Attacking position: [ (Piece ID, Desired position, The number of targeting positions,
                     [The targeting positions], [Outstanding positions] ) ]}

The possible offensive formations:
 [ [(9, 31), (8, 63)],
   [(9, 33), (8, 63)],
   [(8, 33), (9, 32)],
   [(8, 33), (9, 63)],
   [(9, 31), (8, 32)],
   [(9, 33), (8, 32)],
   [(8, 31), (9, 32)],
   [(8, 31), (9, 63)] ]
   {Offensive formation: [ [ (Piece ID, Pinning position), (Piece ID, Striking position) ] ] }

Number of formations : 8                          {Eight attacking formations}
 *** Tactical Agent ***
 The possible offensive plans:
  [ [ (9, [28, 7, 26,14, 33] ), (8, [8, 27, 15, 34, 55, 63] )],
    [ (8, [8, 27, 6, 25, 33] ), (9, [28, 36, 55, 63] )],
    [ (8, [8, 27, 15, 23, 31] ), (9, [28, 36, 55, 63] )] ]
    {Plan: [ (Pinning Piece ID, [Path] ) , (Striking Piece ID, [Path] ) ] }

 Number of plans: 3
```

------------ Computer enters Decision-Making (Plan Selection) ------------
With these three fully connected strategic plans, the planning manager will examine their quality and select the plan with the shortest path as the operational plan and the other two as the stand-by.

Evaluating ......
The best plan:
[(8, [8, 27, 6, 25, 33]), (9, [28, 36, 55, 63])] {7 moves to checkmate}

The stand-by plans:
[(8, [8, 27, 15, 23, 31]), (9, [28, 36, 55, 63])], {7 moves to checkmate}
[(9,[28, 7, 26, 14, 33]), (8, [8, 27, 15, 34, 55, 63])] {9 moves to checkmate}

Strategic plan: pinning with (8, [8, 27, 6, 25, 33]),
striking with (9, [28, 36, 55, 63]), and
the sequence of control is first pin and last strike.

------------ Computer enters C^2 Stage for Plan Execution ------------
Move: 1 Computer (red) moves: H(horse), 8 -> 27
Computer plan: [(8, [27, 6, 25, 33]), (9, [28, 36, 55, 63])] {6 moves to checkmate}
Opponent plan: none

Move: 2 Opponent (blue) moves: c(cannon), 12 -> 17
Opponent plan: none
Computer plan: [(8, [27, 6, 25, 33]), (9, [28, 36, 55, 63])] {Current plan is blocked}

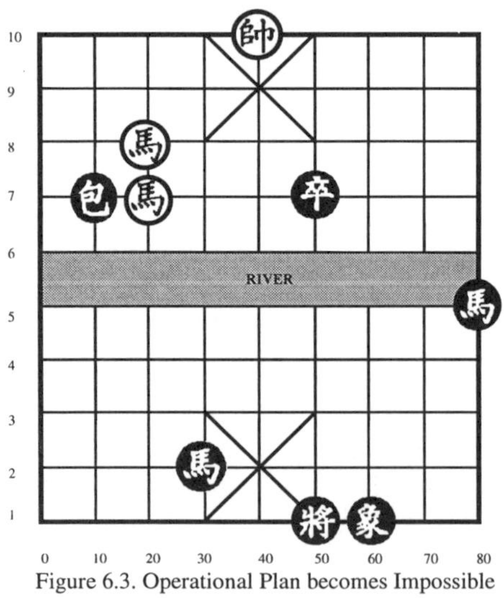

Figure 6.3. Operational Plan becomes Impossible

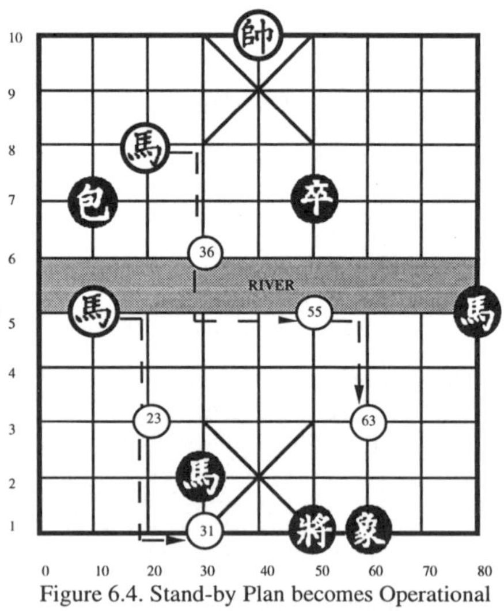

Figure 6.4. Stand-by Plan becomes Operational

In the case study here, the control mechanism is very simple. The objective of the first sub-plan must be achieved before the control is returned to C^2 for the activation of the second sub-plan. The role of C^2 role is to keep the plan as much intact as possible. Failure to do so would often mean remedying the current plan, or switching it to one of the stand-by plan. In here, backtracking to an earlier choice as suggested in O-Plan is not an option in a dynamic environment. This is highlighted in the case study by an event leading to plan modification, a counter-move from the opponent to take the blue cannon from position 12 to 17 has not only deny the red horse 1 from moving to position 06 as planed, but it has also made backtracking to the previous position (27 -> 08), an impossibility as shown in Figure 6.3.

The C^2 will now look for a stand-by plan [(8, [27, 15, 23, 31]), (9, [28, 36, 55, 63])], feasible to proceed from current situation and, at the same time, organise the tactical agent to produce a detour plan from position 27 -> 35 -> 14 -> 6 -> 25 -> 33 (5 moves + 3 moves for the striking sub-plan). Between them, the stand-by plan with 6 moves will be made operational, and the detour plan with 8 moves will then becomes the stand-by plan as shown in Figure 6.4.

------------ Computer enters C2 Stage for Plan Modification ------------
The current plan can not be executed...... {[(8, [27, 6, 25, 33]), (9, [28, 36, 55, 63])]}

The best alternative amongst the stand-by plans:
[(8, [27, 15, 23, 31]), (9, [28, 36, 55, 63])] {6 moves to checkmate}

Looking for an alternatives to the current plan.... {Finding a way to reach position 6}
The best alternative to the current plan:
[(8, [27, 35, 14, 6, 25, 33]), (9, [28, 36, 55, 63])] {8 moves to checkmate}

The best plan:
[(8, [27, 15, 23, 31]), (9, [28, 36, 55, 63])] {6 moves to checkmate}

The stand-by plan:
[[(8, [27, 35, 14, 6, 25, 33]), (9, [28, 36, 55, 63])]] {8 moves to checkmate}

The selection of "the best alternative amongst the stand-by plans" is applicable only to those "ready made" stand-by plans, which means choosing between the plan [(8, [8, 27, 15, 23, 31]), (9, [28, 36, 55, 63])] and the plan [(9, [28, 7, 26, 14, 33]), (8, [8, 27, 15, 34, 55, 63])] . The meaning of "looking for alternatives to the current plan" is to find a path to **detour** around the blockage back to the next state in the current solution path. In this case, the blockage at position 27, with the next position at 6, produces an alternative (solution path) of [27, 35, 14, 6]. However, detour plan often means lengthening the solution path, therefore, a substitute plan if available, is a better remedy for mending the operational plan.

Move: 3 Computer (red) moves: H(horse), 27 -> 15
Computer plan: [(8, [15, 23, 31]), (9, [28, 36, 55, 63])] {5 moves to checkmate}
Opponent plan : none

6.2 The Case Study Two

The co-operative planning in end-game is presented here as an example of the SOP modelled on the proposed problem solving methodology. At the same time, the idea of interleaving planning and execution (IPE) as part of the command and control protocol to modify operational plan or replace existing plan with suitable stand-by plan are also presented in the first case study. However, very little is said about the opponent. Has it a plan? If so, how would both plans interact with each other in battle? We would examine these issues in detail in the second case study, where each side has at least a plan to check the other. Let us start from the planning stage where the red enters.

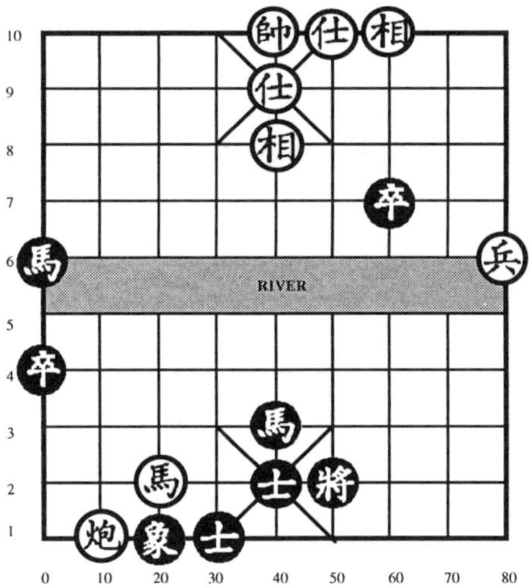

Figure 6.5. The Current Situation

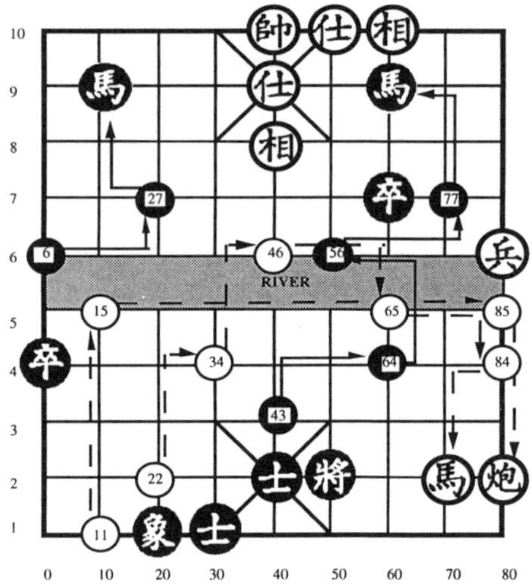

Figure 6.6. The Attack Formations from Both Sides

------------ Computer enters Planning Reasoning (Planning Agent) ------------

*** Strategic Agent ***

Offensive pieces: [8, 10] {8: red horse 1; 10: red cannon 1}

Looking for possible targets.......

Target is opponent general...... {Checkmate}

The targeting positions: [52, 53, 51] {As shown in Figure 6.6}

Formation: Horse_screen formation .... {Special formation}

The possible offensive formations:

[[(8, 72), (10, 82)]]

Number of formations : 1 {One offensive formation}

*** Tactical Agent ***

The possible offensive plans:

[[(8, [22, 34, 46, 65, 84, 72]), (10, [11, 15, 85, 82])]]

Number of plans: 1 {One possible strategic plan}

------------ Computer enters Decision-Making (Plan Selection) ------------
Evaluating ......
The best plan:
[(8, [22, 34, 46, 65, 84, 72]), (10, [11, 15, 85, 82])] {8 moves to checkmate}
The stand-by plans: [ ]

Strategic plan: pinning with (8, [22, 34, 46, 65, 84, 72]),
striking with (10, [11, 15, 85, 82]), and
the sequence of control is first pin and last strike. {As in Figure 6.6}

------------ Computer enters C^2 Stage for Plan Execution ------------
At the end of the planning stage, only one plan is feasible and therefore adopted as the operational plan to move the red horse (ID: 8) from position 22 to the pinning position at 72, and the red cannon (ID: 10) from position 11 to the striking position at 82.

Move: 1 Computer (red) moves: H(horse), 22 -> 34 {As shown in Figure 6.7}
Computer plan: [[(8, [34, 46, 65, 84, 72]), (10, [11, 15, 85, 82])] {7 moves .. }
Opponent plan: none

------------ Opponent enters Situation Analysis ------------
------------ Opponent enters Planning Reasoning (Planning Agent) ------------
*** Strategic Agent ***
Offensive pieces: [24, 25] {24: blue horse 1; 25: blue horse 2}
Looking for possible targets.......
Target is opponent general...... {Checkmate}
The targeting positions: [50, 40] {As shown in Figure 6.6}
Formation: General attacking formation .... {Normal pin and strike}

Offensive piece: 24,
The valid attacking positions:
[(24, 19, 1, [40], [50]),
(24, 28, 1, [40], [50]),
(24, 29, 1, [50], [40]),
(24, 69, 1, [50], [40])]

Offensive piece: 25,
The valid attacking positions:
[(25, 19, 1, [40], [50]),
(25, 28, 1, [40], [50]),
(25, 29, 1, [50], [40]),
(25, 69, 1, [50], [40])]

The possible offensive formations:
[[(25, 19), (24, 69)],
[(25, 28), (24, 69)],
[(24, 28), (25, 69)],
[(24, 19), (25, 69)]]
Number of formations: 4 {Four attack formations}

*** Tactical agent ***
The possible offensive plans:
[[(25, [43, 35, 27, 19]), (24, [6, 25, 44, 65, 57, 69])] ,
[(25, [43, 35, 16, 28), (24, [6, 25, 44, 65, 57, 69])] ,
[(24, [6, 25, 44, 36, 28]), (25, [43, 64, 56, 77, 69])] ,
[(24, [6, 27, 19]), (25, [43, 64, 56, 77, 69])]]
Number of plans: 4 {Four possible strategic plans}

------------ Opponent enters Decision-Making (Plan Selection) ------------
Evaluating ......

The best Plan :
[(24, [6, 27, 19]), (25, [43, 64, 56, 77, 69])] {6 moves to checkmate}

The stand-by plans:
[[(25, [43, 35, 27, 19]), (24, [6, 25, 44, 65, 57, 69])] , {8 moves to checkmate}
[(25, [43, 35, 16, 28]), (24, [6, 25, 44, 65, 57, 69])] , {8 moves to checkmate}
[(24, [6, 25, 44, 36, 28]), (25, [43, 64, 56, 77, 69])]] {8 moves to checkmate}

Strategic plan: pinning with (24, [6, 27, 19]),
striking with (25, [43, 64, 56, 77, 69]), and
the sequence of control is first pin and last strike. {As in Figure 6.6}

------------ Opponent enters C^2 Stage for Plan Execution ------------
Since none of the blue pieces is threatened by the red horse of (8: 22 -> 34), the blue operational plan is put into action by moving (24: 6 -> 27), thus blocking the red horse 1 from position 34 -> 46 and forcing its C^2 to re-examine its operational plan.

Move: 2 Opponent (blue) moves: h(horse), 6 -> 27 {As shown in Figure 6.8}
Opponent plan : [(24, [27, 19]), (25, [43, 64, 56, 77, 69])] {5 moves to checkmate}
Computer plan: [(8, [34,46,65,84,72]), (10, [11,15,85,82])] {Current plan blocked}

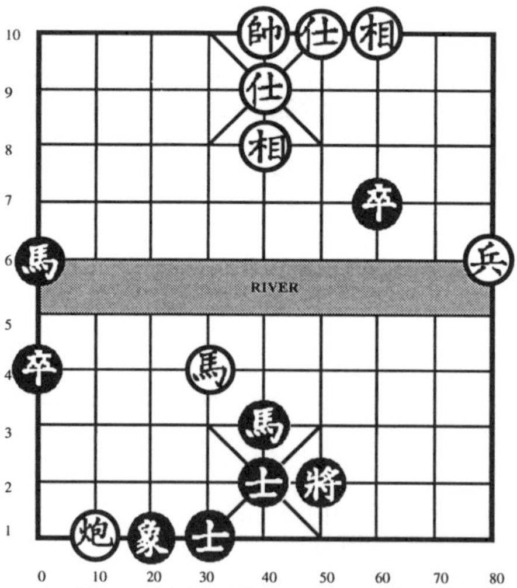

Figure 6.7. Red Horse moves 22 -> 34

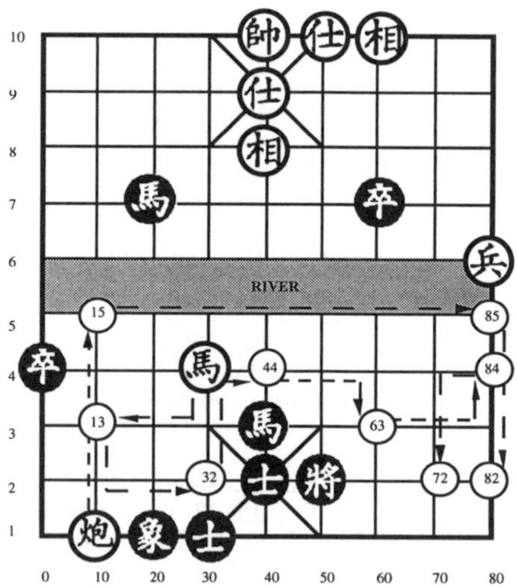

Figure 6.8. Blue Horse moves 6 -> 27

------------ Computer enters C2 Stage for Plan Modification ------------
The current plan can not be executed...... {(8, [34, 46, 65, 84, 72])}
The best alternative amongst the stand-by plans: [ ] {Including stand-by formations}

Looking for alternatives to the current plan.... {Including modifying current formation}
{Using [(8, 72), (10, 82)] as the goal positions, and [(8, 34), (10, 11)] as the current positions}

The best alternative to the current plan: {Detour}
[(8, [34, 13, 32, 44, 63, 84, 72]), (10, [11, 15, 85, 82])] {9 moves to checkmate}

The best plan: [(8, [34, 13, 32, 44, 63, 84, 72]), (10, [11, 15, 85, 82])]
The stand-by plan: [ ]

Strategic plan: pinning with (8, [34, 13, 32, 44, 63, 84, 72]),
striking with (10, [11, 15, 85, 82]), and
the sequence of control is first pin and last strike. {As in Figure 6.8}

Move: 3 Computer (red) moves: H(horse), 34 -> 13 {As shown in Figure 6.9}
Computer plan: [(8, [13, 32, 44, 63, 84, 72]), (10, [11, 15, 85, 82])] {8 moves ...}
Opponent plan : [(24, [27,19]), (25, [43,64,56,77, 69])] {Current plan impossible}

------------ Opponent enters C2 Stage for Plan Modification ------------
The current plan can not be executed...... {(24, [27, 19])}

The best alternative amongst the stand-by plans : {Including stand-by formations}
[(25, [43, 35, 47, 28]), (24, [27, 46, 65, 57, 69])] {7 moves to checkmate}
{Using [(25, 28), (24, 69)] as the goal positions, and [(25, 43), (24, 27)] as the current positions}

Looking for alternatives to the current plan.... {Including modifying current formation}
{Using [(24, 19), (25, 69)] as the goal positions, and [(25, 43), (24, 27)] as the current positions}

The best alternative to the current plan: [ ]

The best plan: [(25, [43,35,47,28]), (24, [27,46,65,57,69])] {7 moves to checkmate}

The stand-by plan: [ ]

Strategic plan: pinning with (25, [43, 35, 47, 28]),
striking with (24, [27, 46, 65, 57, 69]), and
the sequence of control is first pin and last strike. {As in Figure 6.9}

------------ Opponent enters C2 Stage for Plan Execution ------------
Move: 4 Opponent (blue) moves: h(horse), 43 -> 35 {As shown in Figure 6.10}
Opponent plan : [(25, [35,47,28]), (24, [27,46,65,57,69])] {6 moves to checkmate}
Computer plan: [(8, [13, 32, 44, 63, 84, 72]), (10, [11, 15, 85, 82])] {8 moves ...}

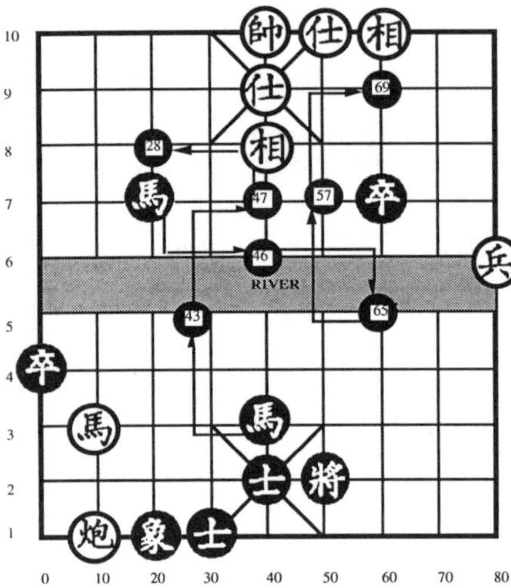

Figure 6.9. Red Horse moves 34 -> 13

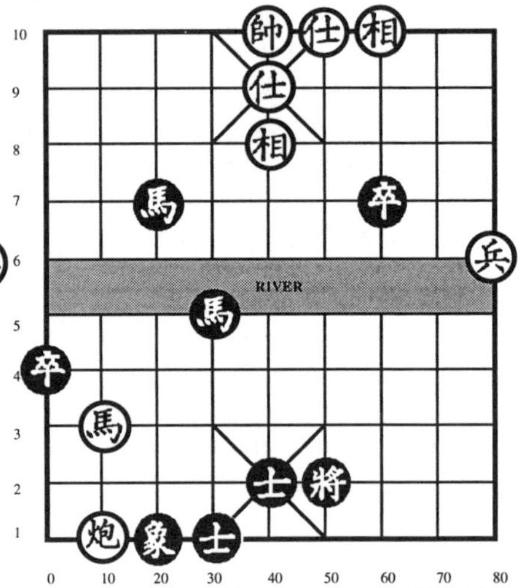

Figure 6.10. Blue Horse moves 43 -> 35

Move: 5 Computer (red) moves: H(horse), 13 -> 32 {As shown in Figure 6.11}
Computer plan: [(8, [32, 44, 63, 84, 72]), (10, [11, 15, 85, 82])] {7 moves....}
Opponent plan : [(25, [35, 47, 28]), (24, [27, 46, 65, 57, 69])] {6 moves...}

Move: 6 Opponent (blue) moves: h(horse), 35 -> 47 {As shown in Figure 6.12}
Opponent plan : [(25, [47, 28]), (24, [27, 46, 65, 57, 69])] {5 moves to checkmate}
Computer plan: [(8, [32, 44, 63, 84, 72]), (10, [11, 15, 85, 82])] {7 moves....}

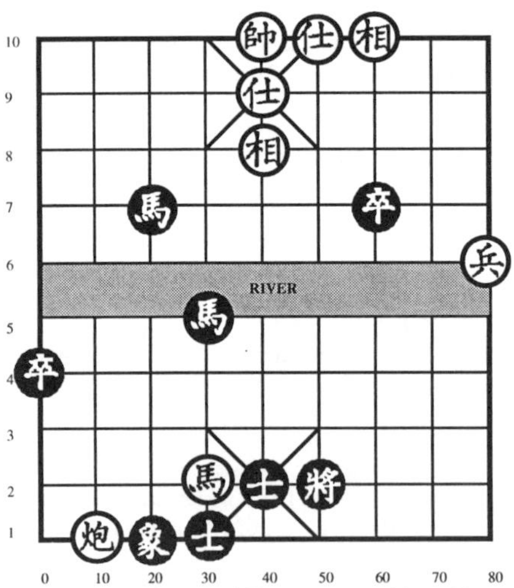

Figure 6.11. Red Horse moves 13 -> 32

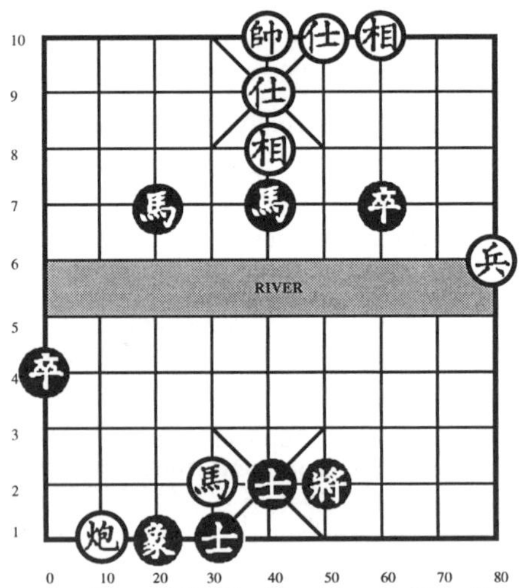

Figure 6.12. Blue Horse moves 35 -> 47

At this stage of the game, an interesting event has emerged when the red horse moves into position 44 and unintentionally creates a checkmate situation unforeseen during the plan construction stage. Although undetectable within the plan, it is picked-up by the tactical agent at the blackboard level, triggering an reactive plan in the form of an elephant defence to protect the general.

Move: 7 Computer (red) moves: H(horse), 32 -> 44 {As shown in Figure 6.13}
Computer plan: [(8, [44, 63, 84, 72]), (10, [11, 15, 85, 82])] {6 moves to checkmate}
Opponent plan : [(25, [47, 28]), (24, [27, 46, 65, 57, 69])] {5 moves to checkmate}

------------ Opponent general is threatened ------------
------------ Opponent enters defensive mode ------------

Move: 8 Opponent (blue) moves: e(elephant), 21 -> 43 {As shown in Figure 6.14}
Opponent plan :[(25, [47, 28]), (24, [27, 46, 65, 57, 69])] {5 moves to checkmate}
Computer plan: [(8, [44, 63, 84, 72]), (10, [11, 15, 85, 82])] {6 moves to checkmate}

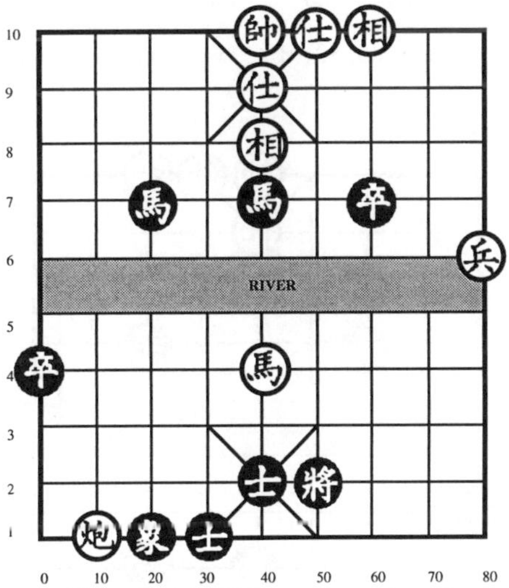

Figure 6.13. Red Horse moves 32 -> 44

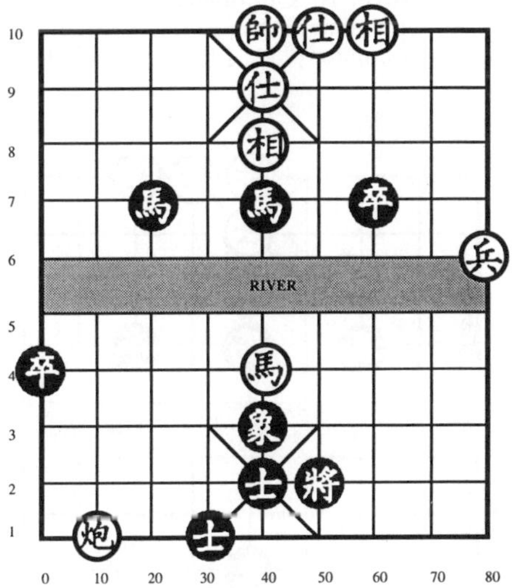

Figure 6.14. Blue Elephant moves 21 -> 43

This event helps underline the weakness in cognitive planning, and the strength of reactive routine in coping with uncertainty in the environment. We can therefore conclude that it is strategically advantageous to integrate both models at different stage of the planning cycle: cognitive model for plan generation and reactive model for plan execution. In other words, comprehensive planning enables plans to be evaluated before execution, and the provision of stand-by plans to cover the changes in the environment, whereas the reactive planing is installed to deal with the discrepancy between the internal cognitive model and the outside world.

Once the threat of checkmate has been removed, the control is returned to implement the operational plan. With the positioning of the blue horse at 28, the only legal move of the red general has now been blocked. What the blue has to do is to activate the striking sub-plan to check mate at position 69. Although in practice, the red general could move away from its current position when its legal move at position 40 is threatened. Such manoeuvring will seriously undermines the assumption of all the plans which targeted at the general in position 50, and resulted in re-planning to focus on new formation with the target now at a new position. This is the issue which we will address later in case study five, but here we are interested in studying how C^2, in the form of "detour" and "stand-by plans", repairs blocked plan in order to realise the goal it has been given.

Move: 9 Computer (red) moves: H(horse), 44 -> 63 {As shown in Figure 6.15}
Computer plan: [(8, [63, 84, 72]), (10, [11, 15, 85, 82])] {5 moves to checkmate}
Opponent plan : [(25, [47, 28]), (24, [27, 46, 65, 57, 69])] {5 moves to checkmate}

Move: 10 Opponent (blue) moves: h(horse), 47 -> 28 {Sub-plan 1 completed}
Opponent plan : [(24, [27, 46, 65, 57, 69])] {4 moves to checkmate}
Computer plan: [(8, [63, 84, 72]), (10, [11, 15, 85, 82])] {5 moves to checkmate}

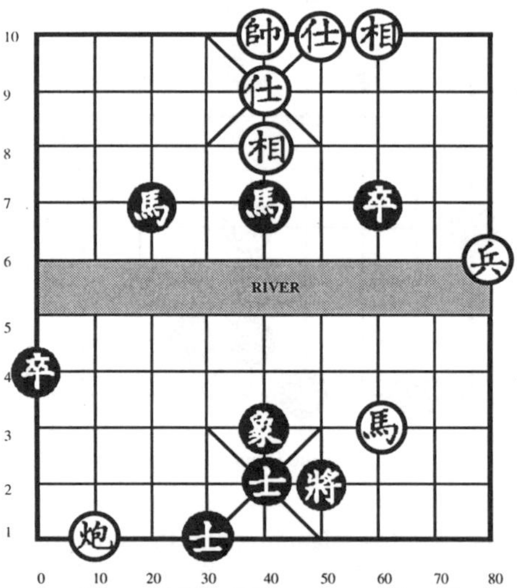

Figure 6.15. Red Horse moves 44 -> 63

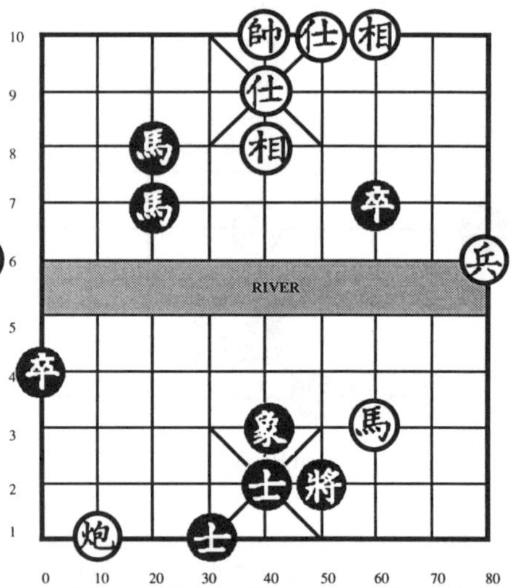

Figure 6.16. Blue Horse moves 47 -> 28

At this stage of the game shown in Figure 6.18, the red horse is now only one step away from completing its goal of pinning down the red general from escaping into position 51 and 53. The attacking potential of the horse in covering two positions [51,

53] here is unique, which enables three targeting positions in this "pin and strike" formation to be covered by only two attacking pieces i.e. a horse and a cannon. However, generally speaking, it takes longer for horse to manoeuvre into positions, and hence, longer solution paths are required. This should be balanced against the strength of cannon and chariot in getting into the desired positions within a shorter time. This is the tactical decision one would have to address in working out an attacking formation.

Move: 11 Computer (red) moves: H(horse), 63 -> 84 {As shown in Figure 6.17}
Computer plan: [(8, [84, 72]), (10, [11, 15, 85, 82])] {4 moves to checkmate}
Opponent plan : [(24, [27, 46, 65, 57, 69])] {4 moves to checkmate}

Move: 12 Opponent (blue) moves: h(horse), 27 -> 46 {As shown in Figure 6.18}
Opponent plan : [(24, [46, 65, 57, 69])] {3 moves to checkmate}
Computer plan: [(8, [84, 72]), (10, [11, 15, 85, 82])] {4 moves to checkmate}

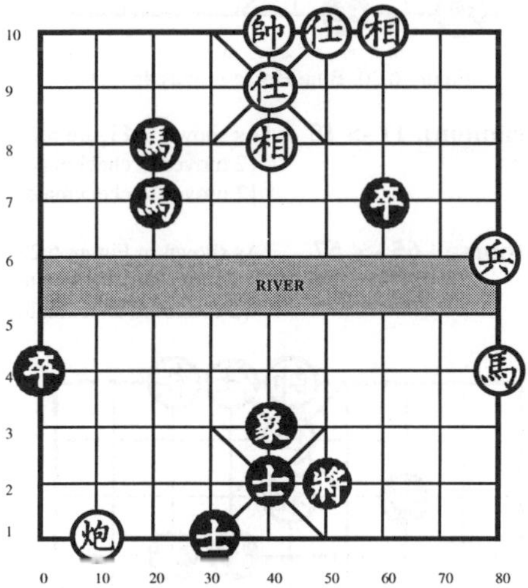

Figure 6.17. Red Horse moves 63 -> 84

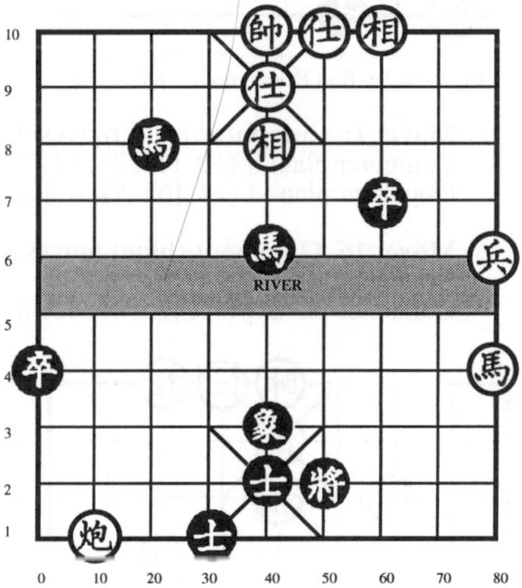

Figure 6.18. Blue Horse moves 27 -> 46

Move: 13 Computer (red) moves: H(horse), 84 -> 72 {Sub-plan 1 completed}
Computer plan: [(10, [11, 15, 85, 82])] {3 moves to checkmate}
Opponent plan : [(24, [46, 65, 57, 69])] {3 moves to checkmate}

Move: 14 Opponent (blue) moves: h(horse), 46 -> 65 {As shown in Figure 6.20}
Opponent plan : [(24, [65, 57, 69])] {2 moves to checkmate}
Computer plan: [(10, [11, 15, 85, 82])] {3 moves to checkmate}

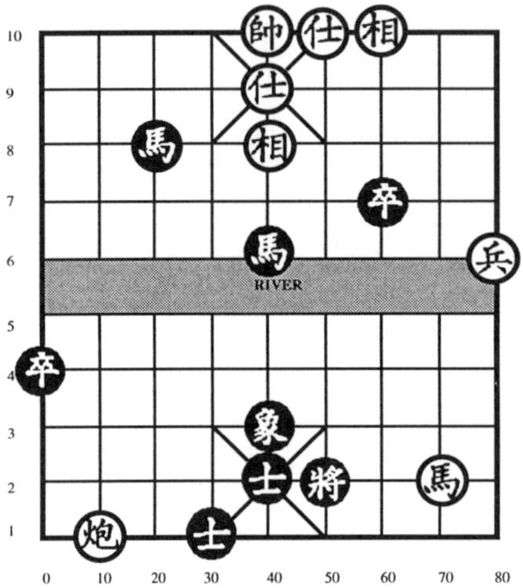

Figure 6.19. Red Horse moves 84 -> 72

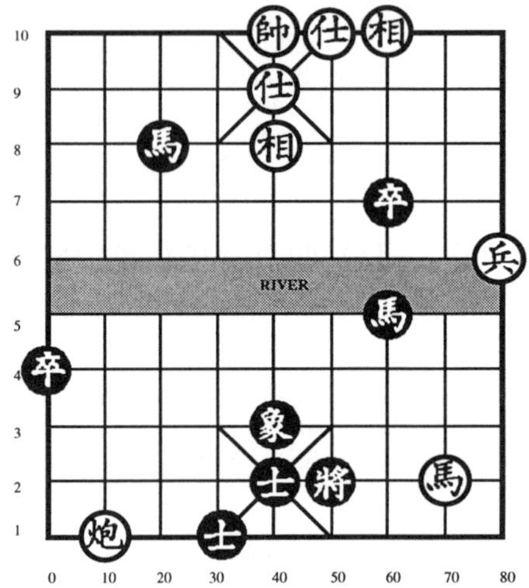

Figure 6.20. Blue Horse moves 46 -> 65

Move: 15 Computer (red) moves: C(cannon), 11 -> 15 {As shown in Figure 6.21}
Computer plan: [(10, [15, 85, 82])] {2 moves to checkmate}
Opponent plan : [(24, [65, 57, 69])] {2 moves to checkmate}

Move: 16 Opponent (blue) moves: h(horse), 65 -> 57 {As shown in Figure 6.22}
Opponent plan : [(24, [57, 69])] {1 moves to checkmate}
Computer plan: [(10, [15, 85, 82])] {2 moves to checkmate}

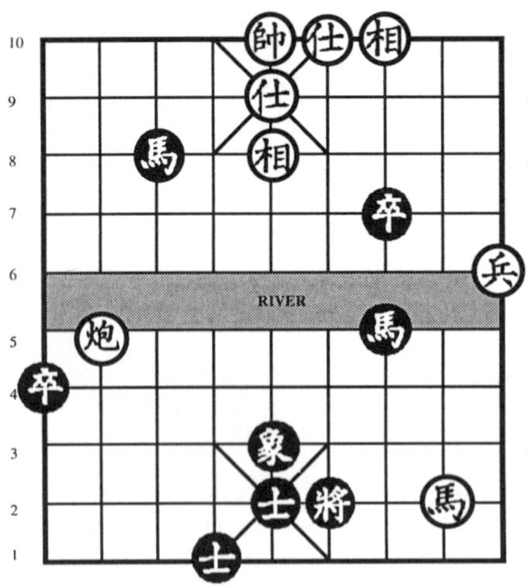

Figure 6.21. Red Cannon moves 11 -> 15

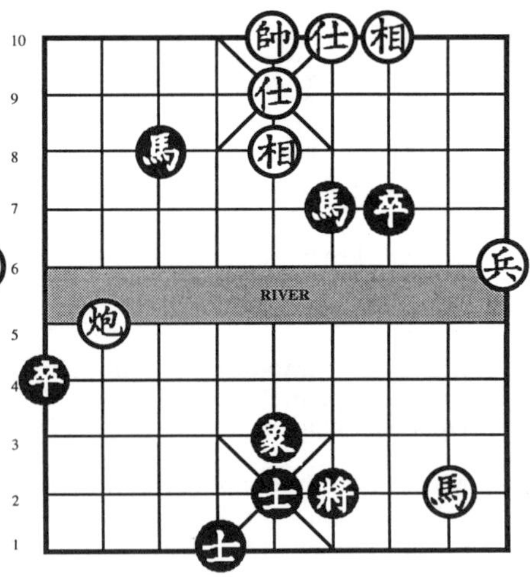

Figure 6.22. Blue Horse moves 65 -> 57

As shown is Figure 6.22, the blue horse is now at the brink to capture the red general, the target (the red general) is pinned down and can not move; the only reactive routine (elephant defence) is unable to protect the general, and the game is literally over. This illustrates the need for more defensive reactive routine together with other agents to detect the threat and protect the general. This issue will be addressed in case study six when the pure recognition, heuristic and exhaustive search agent are integrated together in a multi-agent platform.

------------ Computer enters Decision-Making (System Master) ------------

Evaluating ......

Recognition agent	nil	{Algorithm 2a}
Heuristic agent:	nil	{Algorithm 2b}
Planning agent:	nil	{Algorithm 2c}
Tactical agent:	move (24, 69, 50, 15,976)	{Algorithm 2d}
System master:	move (24, 69, 50, 15,976)	{Checkmate the red general at 50}

Move: 17 Computer (red) moves: C(cannon), 15 -> 85 {As shown in Figure 6.23}

Computer plan: [(10, [85, 82])]	{1 move to checkmate}
Opponent plan : [(24, [57, 69])]	{1 moves to checkmate}

Move: 18 Opponent (blue) moves: h(horse), 57 -> 69 {As shown in Figure 6.24}

Opponent plan : [GAME OVER: OPPONENT WINS]	{Checkmate}
Computer plan: [(10, [85, 82])]	{1 moves to checkmate}

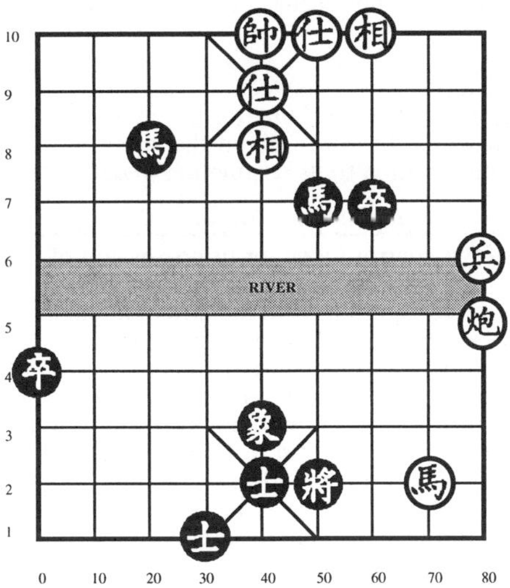

Figure 6.23. Red Cannon moves 15 -> 85

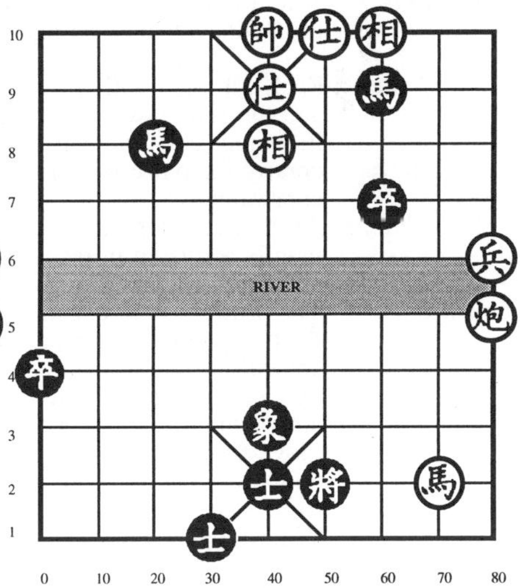

Figure 6.24. Blue Horse moves 57 -> 69

6.3 The Case Study Three

Co-operative planning in the first case study, and the re-routing and plan modification in the second case study are all based on very primitive control mechanism; each sub-plan within a strategic plan is given a desired position as the goal, and constraint is imposed on it to achieve the goal (pinning) before transferring the control back to the C^2 co-ordinator to execute other sub-plans (striking). This has resulted in unnecessary detour and plan modification whenever the operational plan becomes impossible. In an ever-changing world, temporary suspension of the operational sub-plan, while handing the control over to activate other sub-plan on a move-by-move basis, could often offer a more productive strategy. In the third case study, we would investigate the co-operation between sub-plans during the execution stage through local negotiation. The same end-game set-up will be used here to demonstrate the impact on the outcome, when constrains on sub-plans are relaxed sufficiently for control to be temporarily passed for activating COA in other sub-plan.

Following the standard operating procedure (SOP), the desire to win derives from the formulation of checkmate formations, in which a strategic plan with fully connected paths (COAs) will be selected and made operational to realise the goal. In the case of end-game presented above, the "pin and strike" formation consists of two sub-plans.

Strategic plan: pinning with (sub-plan 1),
striking with (sub-plan 2), and
the sequence of control is first pin and last strike.

Pre-condition: All required pieces in the selected formation must be present on the board, while paths between their current positions to the desired positions are feasible.

Constraints: Alteration of the target position must not occur without going through the SOP cycle all over again.

Tactical plans: Each sub-plan with a fully connected path between its current position and the final destination is presented as the COA for the realisation of its objective. Tactical agent which has been given the sub-plan will control the piece from its initial position to its destination under certain constraints.

Pre-condition: All tactical plans must be fully connected from start to end, and each plan is activated in receipt of the control token, or in possession of the control.

Constraints: The order of plan execution is pre-determined in the strategic plan. In the two previous cases, a very simple control mechanism is adopted: the control is passed from one sub-plan to another after the completion of operational sub-plan. In this case study, we will relax this constraints to allow temporary suspension of the current operational sub-plan on a move-by-move basis through local negotiation to allow control to be temporary passed to activate a move in other sub-plans, and the control to be returned to the current operational sub-plan at end of that move. With this relaxation, a pre-condition is inserted to safeguard the proper functioning of the tactical agent at the local level so that each sub-plan will not proceed to their final destination until other sub-plans with the higher priority have duly completed their paths.

Move: 1 Computer (red) moves: H(horse), 22 -> 34 {As shown in Figure 6.7}
Computer plan: [[(8, [34,46,65,84,72]), (10, [11,15,85,82])]{7 moves to checkmate}
Opponent plan: none

Move: 2 Opponent (blue) moves: h(horse), 6 -> 27 {As shown in Figure 6.8}
Opponent plan :[(24, [27,19]), (25, [43,64,76,57,69])] {5 moves to checkmate}
Computer plan: [(8, [34,46,65,84,72]), (10, [11,15,85,82])] {Current plan is blocked}

------------ Computer enters C2 Stage for Plan Execution ------------
The current plan can not be executed ...... {(8, [34, 46, 65, 84, 72])}
Control temporarily pass to other sub-plan: (10, [11, 15, 85, 82]), but not possible.
Move: 3 Computer (red) moves: H(horse), 34 -> 13 {As shown in Figure 6.25}
Computer plan: [(8, [13, 32, 44, 63, 84, 72]), (10, [11, 15, 85, 82])] {8 moves ...}
Opponent plan : [(24, [27, 19]), (25, [43, 64, 76, 57, 69])] {Current plan impossible}

------------ Opponent enters C2 Stage for Plan Execution ------------
The current plan can not be executed ...... {(24, [27, 19])}
Control temporarily pass to other sub-plan: (25, [43, 64, 76, 57, 69]) {Buffering}
Move: 4 Opponent (blue) moves: h(horse), 43 -> 64 {As shown in Figure 6.26}
Opponent plan : [(24, [27, 19]), (25, [64, 76, 57, 69])] {4 moves to checkmate}
Computer plan: [(8, [13, 32, 44, 63, 84, 72]), (10, [11, 15, 85, 82])] {8 moves ...}

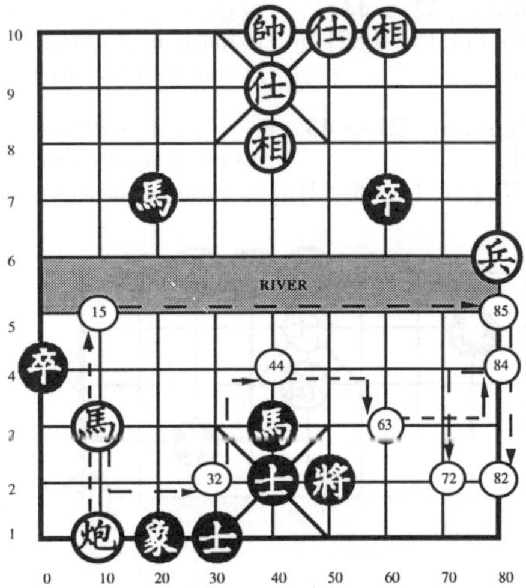

Figure 6.25. Red Horse moves 34 -> 13

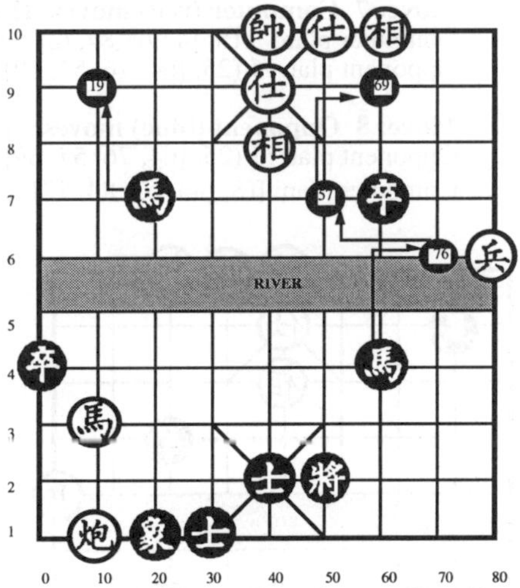

Figure 6.26. Blue Horse_2 moves 43 -> 64

Move: 5 Computer (red) moves: H(horse), 13 -> 32 {As shown in Figure 6.27}
Computer plan: [(8, [32,44,63,84,72]), (10, [11,15,85,82])] {7 moves to checkmate}
Opponent plan : [(24, [27, 19]), (25, [64, 76, 57, 69])] {4 moves to checkmate}

Move: 6 Opponent (blue) moves: h(horse), 27 -> 19 {Sub-plan 1 completed}
Opponent plan : [(25, [64, 76, 57, 69])] {3 moves to checkmate}
Computer plan: [(8, [32,44,63,84,72]), (10, [11,15,85,82])] {7 moves to checkmate}

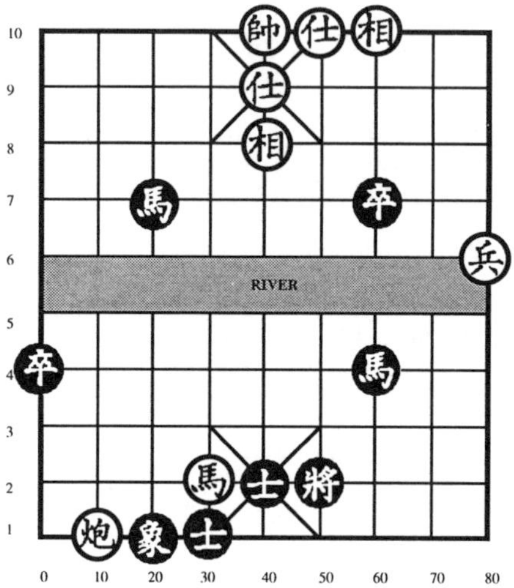

Figure 6.27. Red Horse moves 13 -> 32

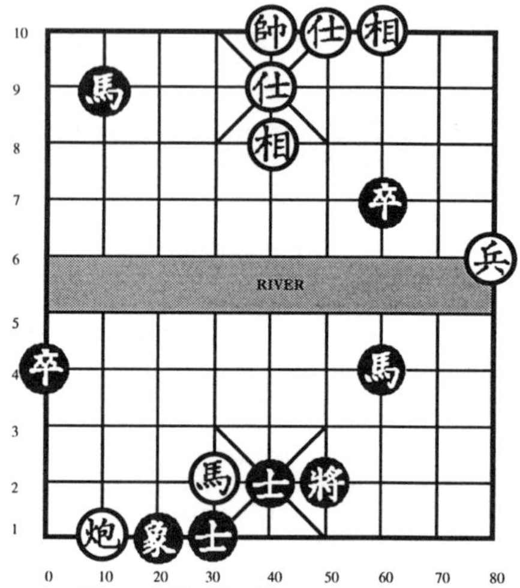

Figure 6.28. Blue Horse_1 moves 27 -> 19

Move: 7 Computer (red) moves: H(horse), 32 -> 44 {As shown in Figure 6.29}
Computer plan: [(8, [44,63,84,72]), (10, [11,15,85,82])] {6 moves to checkmate}
Opponent plan : [(25, [64, 76, 57, 69])] {3 moves to checkmate}

Move: 8 Opponent (blue) moves: e(elephant), 21 -> 43 {Elephant defence}
Opponent plan : [(25, [64, 76, 57, 69])] {3 moves to checkmate}
Computer plan: [(8, [44, 63, 84, 72]), (10, [11, 15, 85, 82])] {6 moves to checkmate}

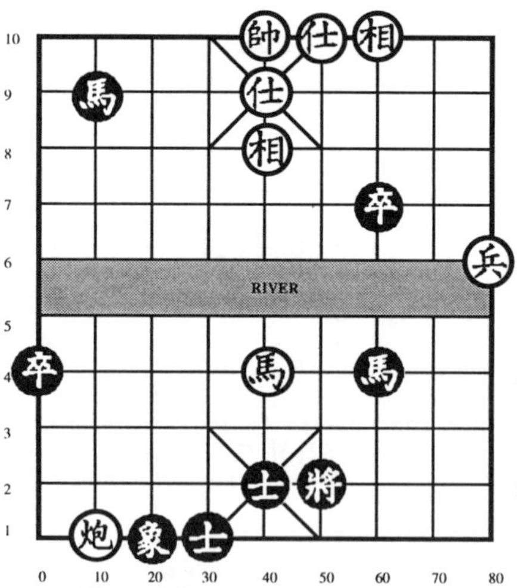

Figure 6.29. Red Horse moves 32 -> 44

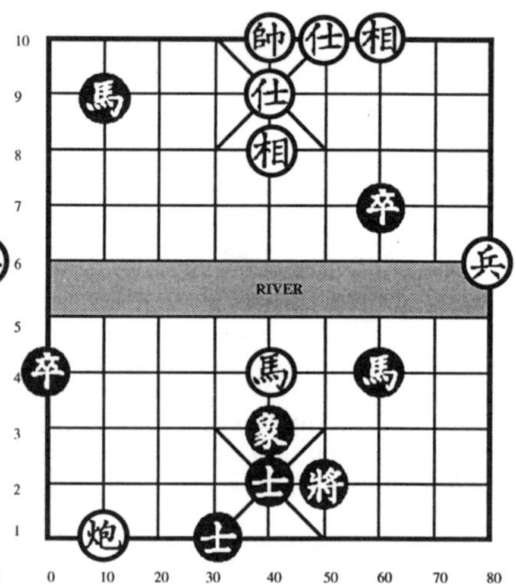

Figure 6.30. Blue Elephant moves 21 -> 43

Move: 9 Computer (red) moves: H(horse), 44 -> 63 {As shown in Figure 6.31}
Computer plan: [(8, [63, 84, 72]), (10, [11, 15, 85, 82])] {5 moves to checkmate}
Opponent plan : [(25, [64, 76, 57, 69])] {3 moves to checkmate}

Move: 10 Opponent (blue) moves: h(horse), 64 -> 76 {As shown in Figure 6.32}
Opponent plan : [(25, [76, 57, 69])] {2 moves to checkmate}
Computer plan: [(8, [63, 84, 72]), (10, [11, 15, 85, 82])] {Current plan is impossible}

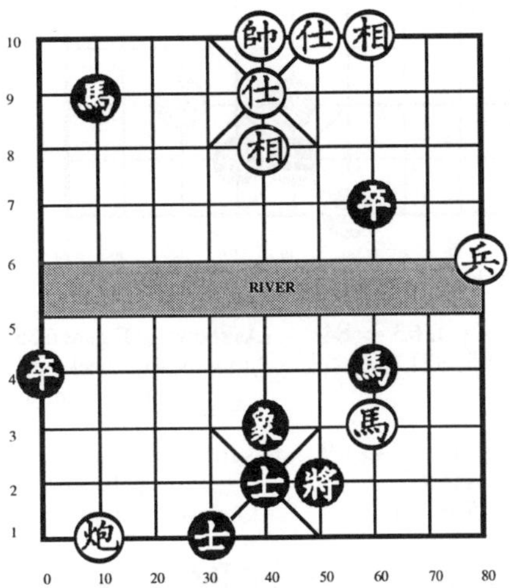

Figure 6.31. Red Horse moves 44 -> 63

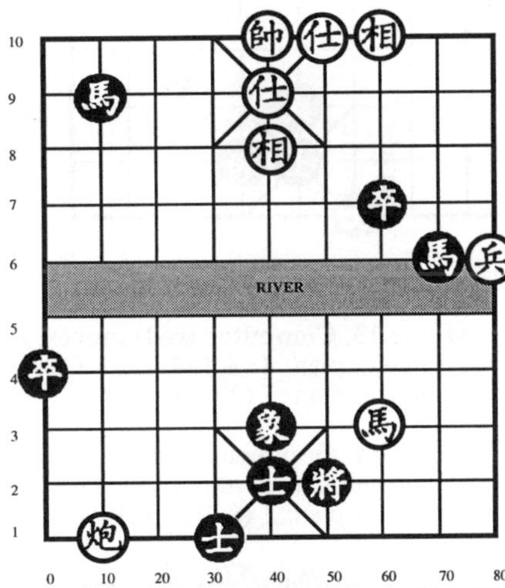

Figure 6.32. Blue Horse_2 moves 64 -> 76

------------ Computer enters C2 Stage for Plan Execution ------------
The current plan can not be executed ...... {(8, [63, 84, 72])}
Control temporarily pass to other sub-plan: (10, [11, 15, 85, 82])
{After the move, the control return back to the operational sub-plan: (8, [63, 84, 72])}

Move: 11 Computer (red) moves: C(cannon), 11 -> 15 {As shown in Figure 6.33}
Computer plan: [(8, [63, 84, 72]), (10, [15, 85, 82])] {4 moves to checkmate}
Opponent plan : [(25, [76, 57, 69])] {2 move to checkmate}

Move: 12 Opponent (blue) moves: h(horse), 76 -> 57 {As shown in Figure 6.34}
Opponent plan : [(25, [57, 69])] {1 move to checkmate}
Computer plan: [(8, [63, 84, 72]), (10, [15, 85, 82])] {4 moves to checkmate}

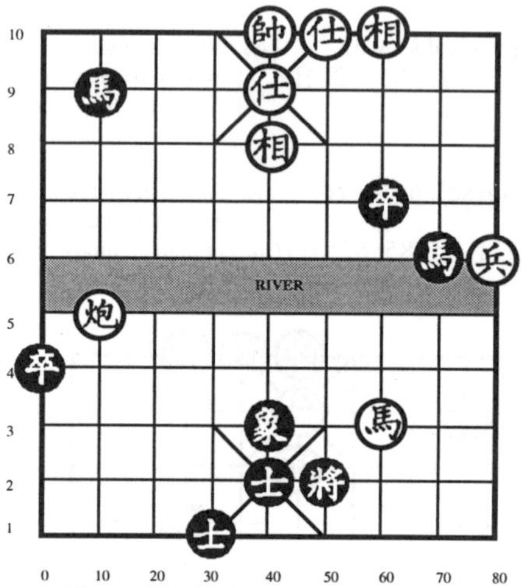

Figure 6.33: Red Cannon moves 11 -> 15

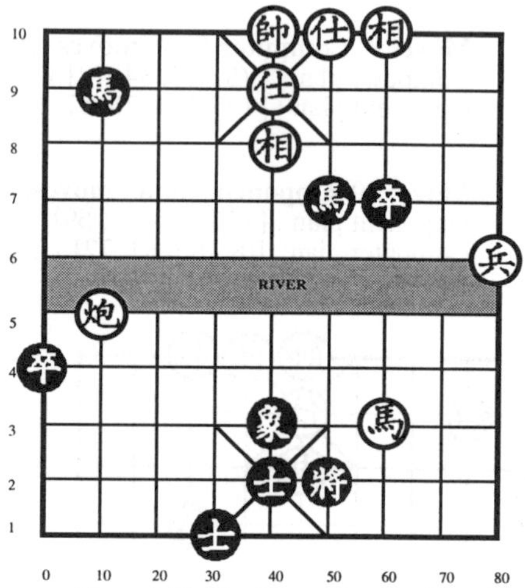

Figure 6.34: Blue Horse_2 moves 76 -> 57

Move: 13 Computer (red) moves: H(horse), 63 -> 84 {As shown in Figure 6.35}
Computer plan: [(8, [84, 72]), (10, [15, 85, 82])] {3 moves to checkmate}
Opponent plan : [(25, [57, 69])] {1 move to checkmate}

Move: 14 Opponent (blue) moves: h(horse), 57 -> 69 {As shown in Figure 6.36}
Opponent plan : [GAME OVER: OPPONENT WINS] {Checkmate}
Computer plan: [(8, [84, 72]), (10, [15, 85, 82])] {3 moves to checkmate}

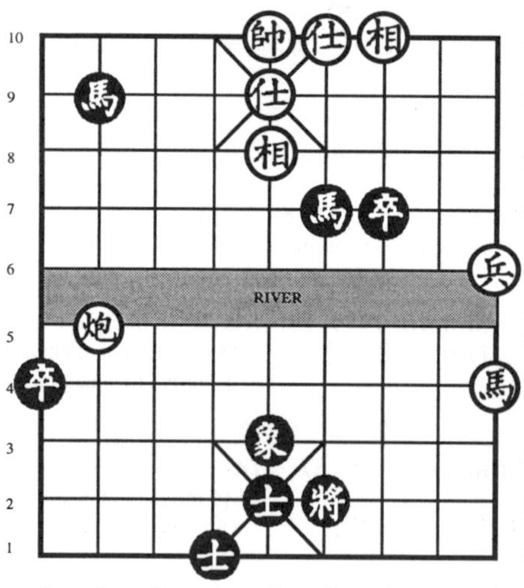

Figure 6.35. Red Cannon moves 11 -> 15

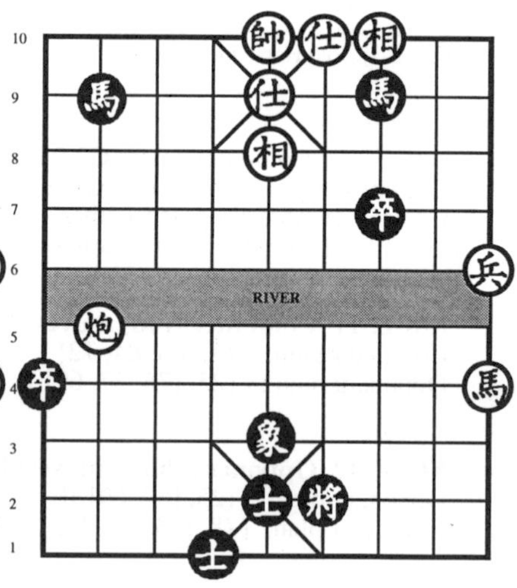

Figure 6.36. Blue Horse_2 moves 57 -> 68

6.4 The Case Study Four

The introduction of buffering in previous case study has reduced the length of the opponent's checkmate plan from nine moves to merely seven moves. However, until now, each sub-plan in the case studies is isolated, and there is no sharing of states or cross-over between solution paths. In the this case study, we intend to address the issues of conflicting paths, where two sub-plans have a common state existing along their solution paths within the same co-operative plan. We shall investigate how constraints could be imposed to synchronise the execution of these sub-plans in order to achieve the desired effect of checkmate.

This case study is again an end-game with two major attacking pieces from both sides, and as far as the red player is concerned, its "pin and strike" formation involves two sub-plans sharing a common state, with two chains of dashed lines tracing their paths from the current positions to their desired positions as shown in Figure 6.37.

```
------------ Computer enters Planning Reasoning (Planning Agent) ------------
***  Strategic Agent  ***
Offensive pieces: [8, 10]                          {8: red horse 1; 10: red cannon 1}
Looking for possible targets.......
Target is opponent general......                                     {Checkmate}
The targeting positions: [52,53, 51]                  {As shown in Figure 6.37}
Formation:  Horse_screen formation ........                  {Special formation}

The possible offensive formations: [ [(8, 72), (10, 82)]]   {One formations only}
Number of formations : 1

***  Tactical Agent  ***
The possible offensive plans:  [ (8, [65, 84, 72] ),  (10, [71, 72, 82] )]
Number of plans: 1

------------ Computer enters Decision-Making (Plan Selection) ------------
Evaluating ......
The best  Plan : [ (8, [65, 84, 72] ),  (10, [71, 72, 82] )]   {4 moves to checkmate}
The stand-by plans: [ ]
```

At the end of the planning stage, only one plan is possible: moving the red horse (ID: 8) from position 65 to 72 and red cannon (ID: 10) from position 71 to 82. However, both sub-plans share a common state at position [72], where a constraint will be imposed on the pinning sub-plan not to move the horse to position [72] before the cannon in the striking sub-plan has reached and moved away from position [72]. Because the striking piece (cannon) is not able to checkmate until a screen (red horse) is in place between the cannon and the blue general, the pre-condition of pinning-before-striking will still apply.

Strategic plan: pinning the target and screening the cannon with (8, [65, 84, 72]),
striking with (10, [71, 72, 82]) and
the sequence of control is pining before striking,
but with the following constraints

{Pinning constraint} activates the pinning sub-plan (8, [65, 84, 72]) to move the horse as far as to position [84], and transfers the control to activate the striking sub-plan (10, [71, 72*, 82]) to move the cannon to position [82], before returning the control to the horse to proceed to position [72].

{Striking constraint} activates (10, [71, 72*, 82]), and returns the control as soon as it moves beyond position [72],
Beyond position [72], both constrains would be removed, and the normal discipline of pin and strike will be applied.

------------ Computer enters C^2 Stage for Plan Execution ------------

Move: 1 Computer (red) moves: H(horse), 65 -> 84 {As shown in Figure 6.38}
Computer plan: [(8, [84, 72*]), (10, [71, 72*, 82])] {3 moves to checkmate}
Opponent plan: none

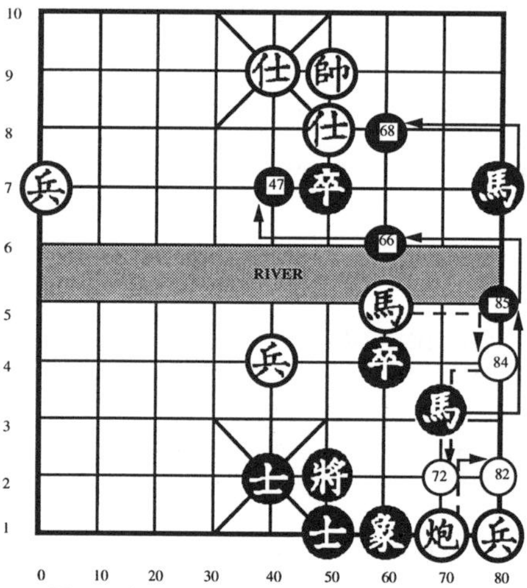

Figure 6.37. Red Plan [(8, 72), (10, 82)], Blue Plan [(25, 68), (24, 47)]

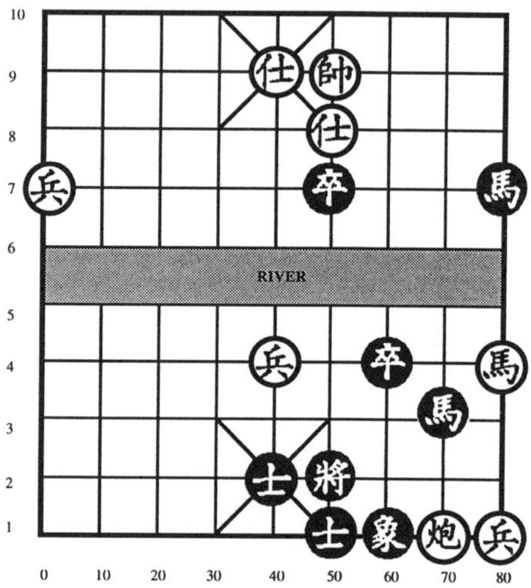

Figure 6.38. Red Horse moves 65 -> 84

------------ Opponent enters Planning Reasoning (Planning Agent) ------------
*** Strategic Agent ***
Offensive pieces: [24, 25] {24: blue horse 1; 25: blue horse 2}
Looking for possible targets.......
Target is opponent general...... {Checkmate}
The targeting positions: [59, 60] {As shown in Figure 6.37}
Formation: General attacking formation .... {Normal pin and strike}

Offensive piece: 24,
The valid attacking positions:
[(24, 47, 1, [59], [60]),
(24, 67, 1, [59], [60]),
(24, 68, 1,[60], [59])]

Offensive piece: 25,
The valid attacking positions:
[(25, 47, 1, [59], [60]),
(25, 67, 1, [59], [60]),
(25, 68, 1,[60], [59])]

The possible offensive formations:
[[(24, 68), (25, 47)],
[(25, 68), (24, 47)]]
Number of formations : 2 {There are two offensive formations}

*** Tactical Agent ***
The possible offensive plans: [[(25, [87, 68]), (24, [73, 85, 66, 47])]]
Number of plans: 1

------------ Opponent enters Decision-Making (Plan Selection) ------------
Evaluating ......
The best Plan : [(25, [87, 68]), (24, [73, 85, 66, 47])] {4 moves to checkmate}
The stand-by plans: [ ]
Strategic plan: pinning with[(25, [87, 68]),
striking with (24, [73, 85, 66, 47]), and
the sequence of control is first pin and last strike.

------------ Opponent enters C^2 Stage for Plan Execution ------------
Move 2: Opponent (blue) moves: h(horse), 87 -> 68 {Pinning is in position }
Opponent plan : [(24, [73, 85, 66, 47])] {3 moves to checkmate}
Computer plan: [(8, [84, 72^*]), (10, [71, 72^*, 82])] {3 moves to checkmate}

------------ Computer enters C^2 Stage for Plan Execution ------------
The constraint on (8, [84, 72^*]) is triggered, and the control is transferred to sub-plan 2 (10, [71, 72^*, 82]).
Move 3: Computer (red) moves: C(cannon), 71 -> 72 {As shown in Figure 6.40}
Computer plan: [(8, [84, 72^*]), (10, [72^*, 82])] {2 moves to checkmate}
Opponent plan : [(24, [73, 85, 66, 47])] {3 moves to checkmate}

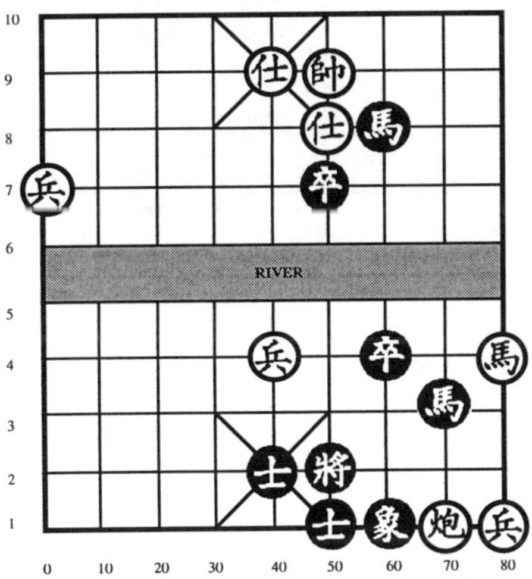

Figure 6.39. Blue Horse moves 87 -> 68

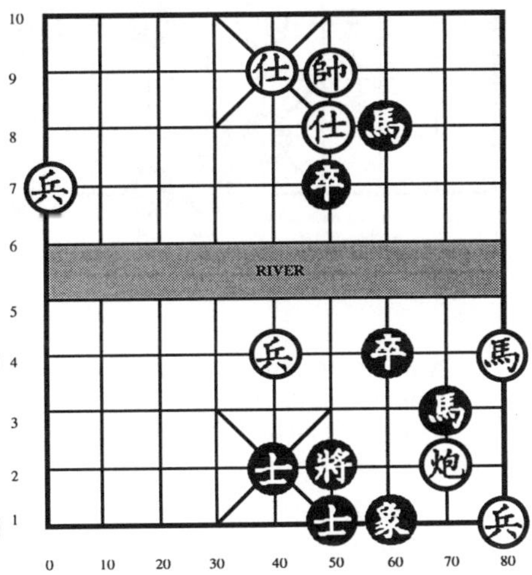

Figure 6.40. Red Cannon moves 71 -> 72*

Move 4: Opponent (blue) moves: h(horse), 73 -> 85 {As shown in Figure 6.41}
Opponent plan : [(24, [85, 66, 47])] {2 moves to checkmate}
Computer plan: [(8, [84, 72*]), (10, [72*, 82])] {2 moves to checkmate}

------------ Computer enters C^2 Stage for Plan Execution ------------
The constraint attached on to (8, [84, 72*]) is removed as soon as the red cannon moves away from position [72] to position [82], and the control then returns to the pinning sub-plan (8, [84, 72]) to signal that the conflict has been resolved.

Move 5: Computer (red) moves: C(cannon), 72 -> 82 {striking piece is in position }
Computer plan: [(8, [84, 72])] {1 move to checkmate}
Opponent plan : [(24, [85, 66, 47])] {2 moves to checkmate}

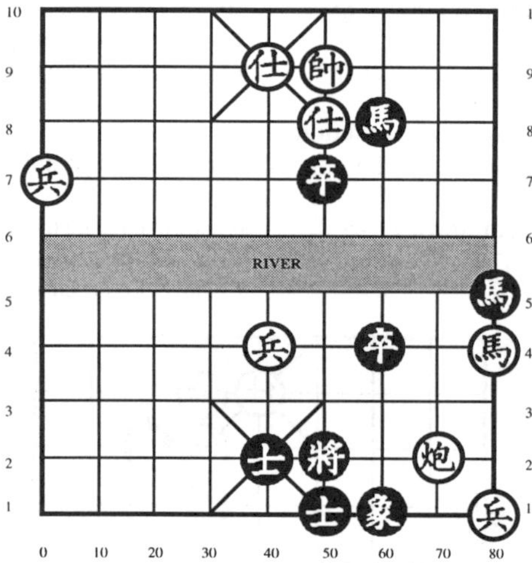

Figure 6.41. Blue Horse moves 73 -> 85

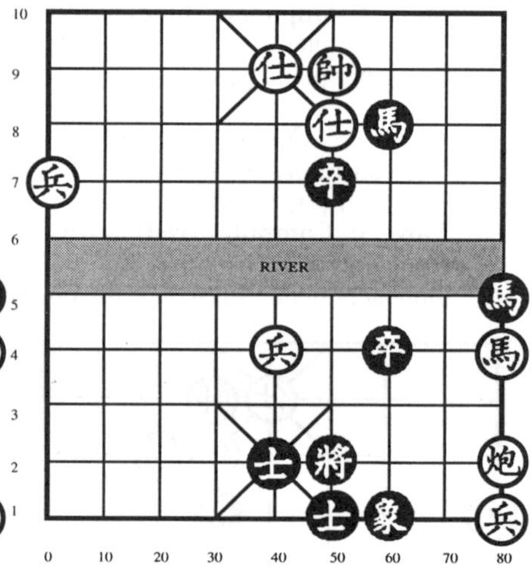

Figure 6.42. Red Cannon moves 72 -> 82

Move 6: Opponent (blue) moves: h(horse), 85 -> 66 {As shown in Figure 6.43}
Opponent plan : [(24, [66, 47])] {1 move to checkmate}
Computer plan: [(8, [84, 72])] {1 move to checkmate}

Move 7: Computer (red) moves: H(horse), 84 -> 72 {Pinning screen is in position}
Computer plan: [GAME OVER: COMPUTER WINS] {Checkmate}
Opponent plan : [(24, [66, 47])] {1 move to checkmate}

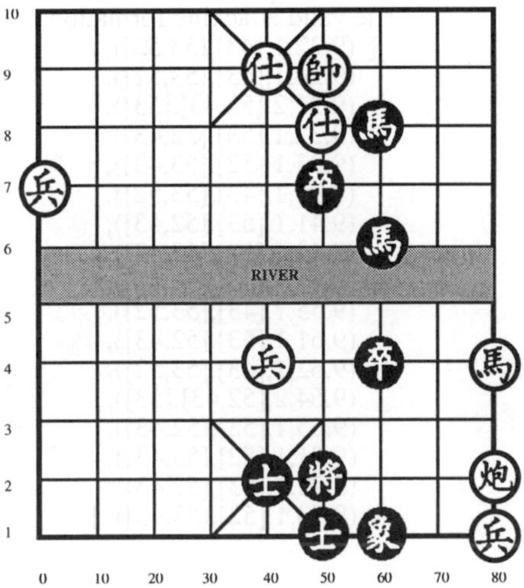

Figure 6.43. Blue Horse moves 85 -> 66

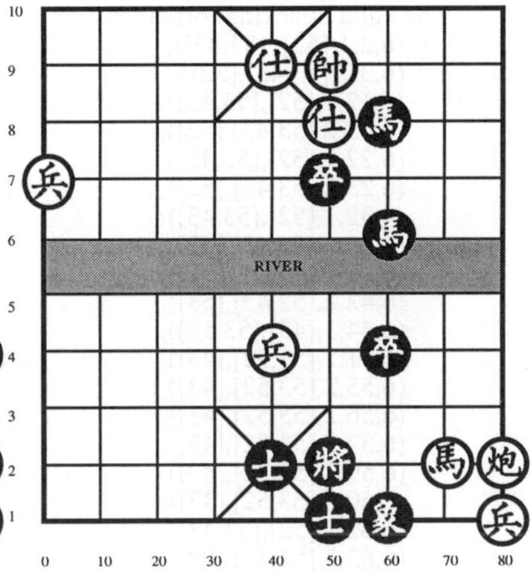

Figure 6.44. Red Horse moves 84 -> 72

6.5 The Case Study Five

Since our decision support system is designed to operate in a dynamic environment, the issue of moving target can hardly be ignored. In the case of Chinese chess, plans are formulated under the assumption that the target remains in the same position throughout the execution. When this condition is no longer true, the re-routing or plan modification become irrelevant, making re-planning the only course of action to focus on the new target position. In the fifth case study, we intends to assess the impact of a moving target by equipping the general with a reactive plan to move into a new position, whenever its mobility has been reduced.

The set-up of this end-game consists of a chariot (rook) and horse on the red side, and two horses on the blue side. This is the first time the chariot is introduced in our simulation, mobility is its major strength, but it does not have the potential of horses in covering two attacking positions at once.

------------ Computer enters Planning Reasoning (Planning Agent) ------------
*** Strategic Agent ***
Offensive pieces: [6,9] {6: red rook 1; 9: red horse 2}
Looking for possible targets.......
Target is opponent general...... {Checkmate}
The targeting positions: [53, 52, 43] {As shown in Figure 6.45}
Formation: General attacking formation .... {Normal pin and strike}

Offensive piece: 6
The valid attacking formations:

```
[ (6,2,1,[52], [53,43]),
  (6,3,2,[53,43],[52]),
  (6,12,1,[52],[53,43]),
  (6,13,2,[53,43],[52]),
  (6,22,1,[52],[53,43]),
  (6,23,2,[53,43],[52]),
  (6,32,1,[52],[53,43]),
  (6,33,2,[53,43],[52]),
  (6,41,1,[43],[53,52]),
  (6,42,2,[52,43],[53]),
  (6,44,1,[43],[53,52]),
  (6,51,2,[53,52],[43]),
  (6,55,2,[53,52],[43]),
  (6,56,2,[53,52],[43]),
  (6,57,2,[53,52],[43]),
  (6,59,2,[53,52],[43]),
  (6,60,2,[53,52],[43]),
  (6,62,1,[52],[53,43]),
  (6,63,2,[53,43],[52]),
  (6,72,1,[52],[53,43]),
  (6,73,2,[53,43],[52]),
  (6,82,1,[52],[53,43]),
  (6,83,2,[53,43],[52]) ]
```

Offensive piece: 9
The valid attacking formations:

```
[ (9,22,1,[43],[53,52]),
  (9,24,1,[43],[53,52]),
  (9,31,2,[52,43],[53]),
  (9,32,1,[53],[52,43]),
  (9,33,1,[52],[53,43]),
  (9,35,1,[43],[53,52]),
  (9,41,1,[53],[52,43]),
  (9,44,1,[52],[53,43]),
  (9,51,1,[43],[53,52]),
  (9,55,1,[43],[53,52]),
  (9,61,1,[53],[52,43]),
  (9,62,1,[43],[53,52]),
  (9,64,2,[52,43],[53]),
  (9,65,1,[53],[52,43]),
  (9,71,1,[52],[53,43]),
  (9,72,1,[53],[52,43]),
  (9,73,1,[52],[53,43]) ]
```

The possible offensive formations:

```
[ [(9,31),(6,83)],
  [(9,64),(6,83)],
  [(9,31),(6,73)],
  [(9,64),(6,73)],
  [(9,31),(6,63)],
  [(9,31),(6,60)],
  [(9,64),(6,60)],
  [(9,31),(6,59)],
  [(9,64),(6,59)],
  [(9,31),(6,57)],
  [(9,64),(6,57)],
  [(9,31),(6,56)],
  [(9,64),(6,56)],
  [(9,31),(6,55)],
  [(9,64),(6,55)],
  [(9,22),(6,51)],
  [(9,24),(6,51)],
  [(9,31),(6,51)],
  [(9,35),(6,51)],
  [(9,55),(6,51)],
  [(9,62),(6,51)],
  [(9,64),(6,51)],
  [(6,42),(9,61)],
```

```
    [(6,42),(9,65)],
    [(6,42),(9,72)],
    [(9,31),(6,33)],
    [(9,44),(6,33)],
    [(9,64),(6,33)],
    [(9,71),(6,33)],
    [(9,73),(6,33)],
    [(9,31),(6,23)],
    [(9,44),(6,23)],
    [(9,64),(6,23)],
    [(9,71),(6,23)],
    [(9,73),(6,23)],
    [(9,31),(6,13)],
    [(9,44),(6,13)],
    [(9,64),(6,13)],
    [(9,71),(6,13)],
    [(9,73),(6,13)],
    [(9,31),(6,3)],
    [(9,44),(6,3)],
    [(9,64),(6,3)],
    [(9,71),(6,3)],
    [(9,73),(6,3)] ]
Number of formations: 45                    {There are 45 attack formations}

***  Tactical Agent  ***
The possible offensive plans:
  [  [(9,[85,77,56,35,23,31]),(6,[10,2,82,83])],
     [(9,[85,77,56,64]),(6,[10,2,82,83])],
     [(9,[85,77,56,35,23,31]),(6,[10,2,72,73])],
     [(9,[85,77,56,64]),(6,[10,2,72,73])],
     [(9,[85,77,56,35,23,31]),(6,[10,5,65,63])],
     [(9,[85,77,56,35,23,31]),(6,[10,7,57,60])],
     [(9,[85,77,56,64]),(6,[10,7,57,60])],
     [(9,[85,77,56,35,23,31]),(6,[10,7,57,59])],
     [(9,[85,77,56,64]),(6,[10,7,57,59])],
     [(9,[85,77,56,35,23,31]),(6,[10,7,57])],
     [(9,[85,77,56,64]),(6,[10,7,57])],
     [(9,[85,77,56,35,23,31]),(6,[10,6,56])],
     [(9,[85,77,56,64]),(6,[10,6,56])],
     [(9,[85,77,56,35,23,31]),(6,[10,5,55])],
     [(9,[85,77,56,64]),(6,[10,5,55])],
     [(9,[85,77,56,35,14,22]),(6,[10,8,38,31,51])],
     [(9,[85,77,69,48,36,24]),(6,[10,8,38,31,51])],
     [(9,[85,77,56,35,23,31]),(6,[10,8,38,31,51])],
     [(9,[85,77,56,35]),(6,[10,8,38,31,51])],
     [(9,[85,77,69,48,36,55]),(6,[10,8,38,31,51])],
     [(9,[85,73,81,62]),(6,[10,8,38,31,51])],
     [(9,[85,77,56,64]),(6,[10,8,38,31,51])],
     [(6,[10,2,42]),(9,[85,73,61])],
     [(6,[10,2,42]),(9,[85,77,65])],
```

[(6,[10,2,42]),(9,[85,77,56,64,72])],
[(9,[85,77,56,35,23,31]),(6,[10,3,33])],
[(9,[85,77,56,44]),(6,[10,3,33])],
[(9,[85,77,56,64]),(6,[10,3,33])],
[(9,[85,77,56,44,63,71]),(6,[10,3,33])],
[(9,[85,73]),(6,[10,3,33])],
[(9,[85,77,56,35,23,31]),(6,[10,3,23])],
[(9,[85,77,56,44]),(6,[10,3,23])],
[(9,[85,77,56,64]),(6,[10,3,23])],
[(9,[85,77,56,44,63,71]),(6,[10,3,23])],
[(9,[85,73]),(6,[10,3,23])],
[(9,[85,77,56,35,23,31]),(6,[10,3,13])],
[(9,[85,77,56,44]),(6,[10,3,13])],
[(9,[85,77,56,64]),(6,[10,3,13])],
[(9,[85,77,56,44,63,71]),(6,[10,3,13])],
[(9,[85,73]),(6,[10,3,13])],
[(9,[85,77,56,35,23,31]),(6,[10,3])],
[(9,[85,77,56,44]),(6,[10,3])],
[(9,[85,77,56,64]),(6,[10,3])],
[(9,[85,77,56,44,63,71]),(6,[10,3])],
[(9,[85,73]),(6,[10,3])]]

Number of plans: 45

------------ Computer enters Decision-Making (Plan Selection) ------------

Due to the large number of possible pinning and striking positions, forty five formations have been identified, and hence, forty five plans are formulated. Amongst them, [(9, [85, 73]), (6, [10, 3])] with the shortest path is selected as the operational plan and the rest as the stand-by plans. The quality of this plan [(9, [85, 73]), (6, [10, 3])] reflexes, to a certain extent, the strength of the chariot (rook) in moving into attacking position faster than any other piece.

Evaluating ......

The best Plan : [(9, [85, 73]), (6, [10, 3])] {2 moves to checkmate}

The stand-by plans:

[[(9,[85,73]),(6,[10,3,33])],
[(9,[85,73]),(6,[10,3,23])],
[(9,[85,73]),(6,[10,3,13])],
[(6,[10,2,42]),(9,[85,73,61])],
[(6,[10,2,42]),(9,[85,77,65])],
[(9,[85,77,56,44]),(6,[10,3])],
[(9,[85,77,56,64]),(6,[10,3])],
[(9,[85,77,56,64]),(6,[10,7,57])],
[(9,[85,77,56,64]),(6,[10,6,56])],
[(9,[85,77,56,64]),(6,[10,5,55])],
[(9,[85,77,56,44]),(6,[10,3,33])],
[(9,[85,77,56,64]),(6,[10,3,33])],
[(9,[85,77,56,44]),(6,[10,3,23])],
[(9,[85,77,56,64]),(6,[10,3,23])],
[(9,[85,77,56,44]),(6,[10,3,13])],
[(9,[85,77,56,64]),(6,[10,3,13])],

[(9,[85,77,56,64]),(6,[10,2,82,83])],
[(9,[85,77,56,64]),(6,[10,2,72,73])],
[(9,[85,77,56,64]),(6,[10,7,57,60])],
[(9,[85,77,56,64]),(6,[10,7,57,59])],
[(6,[10,2,42]),(9,[85,77,56,64,72])],
[(9,[85,77,56,35,23,31]),(6,[10,3])],
[(9,[85,77,56,44,63,71]),(6,[10,3])],
[(9,[85,77,56,35,23,31]),(6,[10,7,57])],
[(9,[85,77,56,35,23,31]),(6,[10,6,56])],
[(9,[85,77,56,35,23,31]),(6,[10,5,55])],
[(9,[85,77,56,35]),(6,[10,8,38,31,51])],
[(9,[85,73,81,62]),(6,[10,8,38,31,51])],
[(9,[85,77,56,64]),(6,[10,8,38,31,51])],
[(9,[85,77,56,35,23,31]),(6,[10,3,33])],
[(9,[85,77,56,44,63,71]),(6,[10,3,33])],
[(9,[85,77,56,35,23,31]),(6,[10,3,23])],
[(9,[85,77,56,44,63,71]),(6,[10,3,23])],
[(9,[85,77,56,35,23,31]),(6,[10,3,13])],
[(9,[85,77,56,44,63,71]),(6,[10,3,13])],
[(9,[85,77,56,35,23,31]),(6,[10,2,82,83])],
[(9,[85,77,56,35,23,31]),(6,[10,2,72,73])],
[(9,[85,77,56,35,23,31]),(6,[10,5,65,63])],
[(9,[85,77,56,35,23,31]),(6,[10,7,57,60])],
[(9,[85,77,56,35,23,31]),(6,[10,7,57,59])],
[(9,[85,77,56,35,14,22]),(6,[10,8,38,31,51])],
[(9,[85,77,69,48,36,24]),(6,[10,8,38,31,51])],
[(9,[85,77,56,35,23,31]),(6,[10,8,38,31,51])],
[(9,[85,77,69,48,36,55]),(6,[10,8,38,31,51])]]

Strategic plan: pinning with (9, [85, 73]),
striking with (6, [10, 3]), and
the sequence of control is first pin and last strike. {As in Figure 6.45}

------------ Computer enters C^2 Stage for Plan Execution ------------

Move 1: Computer (red) moves: H(horse), 85 -> 73 {Pinning in position}
Computer plan: [(6, [10, 3])] {1 move to checkmate}
Opponent plan: none

------------ Opponent general is threatened ------------
------------ Opponent enters defence mode ------------
The placing of red horse at position [73] reduces the mobility of the blue general from [52, 43] to only one legal move at position [43]. This activates the reactive routine to move the general away from its current position [53] to a better position at [43] that have three legal moves [42, 33, 53], and as a result, the red side is forced into re-planning.

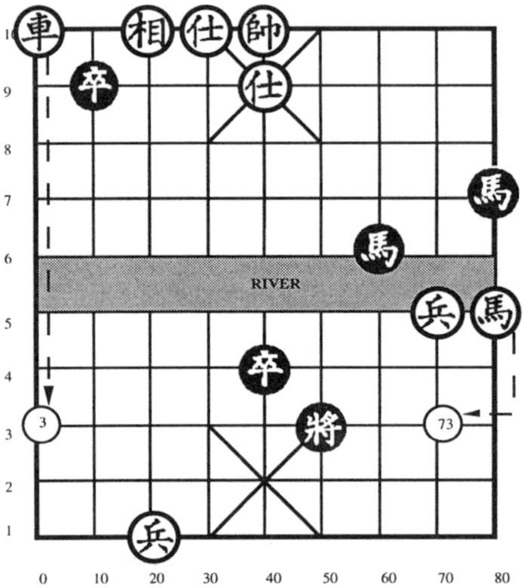

Figure 6.45. Computer Plan [(9, 73), (6, 3)]

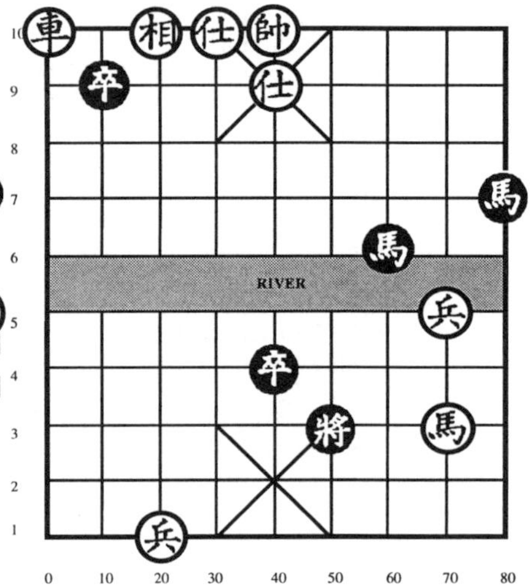

Figure 6.46. Red Horse moves 85 -> 73

Move 2: Opponent (blue) moves: g(general), 53 -> 43 {As shown in Figure 6.47}
Opponent plan: none
Computer plan: [(6, [10, 3])] {1 move to checkmate}

------------ Target has changed position ------------
------------ Computer enters Re-planning Reasoning (Planning Agent) ------------

*** Strategic Agent ***
Offensive pieces: [6,9] {6: red rook 1; 9: red horse 2}
Looking for possible targets.......
Target is opponent general...... {Checkmate}
The targeting positions: [43,53,42,33]
Formation: General attacking formation .... {Normal pin and strike}

Offensive piece: 6
The valid attacking formations:
[(6,2,1,[42],[43,53,33]),
(6,3,3,[43,53,33],[42]),
(6,12,1,[42],[43,53,33]),
(6,13,3,[43,53,33],[42]),
(6,22,1,[42],[43,53,33]),
(6,23,3,[43,53,33],[42]),
(6,31,1,[33],[43,53,42]),
(6,32,2,[42,33],[43,53]),
(6,34,1,[33],[43,53,42]),
(6,35,1,[33],[43,53,42]),

Offensive piece: 9
The valid attacking formations:
[(9,12,1,[33],[43,53,42]),
(9,14,1,[33],[43,53,42]),
(9,22,1,[43],[53,42,33]),
(9,23,1,[42],[43,53,33]),
(9,24,1,[43],[53,42,33]),
(9,25,1,[33],[43,53,42]),
(9,31,1,[43],[53,42,33]),
(9,32,1,[53],[43,42,33]),
(9,34,1,[42],[43,53,33]),
(9,35,1,[43],[53,42,33]),

```
(6,36,1,[33],[43,53,42]),
(6,37,1,[33],[43,53,42]),
(6,38,1,[33],[43,53,42]),
(6,39,1,[33],[43,53,42]),
(6,41,2,[43,42],[53,33]),
(6,44,2,[43,42],[53,33]),
(6,51,1,[53],[43,42,33]),
(6,52,2,[53,42],[43,33]),
(6,55,1,[53],[43,42,33]),
(6,56,1,[53],[43,42,33]),
(6,57,1,[53],[43,42,33]),
(6,59,1,[53],[43,42,33]),
(6,60,1,[53],[43,42,33]),
(6,62,1,[42],[43,53,33]),
(6,63,3,[43,53,33],[42]),
(6,72,1,[42],[43,53,33]),
(6,82,1,[42],[43,53,33]) ]
(9,41,2,[53,33],[43,42]),
(9,51,1,[43],[53,42,33]),
(9,52,1,[33],[43,53,42]),
(9,55,1,[43],[53,42,33]),
(9,61,2,[53,42],[43,33]),
(9,62,1,[43],[53,42,33]),
(9,63,1,[42],[43,53,33]),
(9,64,1,[43],[53,42,33]),
(9,65,1,[53],[43,42,33]),
(9,72,1,[53],[43,42,33]) ]
```

```
The possible offensive formations:
  [ [(9, 61),(6, 23)],
    [(9, 61),(6, 13)],
    [(9, 61),(6, 3)]  ]
Number of formations: 3                    {There are only 3 attack formations}

***  Tactical Agent  ***
The possible offensive plans:
  [ [(9, [73, 61]), (6, [10, 3, 23])],
    [(9, [73, 61]), (6, [10, 3, 13])],
    [(9, [73, 61]), (6, [10, 3])]  ]
Number of plans: 3

------------ Computer enters Decision-Making (Plan Selection) ------------
Evaluating ......
The best Plan : [ (9, [73, 61]), (6, [10, 3])]          {2 moves to checkmate}
The stand-by plans:
  [ [(9, [73, 61]), (6, [10, 3, 23])],
    [(9, [73, 61]),(6, [10, 3, 13])]  ]

Strategic plan: pinning with (9, [73, 61]),
                striking with (6, [10, 3]), and
                the sequence of control is first pin and last strike. {As in Figure 6.48}
```

------------ Computer enters C^2 Stage for Plan Execution ------------

Move 3: Computer (red) moves: H(horse), 73 -> 61 {Pinning in position}

Computer plan: [(6, [10, 3])] {1 move to checkmate}

Opponent plan : none

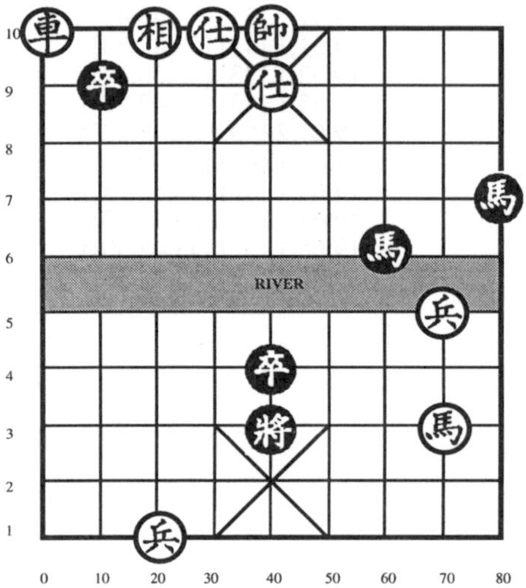
Figure 6.47. Blue General moves 53 -> 43

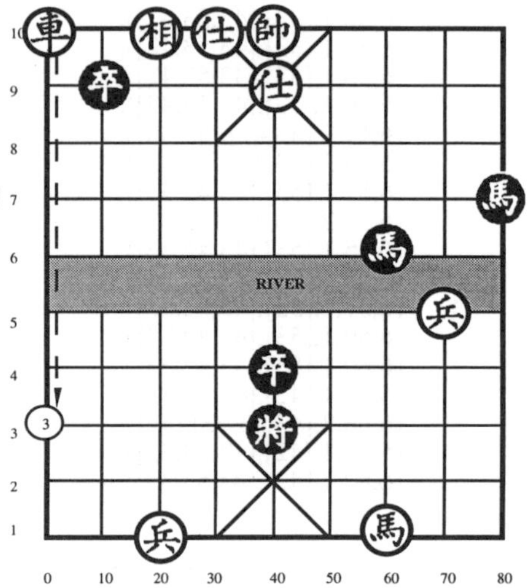
Figure 6.48. Red Horse moves 71 -> 61
Computer Plan: [(9, 61), (6, 3)],

------------ Opponent general is threatened ------------
------------ Opponent enters defence mode ------------
Again, the placing of red horse at position [61] reduces the legal moves of the blue general from [33, 42, 53] to just one at position [33]. Hence, the general moves away from the current position [43] towards a better position at [33] and restores its legal moves respectively to two at [43, 32].

Move 4: Opponent (blue) moves: g(general), 43 -> 33 {As shown in Figure 6.49}
Opponent plan: none
Computer plan: [(6, [10, 3])] {1 move to checkmate}

------------ Target had changed position ------------
------------ Computer enters Re-planning Reasoning (Planning Agent) ------------
*** Strategic Agent ***
Offensive pieces: [6,9] {6: red rook 1; 9: red horse 2}
Looking for possible targets.......
Target is opponent general...... {Checkmate}
The targeting positions: [33,43,32] {As shown in Figure 6.49}
Formation: General attacking formation .... {Normal pin and strike}

Offensive piece: 6
The valid attacking formations:
[(6,2,1,[32],[33,43]),
(6,3,2,[33,43],[32]),
(6,12,1,[32],[33,43]),
(6,13,2,[33,43],[32]),

Offensive piece: 9
The valid attacking formations:
[(9,12,1,[33],[43,32]),
(9,13,1,[32],[33,43]),
(9,14,1,[33],[43,32]),
(9,22,1,[43],[33,32]),

(6,22,1,[32],[33,43]),
(6,23,2,[33,43],[32]),
(6,31,2,[33,32],[43]),
(6,34,2,[33,32],[43]),
(6,35,2,[33,32],[43]),
(6,36,2,[33,32],[43]),
(6,37,2,[33,32],[43]),
(6,38,2,[33,32],[43]),
(6,39,2,[33,32],[43]),
(6,41,1,[43],[33,32]),
(6,42,2,[43,32],[33]),
(6,44,1,[43],[33,32]),
(6,52,1,[32],[33,43]),
(6,53,2,[33,43],[32]),
(6,62,1,[32],[33,43]),
(6,63,2,[33,43],[32]),
(6,72,1,[32],[33,43]),
(6,73,2,[33,43],[32]),
(6,82,1,[32],[33,43]),
(6,83,2,[33,43],[32])]

(9,24,2,[43,32],[33]),
(9,25,1,[33],[43,32]),
(9,31,1,[43],[33,32]),
(9,35,1,[43],[33,32]),
(9,41,1,[33],[43,32]),
(9,44,1,[32],[33,43]),
(9,51,2,[43,32],[33]),
(9,52,1,[33],[43,32]),
(9,53,1,[32],[33,43]),
(9,55,1,[43],[33,32]),
(9,62,1,[43],[33,32]),
(9,64,1,[43],[33,32])]

The possible offensive formations:
[[(9,13),(6,83)],
[(9,24),(6,83)],
[(9,44),(6,83)],
[(9,51),(6,83)],
[(9,13),(6,73)],
[(9,24),(6,73)],
[(9,44),(6,73)],
[(9,51),(6,73)],
[(9,13),(6,63)],
[(9,24),(6,63)],
[(9,44),(6,63)],
[(9,51),(6,63)],
[(9,13),(6,53)],
[(9,24),(6,53)],
[(9,44),(6,53)],
[(9,51),(6,53)],
[(6,42),(9,12)],
[(6,42),(9,14)],
[(6,42),(9,25)],
[(9,24),(6,39)],
[(9,51),(6,39)],
[(9,24),(6,38)],
[(9,51),(6,38)],
[(9,24),(6,37)],
[(9,51),(6,37)],
[(9,24),(6,36)],
[(9,51),(6,36)],
[(9,24),(6,35)],

```
    [(9,51),(6,35)],
    [(9,51),(6,34)],
    [(9,22),(6,31)],
    [(9,24),(6,31)],
    [(9,35),(6,31)],
    [(9,51),(6,31)],
    [(9,55),(6,31)],
    [(9,62),(6,31)],
    [(9,64),(6,31)],
    [(9,51),(6,23)],
    [(9,24),(6,13)],
    [(9,51),(6,13)],
    [(9,24),(6,3)],
    [(9,51),(6,3)]]
Number of formations: 42                 {There are 42 attack formations}

*** Tactical Agent ***
The possible offensive plans:
  [ [(9,[61,53,34,13]),(6,[10,2,82,83])],
    [(9,[61,82,63,55,36,24]),(6,[10,2,82,83])],
    [(9,[61,82,63,44]),(6,[10,2,82,83])],
    [(9,[61,82,63,51]),(6,[10,2,82,83])],
    [(9,[61,53,34,13]),(6,[10,2,72,73])],
    [(9,[61,82,63,55,36,24]),(6,[10,2,72,73])],
    [(9,[61,82,63,44]),(6,[10,2,72,73])],
    [(9,[61,82,63,51]),(6,[10,2,72,73])],
    [(9,[61,53,34,13]),(6,[10,5,65,63])],
    [(9,[61,82,63,55,36,24]),(6,[10,5,65,63])],
    [(9,[61,82,63,44]),(6,[10,5,65,63])],
    [(9,[61,82,63,51]),(6,[10,5,65,63])],
    [(9,[61,53,34,13]),(6,[10,7,57,53])],
    [(9,[61,82,63,55,36,24]),(6,[10,7,57,53])],
    [(9,[61,82,63,44]),(6,[10,7,57,53])],
    [(9,[61,82,63,51]),(6,[10,7,57,53])],
    [(6,[10,2,42]),(9,[61,42,23,4,12])],
    [(6,[10,2,42]),(9,[61,53,34,26,14])],
    [(6,[10,2,42]),(9,[61,82,63,44,25])],
    [(9,[61,82,63,55,36,24]),(6,[10,8,38,39])],
    [(9,[61,82,63,51]),(6,[10,8,38,39])],
    [(9,[61,82,63,55,36,24]),(6,[10,8,38])],
    [(9,[61,82,63,51]),(6,[10,8,38])],
    [(9,[61,82,63,55,36,24]),(6,[10,7,37])],
    [(9,[61,82,63,51]),(6,[10,7,37])],
    [(9,[61,82,63,55,36,24]),(6,[10,6,36])],
    [(9,[61,82,63,51]),(6,[10,6,36])],
    [(9,[61,82,63,55,36,24]),(6,[10,5,35])],
    [(9,[61,82,63,51]),(6,[10,5,35])],
    [(9,[61,82,63,51]),(6,[10,4,34])],
    [(9,[61,53,41,22]),(6,[10,7,57,51,31])],
    [(9,[61,82,63,55,36,24]),(6,[10,7,57,51,31])],
```

```
    [(9,[61,42,23,35]),(6,[10,7,57,51,31])],
    [(9,[61,82,63,51]),(6,[10,7,57,51,31])],
    [(9,[61,82,63,55]),(6,[10,7,57,51,31])],
    [(9,[61,53,41,62]),(6,[10,7,57,51,31])],
    [(9,[61,53,72,64]),(6,[10,7,57,51,31])],
    [(9,[61,82,63,51]),(6,[10,3,23])],
    [(9,[61,82,63,55,36,24]),(6,[10,3,13])],
    [(9,[61,82,63,51]),(6,[10,3,13])],
    [(9,[61,82,63,55,36,24]),(6,[10,3])],
    [(9,[61,82,63,51]),(6,[10,3])] ]
Number of plans: 42


------------ Computer enters Decision-Making (System Master) ------------
Evaluating ......
The best  Plan : [ (9, [61, 82, 63, 51]),(6,[10, 3])]            {4 moves to checkmate}
The stand-by plans:
  [ [(9,[61,82,63,51]),(6,[10,8,38])],
    [(9,[61,82,63,51]),(6,[10,7,37])],
    [(9,[61,82,63,51]),(6,[10,6,36])],
    [(9,[61,82,63,51]),(6,[10,5,35])],
    [(9,[61,82,63,51]),(6,[10,4,34])],
    [(9,[61,82,63,51]),(6,[10,3,23])],
    [(9,[61,82,63,51]),(6,[10,3,13])],
    [(9,[61,53,34,13]),(6,[10,2,82,83])],
    [(9,[61,82,63,44]),(6,[10,2,82,83])],
    [(9,[61,82,63,51]),(6,[10,2,82,83])],
    [(9,[61,53,34,13]),(6,[10,2,72,73])],
    [(9,[61,82,63,44]),(6,[10,2,72,73])],
    [(9,[61,82,63,51]),(6,[10,2,72,73])],
    [(9,[61,53,34,13]),(6,[10,5,65,63])],
    [(9,[61,82,63,44]),(6,[10,5,65,63])],
    [(9,[61,82,63,51]),(6,[10,5,65,63])],
    [(9,[61,53,34,13]),(6,[10,7,57,53])],
    [(9,[61,82,63,44]),(6,[10,7,57,53])],
    [(9,[61,82,63,51]),(6,[10,7,57,53])],
    [(6,[10,2,42]),(9,[61,42,23,4,12])],
    [(6,[10,2,42]),(9,[61,53,34,26,14])],
    [(6,[10,2,42]),(9,[61,82,63,44,25])],
    [(9,[61,82,63,51]),(6,[10,8,38,39])],
    [(9,[61,82,63,55,36,24]),(6,[10,3])],
    [(9,[61,82,63,55,36,24]),(6,[10,8,38])],
    [(9,[61,82,63,55,36,24]),(6,[10,7,37])],
    [(9,[61,82,63,55,36,24]),(6,[10,6,36])],
    [(9,[61,82,63,55,36,24]),(6,[10,5,35])],
    [(9,[61,53,41,22]),(6,[10,7,57,51,31])],
    [(9,[61,42,23,35]),(6,[10,7,57,51,31])],
    [(9,[61,82,63,51]),(6,[10,7,57,51,31])],
    [(9,[61,82,63,55]),(6,[10,7,57,51,31])],
    [(9,[61,53,41,62]),(6,[10,7,57,51,31])],
```

[(9,[61,53,72,64]),(6,[10,7,57,51,31])],
[(9,[61,82,63,55,36,24]),(6,[10,3,13])],
[(9,[61,82,63,55,36,24]),(6,[10,2,82,83])],
[(9,[61,82,63,55,36,24]),(6,[10,2,72,73])],
[(9,[61,82,63,55,36,24]),(6,[10,5,65,63])],
[(9,[61,82,63,55,36,24]),(6,[10,7,57,53])],
[(9,[61,82,63,55,36,24]),(6,[10,8,38,39])],
[(9,[61,82,63,55,36,24]),(6,[10,7,57,51,31])]]

Strategic plan: pinning with (9, [61, 82, 63, 51]),
striking with (6, [10, 3]), and
the sequence of control is first pin and last strike. {As in Figure 6.49}

------------ Computer enters C^2 Stage for Plan Execution ------------

Move 5: Computer (red) moves: H(horse), 61 -> 82 {As shown in Figure 6.50}
Computer plan: [(9, [82, 63, 51]),(6,[10, 3])] {3 moves to checkmate}
Opponent plan : none

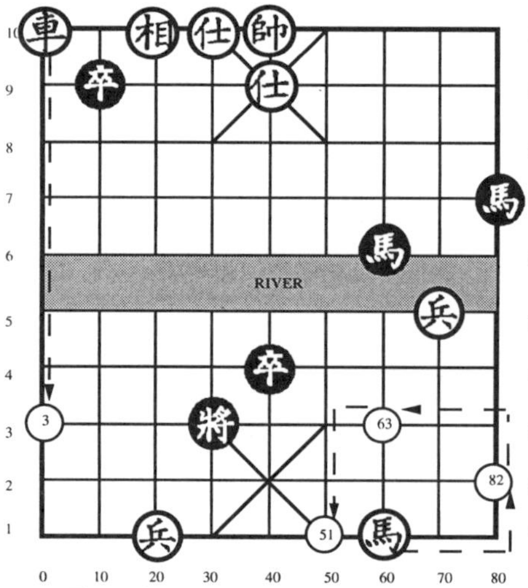

Figure 6.49. Blue General moves 43 -> 33
Computer Plan: [(9, 51), (6, 3)],

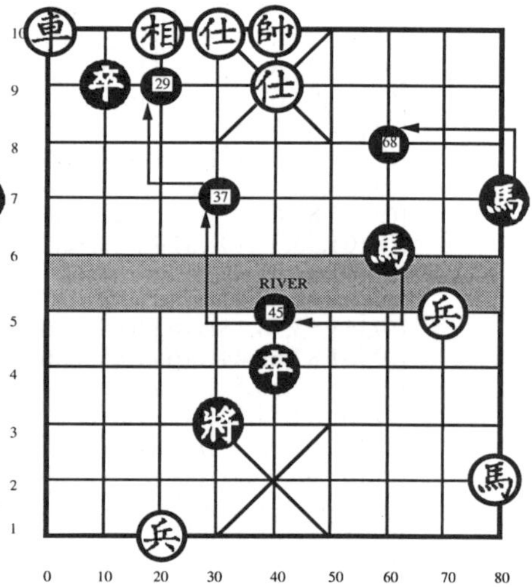

Figure 6.50. Red Horse moves 61 -> 82
Opponent Plan: [(25, 68]), (24, 29)]

------------ Opponent enters Planning Reasoning (Planning Agent) ------------
*** Strategic Agent ***
Offensive pieces: [24, 25] {24: blue horse 1; 25: blue horse 2}
Looking for possible targets.......
Target is computer general...... {Checkmate}
The targeting positions: [50, 60] {As shown in Figure 6.50}
Formation: General attacking formation .... {Normal pin and strike}

Offensive piece: 24
The valid attacking formations:
[(24,29,1,[50],[60]),
(24,68,1,[60],[50]),
(24,69,1,[50],[60]),
(24,79,1,[60],[50])]

Offensive piece: 25
The valid attacking formations:
[(25,29,1,[50],[60]),
(25,68,1,[60],[50]),
(25,69,1,[50],[60]),
(25,79,1,[60],[50])]

The possible offensive formations:
[[(24,79),(25,29)],
[(24,68),(25,29)],
[(25,68),(24,29)],
[(25,79),(24,29)]]
Number of formations: 4 {There are 4 attack formations}

*** Tactical Agent ***
The possible offensive plans:
[[(24,[66,78,59,67,79]),(25,[87,68,56,37,29])],
[(24,[66,47,68]),(25,[87,68,56,37,29])],
[(25,[87,68]),(24,[66,45,37,29])],
[(25,[87,79]),(24,[66,45,37,29])]]
Number of plans: 4

------------ Opponent enters Decision-Making Stage (Plan Selection) ------------
Evaluating ......

The best plan: [(25, [87, 68]),(24, [66, 45, 37, 29])] {4 moves to checkmate}

The stand-by plans:
[[(25,[87,79]),(24,[66,45,37,29])],
[(24,[66,47,68]),(25,[87,68,56,37,29])],
[(24,[66,78,59,67,79]),(25,[87,68,56,37,29])]]

Strategic plan: pinning with (25, [87, 68]),
striking with (24, [66, 45, 37, 29]), and
the sequence of control is first pin and last strike. {As in Figure 6.50}

------------ Opponent enters C^2 Stage for Plan Execution ------------
Move 6: Opponent (blue) moves: h (horse), 87 -> 68 {Pinning in position}
Opponent plan : [(24, [66, 45, 37, 29])] {3 moves to checkmate}
Computer plan: [(9, [82, 63, 51]),(6,[10, 3])] {3 moves to checkmate}

Move 7: Computer (red) moves: H(horse), 82 -> 63 {As shown in Figure 6.52}
Computer plan: [(9, [63, 51]),(6,[10, 3])] {2 moves to checkmate}
Opponent plan : [(24, [66, 45, 37, 29])] {3 moves to checkmate}

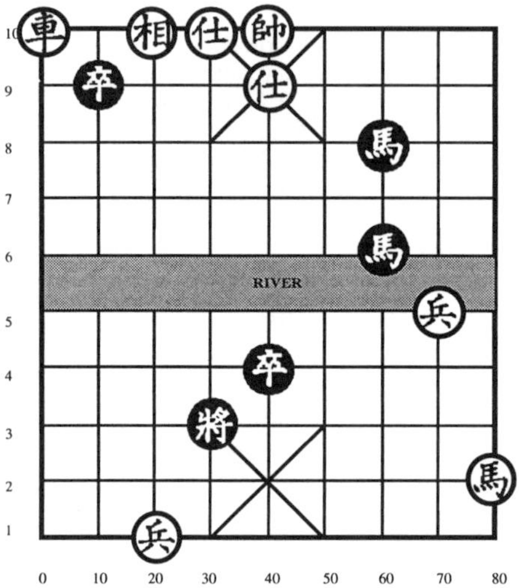

Figure 6.51. Blue Horse_2 moves 87 -> 68

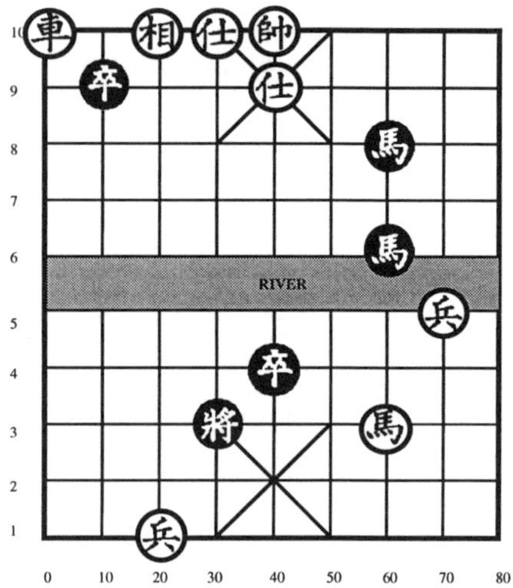

Figure 6.52. Red Horse moves 82 -> 63

Move 8: Opponent (blue) moves: h (horse), 66 -> 45 {As shown in Figure 6.53}
Opponent plan : [(24, [45, 37, 29])] {2 moves to checkmate}
Computer plan: [(9, [63, 51]),(6,[10, 3])] {2 moves to checkmate}

Move 9: Computer (red) moves: H(horse), 63 -> 51 {Pinning piece in place}
Computer plan: [(6,[10, 3])] {1 move to checkmate}
Opponent plan : [(24, [45, 37, 29])] {2 moves to checkmate}

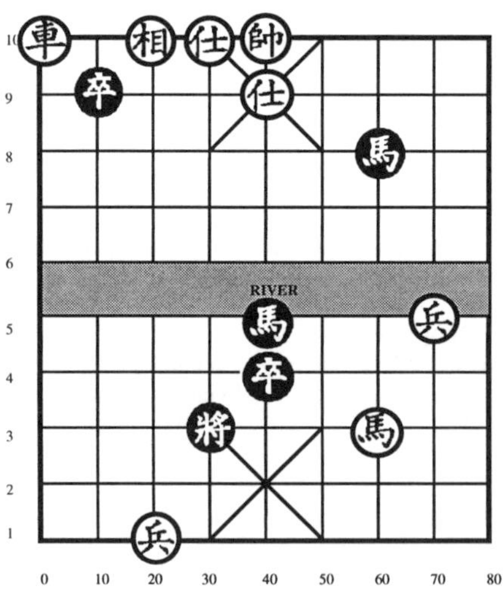

Figure 6.53. Blue Horse_1 moves 66 -> 45

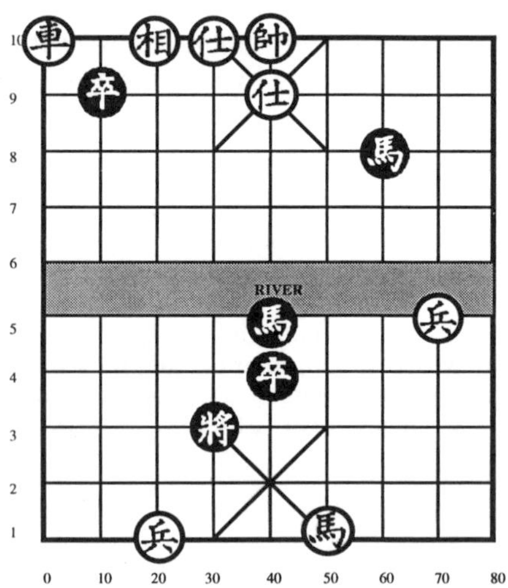

Figure 6.54. Red Horse moves 63 -> 51

In here, as the red horse moves into position [51], the mobility of the blue general will be lost, leaving it as a trapped target, for the red rook moving into position [3] to capture.

Move 10: Opponent (blue) moves: h(horse), 45 -> 37 {As shown in Figure 6.55}
Opponent plan : [(24, [37, 29])] {1 move to checkmate}
Computer plan: [(6,[10, 3])] {1 move to checkmate}

Move 11: Computer (red) moves: R(rook), 10 -> 3 {Striking piece in position}
Computer plan: [GAME OVER: COMPUTER WINS] {Checkmate}
Opponent plan : [(24, [37, 29])] {1 move to checkmate}

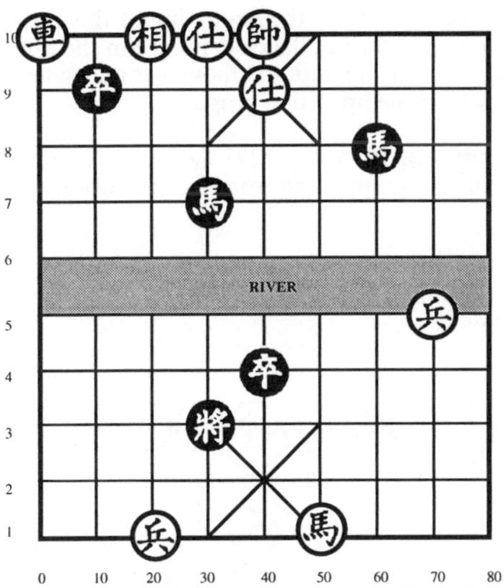

Figure 6.55. Blue Horse_1 moves 45 -> 37

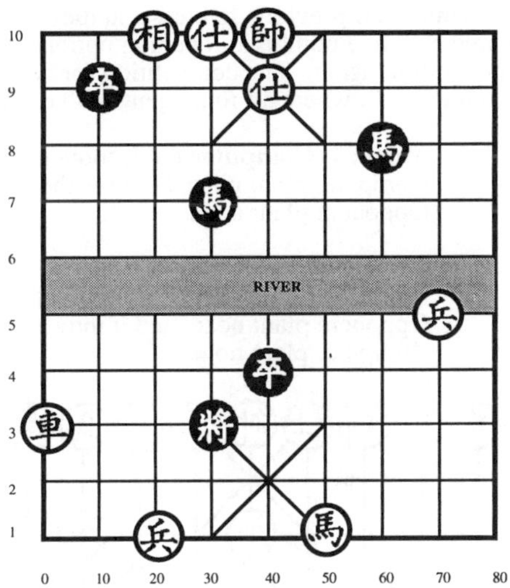

Figure 6.56. Red Horse moves 10 -> 3

The case studies presented so far demonstrate the goal-oriented approach in planning for a solution path once the desired formation has been identified. This approach underlines the strength and impact when recognition and search paradigms are combined to formulate and generate plans. The methodology of decomposing goal into a partial plan lays the foundation for plan modification during the execution stage, in which detour means searching for an alternative path for the same partial plan, and stand-by plans mean alternative formation to achieve the same goal. The IPE (Interleaving of Planning and Execution) is applicable here only at the tactical level to search for an alternative path for the same strategic plan.

6.6 The Case Study Six

Given that the identification of the attacking formation as the pre-condition for a strategic plan, it is not difficult to come to a conclusion that in the absence of these desired formations, other means would have to be pursued in order to come up with the decision for the next move. Case Study Six is intended to broaden the scope of problem solving by taking into account the contribution from all four agents in the system (i.e. 2a, 2b, 2c and 2d of the algorithm outlined in the previous chapter). The choice of move is strongly influenced by the progress of the game. At the opening, the recognition paradigm scores very well with a high chances of match with its case library. However, as the game enters into the later stage, solution from planning agent would become more likely. Failure of the pure recognition agent (2a), heuristic agent (2b) or planning agents (2c), would often lead to the next move being decided by the search agent (2d), based on purely gains and losses in terms of material and/or positional advantages.

Unlike all previous five case studies, Case Six starts from the beginning of the chess game, where a number of opening options can be picked from the case library in the pure recognition agent. The competition for consideration as operational move get under-way from move 2, where all four agents will each try to come up with a proposal.

Move: 1 Computer (red) moves: C(cannon), 18 -> 48 {As shown in Figure 6.57}
Computer plan: none, but uses the central cannon opening from the case library
Opponent plan: none

Move 2: Opponent (blue) moves: c(cannon), 13 -> 43 {As shown in Figure 6.58}
Opponent plan: none, and it moves manually.
Computer plan: none

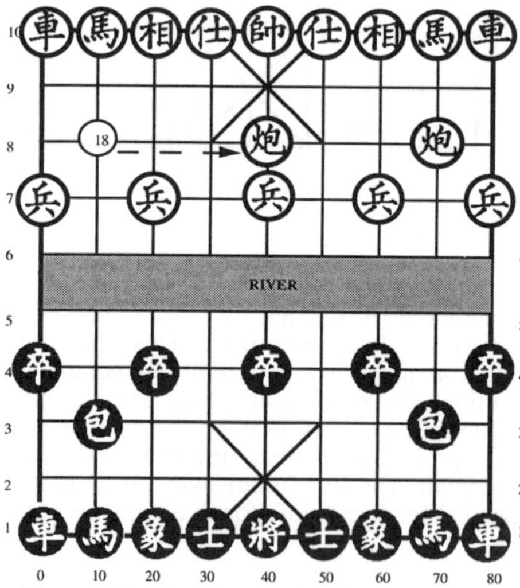

Figure 6.57. Move from book: C(cannon), 18 -> 48

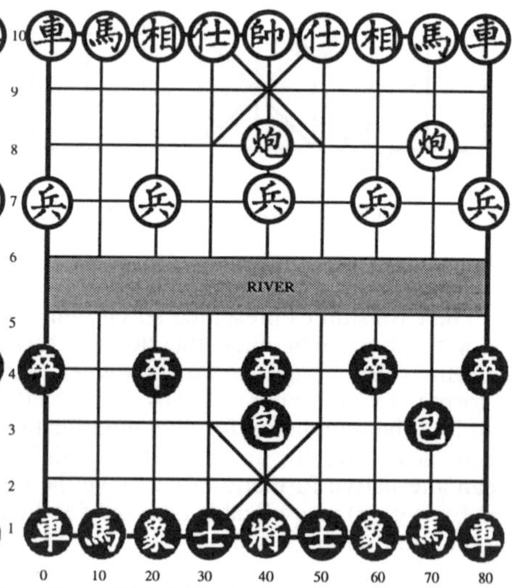

Figure 6.58. Blue Cannon moves from 13 -> 43

------------ Computer enters Decision-Making (System Master) ------------

Evaluating		
Recognition agent:	move (8, 20, 28, 6000)	{Algorithm 2a}
Heuristic agent:	nil	{Algorithm 2b}
Planning agent:	nil * nil	{Algorithm 2c}
Tactical agent:	move (10, 48,44, 20)	{Algorithm 2d}
System master:	move (8, 20, 28, 6000)	{This refers to 8: red horse 1}

At the decision-making stage, the pure recognition agent has returned with a perfect match from its case library, while the tactical agent has identified an advantage of moving red cannon 1 from position [48] to position [44] in order to capture a blue soldier. No plan is forthcoming. In here, the opponent is assumed to play manually.

Move: 3 Computer (red) moves: H(horse), 20 -> 28 {As shown in Figure 6.59}
Computer plan: none, moves (8, [20, 28]).
Opponent plan: none

Move 4: Opponent (blue) moves: h(horse), 11 -> 23 {As shown in Figure 6.60}
Opponent plan: none, and it moves manually.
Computer plan: none

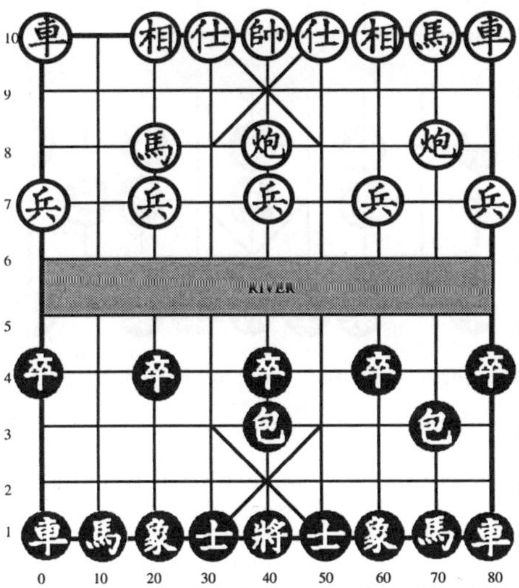

Figure 6.59. Red Horse moves from 20 -> 28

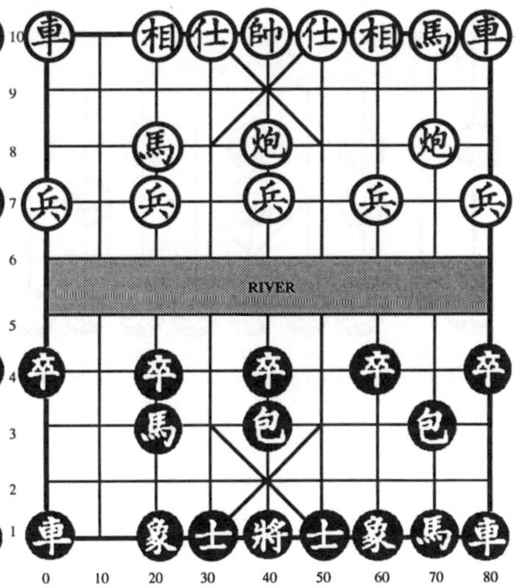

Figure 6.60. Blue Horse moves from 11 -> 23

------------ Computer enters Decision-Making stage (System Master) ------------
Evaluating ......

Recognition agent	move (6, 10, 20, 6000)	{Algorithm 2a}
Heuristic agent:	nil	{Algorithm 2b}
Planning agent:	nil * nil	{Algorithm 2c}
Tactical agent:	move (6, 10, 20, 12)	{Algorithm 2d}
System master:	move (6, 10, 20, 6012)	{values of red rook 1 are combined}

Move: 5 Computer (red) moves: R(rook), 10 -> 20 {As shown in Figure 6.61}
Computer plan: none, moves (6, [10, 20]).
Opponent plan: none

Move 6: Opponent (blue) moves: h(horse), 71 -> 63 {As shown in Figure 6.62}
Opponent plan: none, and it moves manually.
Computer plan: none

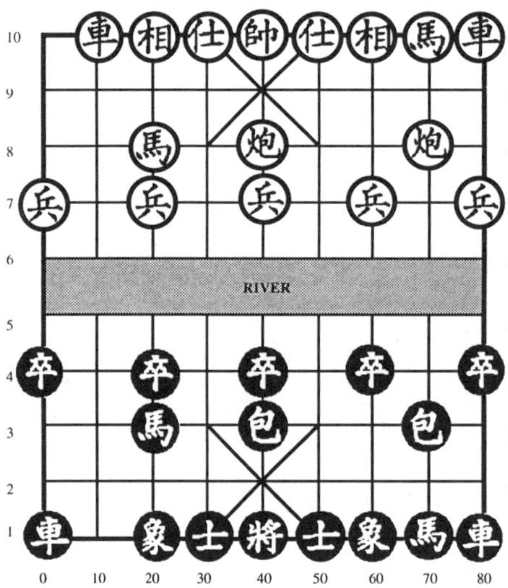

Figure 6.61. Red Rook moves from 10 -> 20

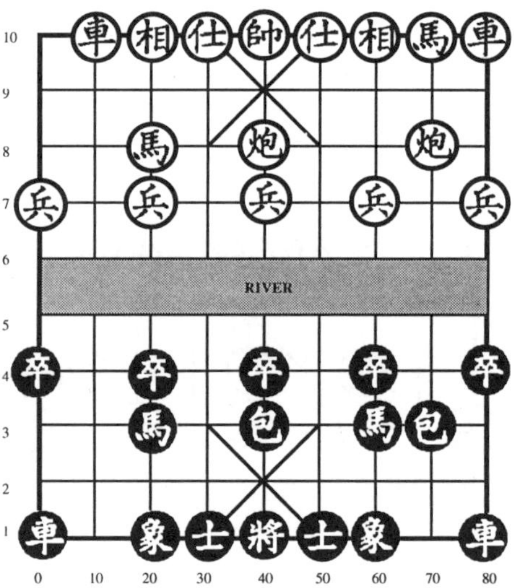

Figure 6.62. Blue Horse moves from 71 -> 63

At this point of the game, perfect match with cases in the library is unlikely. However, pattern matching red rook 1 at position [20], blue horse 1 at position [23] and soldier 2 at position [24] produces a hit within the heuristics agent, but yields only 100 points. No capture or plan is possible here. Only the tactical move of red rook 1 from position [20] to position [12] would generate a positional gain of 10 points.

------------ Computer enters Decision-Making (System Master) ------------

Evaluating ......

Recognition agent	nil	{Algorithm 2a}
Heuristic agent:	move (6, 20, 14, 100)	{Algorithm 2b}
Planning agent:	nil * nil	{Algorithm 2c}
Tactical agent:	move (6, 20, 12, 10)	{Algorithm 2d}
System master:	move (6, 20, 14, 100)	{This refers to 6: red rook 1}

Move: 7 Computer (red) moves: R(rook), 20 -> 14 {As shown in Figure 6.63}
Computer plan: none, move (6, [20, 14]).
Opponent plan: none

Move 8: Opponent (blue) moves: r(rook), 81 -> 82 {As shown in Figure 6.64}
Opponent plan: none, and it moves manually.
Computer plan: none

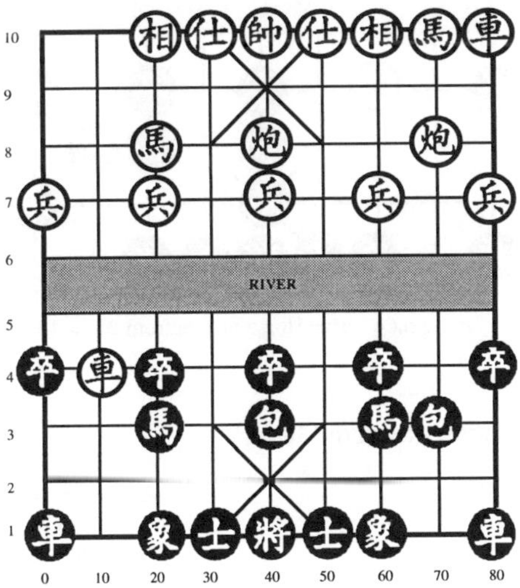

Figure 6.63. Red Rook moves from 20 -> 14

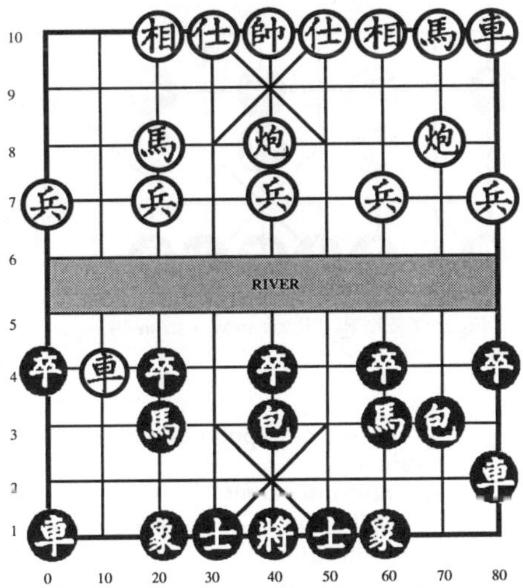

Figure 6.64. Blue Rook moves from 81 -> 82

------------ Computer enters Decision-Making (System Master) ------------

Evaluating ......

Recognition agent	nil	{Algorithm 2a}
Heuristic agent:	move (13, 27, 26, 15)	{Algorithm 2b}
Planning agent:	nil * nil	{Algorithm 2c}
Tactical agent:	move (6, 14, 24, 18)	{Algorithm 2d}
System master:	move (6, 14, 24, 18)	{This refers to 6: red rook 1}

Move: 9 Computer (red) moves: R(rook), 14 -> 24 {As shown in Figure 6.65}
Computer plan: none, moves (6, [14, 24]).
Opponent plan: none

Move 10: Opponent (blue) moves: h(horse), 23 -> 42 {As shown in Figure 6.66}
Opponent plan: none, and it moves manually
Computer plan: none

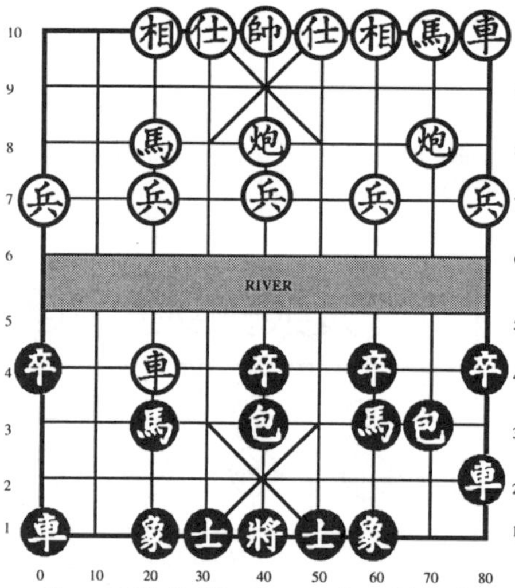

Figure 6.65. Red Rook moves from 14 -> 24

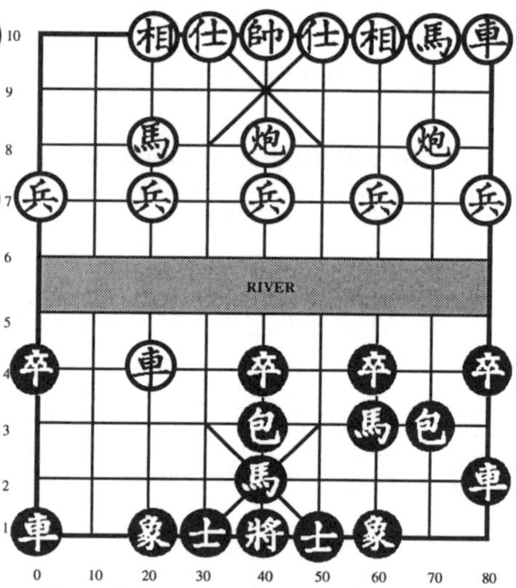

Figure 6.66. Blue Horse moves from 23 -> 42

------------ Computer enters Decision-Making (System Master) ------------
Evaluating ......

Recognition agent	nil	{Algorithm 2a}
Heuristic agent:	move (13, 27, 26, 15)	{Algorithm 2b}
Planning agent:	nil * nil	{Algorithm 2c}
Tactical agent:	move (13, 27, 26, 10)	{Algorithm 2d}
System master:	move (13, 27, 26, 25)	{This refers to 13: red soldier 2}

Move: 11 Computer (red) moves: S(soldier), 27 -> 26 {As shown in Figure 6.67}
Computer plan: none, moves (13, [27, 26]).
Opponent plan: none

Move 12: Opponent (blue) moves: r(rook), 82 -> 52 {As shown in Figure 6.68}
Opponent plan: none, and it moves manually.
Computer plan: none

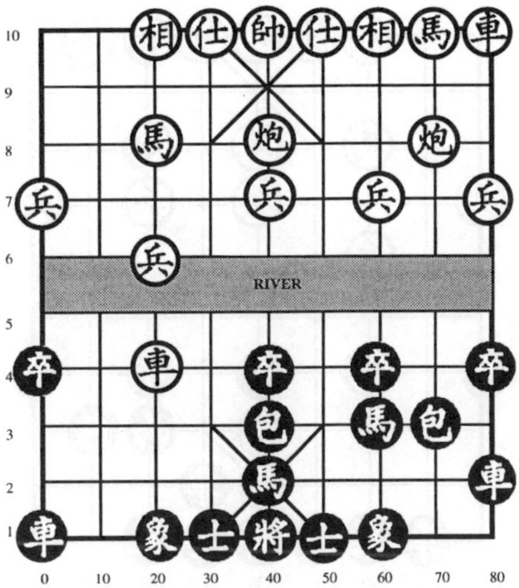

Figure 6.67. Red Soldier moves from 27 -> 26

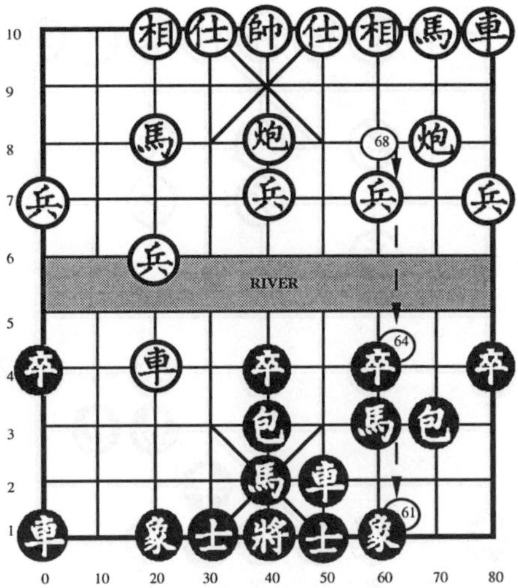

Figure 6.68. Blue Rook moves from 82 -> 52
Computer Plan:[(11,[78,68,64,61])]

A plan to checkmate as shown in Figure 6.68, will take three moves to capture the blue general, and hence generate an attached value of 1500 point for the proposed move ($6000 / 2^2 = 1500$). This attached value will gradually increase as the path gets shorter. Notice that the plan here is only a single striking plan without the need for any pinning sub-plan, because the blue general has no more legal move when the blue horse moves into position [42]. This situation is created in order to shorten the game, but in practice there is no reason not to generate a pinning sub-plan to target at position [42], and hence, a "pin and strike" formation can be made like the previous five case studies.

------------ Computer enters Decision-Making (System Master) ------------
Evaluating ......
Recognition agent nil {Algorithm 2a}
Heuristic agent: move (8, 28, 36, 100) {Algorithm 2b}
Planning agent: move (11,78,68,1500) * [(11, [78,68,64,61])] {Algorithm 2c}
Tactical agent: move (13, 26, 25, 10) {Algorithm 2d}
System master: move (11, 78, 68, 1500) {This refers to 11: red cannon 2}

Move: 13 Computer (red) moves: C(cannon), 78 -> 68 {As shown in Figure 6.69}
Computer plan: [(11, [68, 64, 61])] {2 moves to checkmate}
Opponent plan: none

Move 14: Opponent (blue) moves: r(rook), 1 -> 11 {As shown in Figure 6.70}
Opponent plan: none, and it moves manually.
Computer plan: [(11, [68, 64, 61])] {2 moves to checkmate}

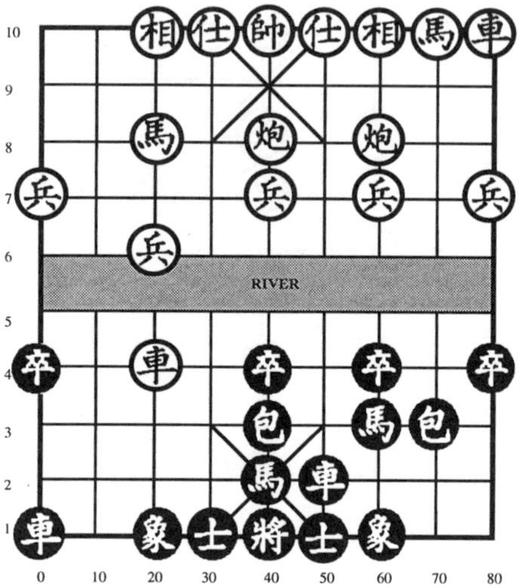

Figure 6.69. Red Cannon moves from 78 -> 68

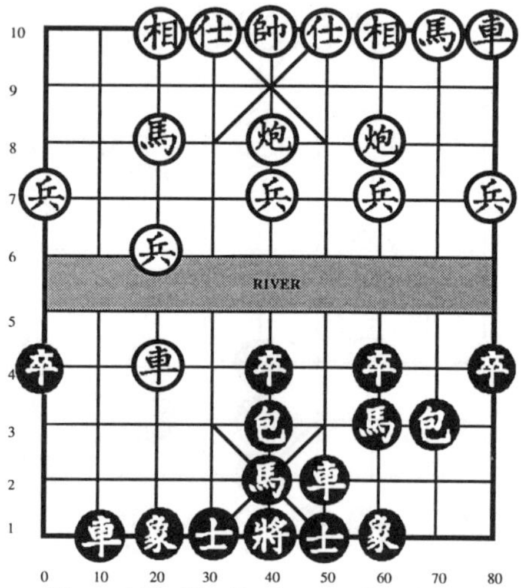

Figure 6.70. Blue Rook moves from 1 -> 11

------------ Computer enters Decision-Making (System Master) ------------

Evaluating		
Recognition agent	nil	{Algorithm 2a}
Heuristic agent:	move (8, 28, 36, 100)	{Algorithm 2b}
Planning agent:	move (11, 68, 64, 3000) * [(11, [68, 64, 61])]	{Algorithm 2c}
Tactical agent:	move (6, 24, 4, 16)	{Algorithm 2d}
System master:	move (11, 68, 64, 3000)	{This refers to 11: red cannon 2}

Move: 15 Computer (red) moves: C(cannon), 68 -> 64 {As shown in Figure 6.71}
Computer plan: [(11, [64, 61])] {1 move to checkmate}
Opponent plan: none

Move 16: Opponent (blue) moves: r(rook), 11 -> 19 {As shown in Figure 6.72}
Opponent plan: none, and it moves manually.
Computer plan: [(11, [64, 61])] {1 move to checkmate}

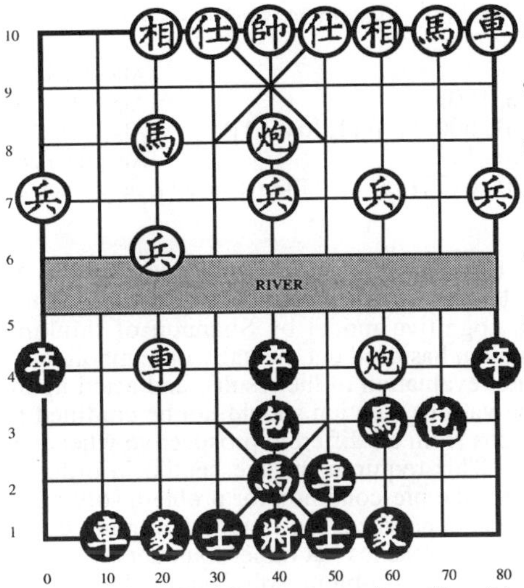

Figure 6.71. Red Cannon moves from 68 -> 64

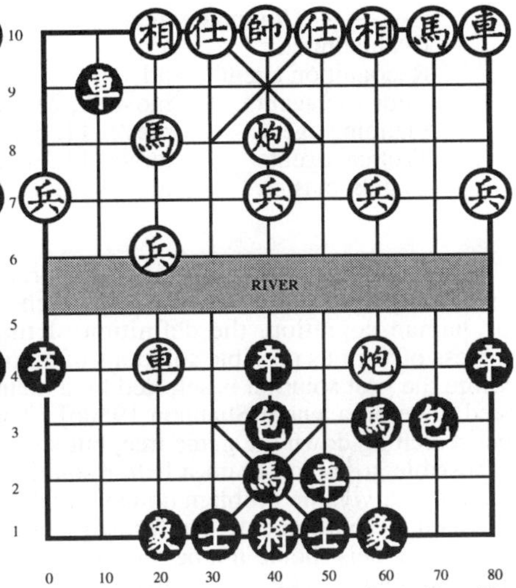

Figure 6.72. Blue Rook moves from 11 -> 19

Move: 17 Computer (red) moves: C(cannon), 64 -> 61 {As shown in Figure 6.73}
Computer plan: [GAME OVER: COMPUTER WINS] {Checkmate}
Opponent plan: none

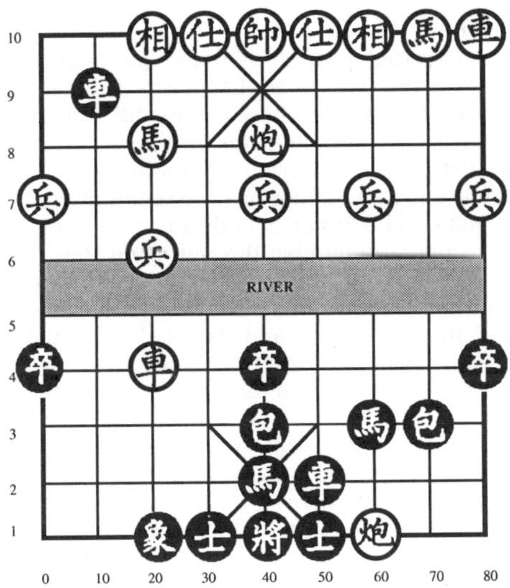

Figure 6.73. Red Cannon moves from 64 -> 61

------------ Computer enters Decision-Making (System Master) ------------

Evaluating		
Recognition agent	nil	{Algorithm 2a}
Heuristic agent:	move (8, 28, 36, 100)	{Algorithm 2b}
Planning agent:	move (11, 64, 61, 6000) * [(11, [64, 61])]	{Algorithm 2c}
Tactical agent:	move (11, 64, 61, 122)	{Algorithm 2d}
System master:	move (11, 64, 61, 6122)	{This refers to 11: red cannon 2}

Playing chess with goal-oriented approach has never been seriously taken by the AI community ever since Newell and Church. However, as we come nearer to understand the human cognition, the definition of the cognitive model by Shannon of thinking process of various possible solutions of a problem has tried out mentally or symbolically, before the best solution is selected by a mental evaluation of the results, and acted upon, need to be broadened [Shannon 1950b]. The various solution should not be confined to just searching down the game tree, but solutions from all different prospective whenever is possible so as to obtain a better solution. This requirement is essential in order to operate in a volatile problem domain, making it the pre-condition for problem solving in a dynamic environment. As far as planning is concerned, the issue of cognitive and reactive models should not be seen as choice of approaches but rather to understand their strength and weakness at different stage of the problem solution cycle so that comprehensive planning is complemented with the help of reactive measure to enhance and improve the surviving rate of the operational plan in dynamic environment. We sincerely hope that our investigation have helped to bring both approaches closer together for a better planning of tomorrow.

6.7 The Summary

In this chapter, the proposed problem-solving methodology with its multi-agent platform has been evaluated in six case studies, each designed to examine a particular aspect of the model in order to highlight its strength and weakness as a decision support system. We start with two very simple cases equipped with only stand-by plans and detour in the event of failed plans. Buffering is then introduced in the next case study to demonstrate how the temporally switching of the execution order could remedy the plan without lengthening its path. This point is underlined by using the same end-game but with buffering to steer the operational plan through from start of finish without the need for additional stage. Case study four assesses the mechanism to handle conflicting state between sub-paths within the same formation. The issue of re-planning is addressed in Case Five in the light of moving target, and the final case study integrates all the four agents together on the multi-agent platform to demonstrate how agents interact with each others to advise the player to come up with the best possible solution.

So far, we have presented a problem solving methodology and its architectural platform to provide decision support in a dynamic environment, but could such a system be capable of operating in a battlefield environment? have we made a sufficient probe in the foundation for the design of a battlefield management system? We will examine the issues in the next chapter.

CHAPTER SEVEN

DECISION SUPPORT FOR BATTLEFIELD SYSTEMS

For a military commander, a machine that could offer decision support in battlefield has always been a dream, and its presence in reality is beyond comprehension. This is not only due to the complexity of the problem domain but also because of the difficulty in obtaining a workable deliberation with the time constraint and volatility of the battlefield environment. This futuristic system, if successful, would no doubt transform the conduct of the modern day warfare and fundamentally enhance the chance of winning the war. This chapter intends to discuss a number of war game systems and to draw up a list of features and requirements before assessing the feasibility of a battlefield system based on the proposed multi-agent decision support platform.

7.1 The Background

Leaving the human emotion aside, battlefield is by far the most time-critical, chaotic and complex domain that one could ever have to work in. Firstly, it requires the understanding and comprehension of the ever-changing battlefield environment. Secondly, it demands a solution in the form of strategy and tactics within the time constraint. The former is a matter of plan deliberation, choice and decision making. As for the latter, it is often made up of incomplete and patchy intelligence report covering weather, terrain, road, river, obstacles, the deployment of the hostile units, their possible movements and plans.

The demanding nature of the battlefield environment requires solutions to be in place before the conflict begins. On the other hand, if the solution would have to be formulated from scratch, the know-how and expertise of the subject would no doubt help speed up the planning process. Furthermore, being in a multi-reasoning environment, a protocol for consolidation and criteria for selection would have to be provided so as to arrive at a "sensible" decision quickly. For centuries, military men and their civilian associates have always sought ways of modelling this decision making process as they prepare for the war.

In the 19th Century, the Prussian Army invented a formal model of "war game" known as "kriegspiel" for training purposes, and later it was improved and refined by the German army as the platform for battlefield planning. For instance: on 10 May 1940, when General Heinz Guderian, the commander of the XIX corps, took his action successfully to cross the Meuse against the British and French. He said ....

> *In view of the very short time at our disposal, we were forced to take the orders used in the war games at Koblenz from our files and, after changing the dates and times, issue these as the orders for the attack. They were perfectly fitted to the reality of the situation... The divisions [then] issued orders to their unit commanders which began: "Attack in accordance with map exercise carried out on........" [Guderian 1952]*

On the other hand, during the World War II, the British initiated the "operations research" or "operations analysis" for anti-submarine warfare in the sea and the modelling fighters in the air. The operation research models the phenomena and events of warfare in the form of probability theory, among which the Lanchester's equation is the most famous mathematics model in those days.

After the Second World War, as the development of Lanchester's equation has become more complex, the pressure for mechanisation has therefore intensified in the light of real-time simulation, which has led to the link up with the Von Neumann computer unearth at about the same time. These "computer warfare simulation" and "computer war game" were mainly designed to study the simulation of plans, other than the deliberation of them. In recent years, the battlefield management systems have been developed mainly in the C^2 (command and control) or C^3I (command, control, communication, and intelligence) systems, where human formulated plans (commands) are decomposed into a list of course of actions to be executed in a pre-determined order and fashion (control). Nonetheless, with the advance in decision support systems, the trend for applying AI into the plan deliberation and decision making has begun to emerge. As the computer is becoming cheaper in price and faster in speed, the progress of decision support system is undoubtedly getting closer to the desired reality.

7.2 Some Battlefield Management Systems

Although a battlefield management system normally requires for support of both plan deliberation and plan simulation, most early day battlefield systems have focused mainly on the latter rather than the former. This is due mainly to the mistrust of computer in taking charge of the decision of life and death in the complex environment of a battlefield. Hence, the early battlefield management systems were designed primarily for two purposes: firstly, to examine the operational complexity of each potential COA and the trade-offs among them under time constraint before the battle; secondly, to use it as the tool for the training of battlefield management, where various aspects of strategy and tactics could be simulated on machine, instead of using sand table or map exercises [Bonasso 1988] and [Liebowitz 1990].

7.2.1 First Battle

First Battle is a manually operated and low resolution battlefield simulation system, designed by the US Army Command and General Staff College for exercises from battalion to corps level [First Battle 1987]. Its development can be traced back to those days when LG. John H. Cushman was the commandant in the college. First Battle provides commanders and their staff with realistic, free-play events requiring time-based analysis, evaluation and decisions in the environment of command post exercise. In which, any scenario, terrain, or organisation of forces could be simulated.

First Battle is a rule-based system with a number of quantified factors. It consists of abundant basic rules from experience of real battle. These basic rules involve the play, manoeuvre, direct fire (DF), indirect fire (IDF), close combat (CC), aid defence artillery (ADA), tactical air (TACAIR), and other supplementary modules for indicating the units, strength, capabilities, terrain effects, and casualties assessment. Engagement is simulated on “Monte Carlo” to determine the chances (numeric) of wining, losing, or stalemate.

To the best of our knowledge, the First Battle system was implemented on HP-41 CV in the US Army Command and General Staff College, and had played a successful role as a battlefield simulation tool, although its functionality is too primitive and out of date for modern day warfare. Nevertheless, its rule-based reasoning approach to capture the battlefield environment and the use of quantified factors in simulation would no doubt set an useful precedence for the development of modern battlefield system.

7.2.2 COMBAT-SIM

COMputerized BATtle SIMulation (COMBAT-SIM)[COMBAT-SIM 1989], a command and control training system for military commanders and their staff, was produced by Perceptronics company under the directions of a number of retired military officers, who were themselves trained with First Battle, and therefore, many traces of First Battle features have found their ways into COMBAT-SIM.

COMBAT-SIM is a distributed microcomputer-based system, networked with high speed graphics to support real-time simulation in combat. However, its most important feature is its conflict-resolving method between the two opposing forces. Unlike the common Lanchester models, COMBAT-SIM uses performance profiles for each weapon, vehicle, or system. The profile is a function of range, which covers the actual firing results against various types of targets and learning from the terminal effects of each weapon, their hit records, and their ability in detecting and identifying targets. Collectively, these results and information are used to compile a matrix of effectiveness under a wide spectrum of possible conditions for all weapon types. This weapon's effectiveness matrix is at the heart of the COMBAT-SIM conflict algorithm.

To date, COMBAT-SIM have been adopted by many countries as a CAD military training tool. However, apart from the extensive use of modern technology in its implementation, flexible microcomputer networking (hardware), advanced imperative language Modular-2 (software) and video-map digitizer for military map display, its underlined problem-solving methodology are all knowledge-based, which keep the planning and decision making in battlefield still under human control.

7.2.3 KOMPASS

While the First Battle and COMBAT-SIM was regarded as the land-marked systems for the US developers, Europe was pursuing her own development in computer war game. The typical model was the KOMPASS [Marty 1982], originated from a research project in the Swiss Military Department before being developed into a formal training system for the Swiss Army.

The main feature of KOMPASS is to simulate the engagements between tanks and anti-tank forces, with artillery, infantry, and helicopter support on both sides over a real stretch of terrain. The winning criterion is to destroy as many enemy tanks as possible or to build up defensive position to delay the defeat as long as possible in a superior enemy tank offensive. In this set-up, different weapon systems and tactical plans are evaluated under the conditions of terrain, weapon-mix and mission.

Putting KOMPASS alongside both First Battle and COMBAT-SIM, it is very much a piece of out-dated system, although there are no doubt some interesting features which could be "cherry picked" into a more advanced system, and its focus point remains squarely in the area of battlefield simulation other than that of plan deliberation and decision making.

Finally, beside these three systems outlined above, there are a number of similar military systems, such as ROSIE (a programming environment for expert systems), ROSS (an object-oriented language for constructing simulations), TATR (a prototype expert system for tactical air targeting) and TWIRL (tactical warfare in the ROSS language) of the Rand company [Klahr and Waterman 1986]. They are all developed for battlefield simulation in one form or another, but no serious attempt has been made to incorporate plan deliberation, plan evaluation and plan execution into the battlefield system.

7.3 The Functionality of a Battlefield Management System

In view of the systems presented above, we will attempt to map out the functionality of a futuristic system for battlefield management. As an aid to the military commander, the proposed decision support system should provide an overview of the situation, should process and analyse the situation as events unfolds in the battlefield, and should offer a reasonable advice under time constraint that could form part of a strategic plan from the current situation to a desired situation (ultimate goal). The generation of advice should be based on some kind of the military decision-making procedure, with a suitable control mechanism to evaluate and select plans from proposals formulated either strategically or tactically. Finally, as a by-product, support should also be provided for analysis and training purposes. In other words,

- For decision support purpose:
  - To offer an advice (a course of action or a plan)
  - To explain the reasoning behind the proposed advice

- For analysis purpose:
  - Weapon evaluation (cost-effectiveness analysis)
  - Operational plan analysis (force structure analysis)
  - Combat development understanding (tactics analysis)

- For training purpose:
  - To learn the standard operating procedure in command post excise
  - To study the possible effects of selected factors in the battlefield
  - To understand how to organise an operation plan
  - To learn the decision making in the battlefield
  - To allow rapid successive iterations of the same phenomena

Putting this functionality in the context of the proposed multi-agent decision support platform, a closed correspondence could be drawn between the chess and battlefield domains, whose differences mainly arise from the level of details required in the battlefield system. We will discuss the problem-solving methodology stage by stage to highlight the gaps between the two kinds of environments.

7.3.1 The Situation Analysis

In here, we are not talking about a chess board with a river and two fortress, but data acquisition from sensors, interpretation or even decoding of intelligence reports, and data fusion in the real battlefield. In addition, the environmental data now includes topographical, meteorological and combat-related information.

The topographical environment is used to define part of the desired battlefield with the following features:

- Terrain relief
- Elevation
- Unit speeds and fuel consumption (based on terrain type)

In here, the line of sight (LOS) between any two given units can be determined by terrain type, elevation and weather conditions. Similarly, the movement rates of various units across different terrain types can also be indicated.

The meteorological environment is defined at the initialisation and modified by commander during each run, according to the realistic situation or the demanding simulation, in terms of weather classes and their meteorological visibility :

- Cloud (nil/light/medium/heavy)
- Rain (nil/light/medium/heavy)
- Sleet
- Snow
- Fog (light/dense)
- Light (daylight/twilight/full-moon/half-moon/no-moon)

The combat-related environment is given by the commander to indicate changes and actions introduced for each run. They shall include:

- Control measure required in partitioning of the tactical environment.
  Tactical descriptions such as axis of advance, boundary line, direction of attack, fire support co-ordination line, line of contact, main supply route, assembly area, objective, etc.
- Obstacle emplacement and reduction, in terms of minefield and obstacles
- Smoke and illumination introduction

Based on the information of these three environments, several manipulation tables could be constructed for situation analysis depending on the **Tactical Command and Control (TCC)** scenarios, for both the friendly and enemy forces. Two simplified tables of terrain effects on movement (mounted and dismounted) are presented as examples for the understanding about the influences from these environments. If we assume that the standard rate for the unit of tracked vehicle is 8 kilometres in a 30 minutes game turn (GT), by consulting the "Mounted" table the unit could move 8 KM (8/1) during the day time or 4 KM (8/2) during the night time over an open terrain or trails in each run. Estimations of mobility on different terrains are in shown Table 7.1 for situation analysis

Table 7.1 Terrain Effects on Movement-Mounted

Terrain	**Cost in Movement Value (MV) per KM**	
	Day	Night
Open & Trails	1	2
Forested	3	6
Built-up	3	6
Improved Roads	1/2	1
Steep Slopes (over 30%)		
Open 30% - 50%	3	6
Open over 50%	Impassable	
Forested 30% - 40%	5	10
Forested over 40%	Impassable	
Marshes & Wetlands	Impassable	
Stream & Rivers Crossing		
(Unopposed by either direct/indirect fires)		
Open & Trails	3	6
Forested & Built-up	5	10
Man Made Obstacles	Halt	
*	*	*
*	*	*

The following table provides the estimation of terrain effects on movement as an indication of the impact of terrain on mobility. The tables here provide information covering various components of the tactical environment. Graphically, a desired battlefield encompasses a rectangular surface of certain square kilometres to a limited altitude, which is further divided into suitable grids, supported by data related to the meteorological condition and combat-related environments. In some way, we could visualise the battlefield as a 3 dimensional chessboard, further compounded by weather and meteorological visibility.

Table 7.2 Terrain Effects on Movement-Dismounted

Terrain	**Cost in Movement Value (MV) per KM**	
	Day	Night
Tactical Approach March		
Open & Trails	1	1
Forested	1	2
Built-up	2	4
Improved Roads	1	1
Steep Slopes (over 40%)		
Open & Trails	2	3
Forested	3	5
Water Obstacle, Crossing with		
Engineering Assistance		
(Unopposed by direct/indirect fires)		
Open & Trails	2	3
Forested & Built-up	3	5
Man made Obstacles (Minefields only)	1	1
*	*	*
*	*	*

At the start of each run, the TCC values for the friendly forces are determined by commander to establish a simulated battlefield environment, while data for enemy forces are generated by an appropriate mathematical model or a pre-defined assumption according to the events in the battlefield or simulated environment. The content includes:

- Unit position, movement, and combat readiness attributes
- Unit composition and resource management
- Weapon fire control
- Environment conditions

Each unit in the system is defined as a collections of personnel, equipment and supplies located within a definable area, which operate as individual entities with quantified strength, responding to commander's instructions and/or model's calculations. It has a set of unit attributes, which are divided into two categories: static and dynamic attributes as shown in the following. The static attributes do not change during the run, while the dynamic attributes are changing during the run in response to either commander orders or the simulation itself.

1) Static Attributes:
 - Name
 - Colour (blue and red)
 - Type (combat and combat support)
 - Tactical Command and Control (TCC)

2) Dynamic Attributes:
 - Movement Value (KM per GT)
 - Maximum Engagement Range (MER) (KM)
 - Close Combat Strength (CCS)
 - Direct Fire Strength (DFS)
 - Indirect Fire Strength (IFS) (per tube or rocket)
 - Mission Capabilities (for combat support units)
 - Current Location
 - Current Control Zone
 - Current Operation State

These levels of complexity could go on to cover manoeuvre capabilities, weapon types and logistical supports. Hence, there is a gulf of difference between chess board and the simulated battlefield in terms of information capture and situation analysis. It is an area which has attracted the minds of many people over the years in the research and development of military system in all shapes and sizes. In fact, most advances in war game systems have been attributed to information capture for the battlefield other than planning. Therefore, as far as situation analysis is concerned, what the proposed multi-agent system can provide is the architectural platform, where information capture (basic blackboard database), data fusion (objective analysis), and situation interpretation (subjective analysis) from other systems could be integrated together for the construction of situation map.

7.3.2 The Strategic Planning

In here, the strategic agent, as in the chess domain relies on pure recognition to look for text-book solution where "Meuse Crossing" is a typical and classic example [Guderian 1952] of the recognition paradigm. Planning is attempted as a matter of routine in order to work out a strategic plan and related tactical plans from start to finish. In the battlefield, tactical and heuristic agents are still coming into play in the absence of any plan. They involve the heuristics of strengthening defensive positions or occupying advantageous position before seeking an opportunity for short-term advantage.

Realistically speaking, the knowledge base needed to support the strategic planning agent in the battlefield should be more comprehensive than the Moltke's "outer line strategy" of encirclement and "pin and strike" tactics used in our chess simulation. However, the methodology of co-operative planning and plan execution would still be relevant and applicable in the battlefield domain, although planning to win a battle is a lot harder than targeting on the opponent's general. Therefore, a combination of capturing a number of targets together with occupation of a number of key positions could be encapsulated in strategic plan, and hence a battlefield might consist a large number of objectives than a simple chess game that need to be achieved before declaring that the war is over. This fuzzy mapping of objective fulfilment to declare it win, loss or stalemate is an issued not addressed in the chess domain, and will undoubtedly form an extension to the existing framework.

7.3.3 The Tactical Planning

Since tactical planning involves the actual formulating of solution path, the contrast in environment between chess and battlefield could not have been more striking. The legal move generator in the chess domain is now given way to a set of mobility and engagement rules, i. e. surface-surface close combat engagements, surface-surface direct fire engagements, surface-surface indirect fire missions, or surface-air engagements. In the battlefield environment, even the evaluation of risk and reward is in the form of casualty and damage assessment.

1) Random Number Generator (RNG):
   RNG is used to generate a RN between 0 and 100.

2) The Casualty and Damage Assessment Databases (CDADs):
   - Database for close combat losses (CC)
   - Database for direct fire into moving target/returns fire (DF)
   - Database for direct fire into stationary target/returns (DF)
   - Database for HE (High Explosive) ammunition against exposed personnel (IDF)
   - Database for HE ammunition against soft targets (IDF)
   - Database for HE ammunition against protected personnel (IDF)
   - Database for ICM (Improved Conventional Munition) ammunition against soft targets (IDF)
   - Database for ICM ammunition against exposed personnel (IDF)
   - Database for ICM ammunition against protected personnel (IDF)
   - Database for attack helicopter with close assault (rockets)
   - Database for attack helicopter with direct fire
   - Database for threat attack helicopter bomb assessment

The casualty and damage assessments for various types of combat are based upon the effectiveness of the weapon systems and the vulnerability of the targets, which are further incorporated into different engagement knowledge sources using Random Number Generator (RNG) to simulates all of the unquantifiable or non-measurable aspects of the battlefield. Furthermore, some databases have additional parameters which could be set up to affect the simulation, for instance:

1) Modification to DF:
   - Status of position (i.e., hasty, protected, and prepared)
   - Status of engagement (i.e., front, flank, and rear)

2) Modification to IDF:
   - Exposed personnel (i.e., 1st volley, 2nd volley, and successive volleys)
   - Personnel/material in prepared/protected position (1st volley, 2nd volley, and successive volleys)

7.3.4 The Plan Selection

In the battlefield, the criteria and parameters used for evaluating and selecting operational plan are much more complex than the chess domain, which involve weapon evaluation, operational plan analysis and tactical analysis, so much so that the involvement of so many parameters in the evaluation, requires simulation "dry run" to assess the impact when various parameters are combined.

At the beginning of each simulation run, each unit in terms of assumed strength (e.g. MV, CCS, DFS, IFS, etc.) is given to the machine with its related tactical orders (e.g., Who, When, Where, What and How) from the commander as the execution order. However, for the enemy units, no order is given but considering all of their possible alternatives arrive at the simulation. In addition, during the run, each unit is given its related current environment data (e.g., terrain and man-made obstacles, etc.) from the environment model for the computation of mobility.

7.3.5 The Planning Execution (Command and Control)

Like all unbounded problem domain, the simulation of battlefield plans could only take into account whatever parameters included in the model. This implies that under certain circumstances, operational plan needs to be adjusted, modified, or even be replaced by other plans due to unexpected events. The role of the C^2 is certainly evident to ensure the smooth execution of the plan. However, detour and buffering only deal with terrain changes and man-made obstacles and they do not address the problem of meteorological, combat-related issues, resource management, weapon fire control and the men and units under command. In here, the issue of synchronisation in a battlefield is so complex that a comprehensive communication infrastructure is required to cope with the plan co-ordination of the number of men and units under command. As a result, the C^2 would have to be expanded into C^3 (Command, Control and Communication) or even C^3I (Command, Control, Communication and Intelligence) systems. In other words, the methodology of constantly checking and verifying associated condition of each plan during plan execution is as essential as its role in the chess domain. However, communication and the intelligence are now the vital components in the battlefield situation.

7.4 The Summary

At a first glance, both chess and battlefield domains may seem to have many features in common, one might be misled to the thought that chess domain is just a simplified battlefield, with almost one-to-one mapping between them.

Battlefield system		Chinese chess
units	---------->	pieces
environment	---------->	board
manoeuvre movement	---------->	legal move generator
detection probabilities	---------->	none
engagement	---------->	legal move
damage assessment	---------->	legal move
judgement	---------->	legal move
update the parameters of units and environment	---------->	none

However, detailed examination has revealed that a the colossal gap exists between them and it would be naive to think that because of these similarity, the multi-agent decision support platform that we have developed could be turned into a practical battlefield system overnight. On the other hand, given the complexity of the domain and the work and efforts done before us, and short of re-invention of the wheel, our problem-solving methodology should be integrated into the existing battlefield systems to enhance their planning ability on the multi-agent architectural framework. In other words, the proposed battlefield system:

- should model the tactical environment on a real-time basis simulating the interaction between friendly (blue) and enemy (red) units. It shall calculate the current tactical situation, generate the workable plan(s), offer the best advice, and provide the possible strategic plan or solution;

- should take into account the physical environment, unit movement, detection probabilities, engagements including weapon firing, effects, and damage assessment, supporting arms such as artillery and air support, as well as considerations of engineering, maintenance and logistical support;

- should have a user interface to facilitate the control and set up the system supporting operations such as PLAY, FINISH, UNDO and RENEW, etc. It should also provide means for the commander to input the suitable modifications (called tactical command and control), in terms of environment and the units attributes, with these information updated at certain time interval (e.g. every half an hour). At the end of each run, the system should offer the advice, the related plan, and the details of its reasoning/calculation process.

CHAPTER EIGHT

LEARNING IN A DYNAMIC ENVIRONMENT

The initial task to understand human cognition has enabled us to develop a planning methodology by combining search and recognition paradigms in a non-monotonic fashion, where more than one thread of reasoning can be pursued to find a better solution. More significantly, investigation has revealed that reasoning might operate on two levels of abstraction. On one level, we could visualise the problem from start to finish at a very discrete level by ignoring most of the details within a state, or even between states. On the other level, only when we are satisfied with the overall plan that is feasible will we concentrate on finding the path, which joins all the intermediate states together, so that recognition is used to construct the partial plan before search is mobilised to establish links between states to complete the solution path. The idea of co-operative planning is an attempt to emulate this hierarchical human problem solving methodology, and to enable the machine to deal with a more complex problem domain other than just the "block's world".

If the human thinking process is as what Shannon described, then the various solutions under consideration should not be confined to just searching down the game tree, but in all directions so as to obtain the best solution. However, the knowledge bases used in the chess domain are all static knowledge programmed by the human, and there is no provision for learning. In this chapter, we shall look at the issue of learning and machine adaptability in a dynamic environment.

8.1 Learning Sequence by Backward Chaining

If problem solving can be characterised by a sequence of states linking the initial state to the goal state, then learning a solution could be achieved by backward chaining [Fulcher 89]. Simulation employs artificial neural network had been set up to learn a number of mazes as a series of left and right turn by reinforcing stimulus-response. This unsupervised learning is reliant on either positive or negative feedback to reinforce the input/output connections. This simulation is about finding "food" in a "maze". Each location of the maze will be learned as a state in the sequence, and for each location the net has to associate the correct move that will take it one state nearer to its destination and eventually to the "food" (goal state).

The simulation was set up on a three layer network, with the first net being the move generator (MG) to learn the input-output association, and the second net being a reinforcement discriminator (RD). When the system moves from location **H** to location **I**, which yields a reward, the RD will reinforce the move the MG has just made. The result of this stimulus-reinforcement is that location **H** is now presented as an input to the RD to output **I**. This learning is repeated in a backward fashion from goal location **H** to the home location **A**, until the solution path for the maze has been learned, as displayed on the left hand side of Figure 8.1.

The network must, this time, be able to "think ahead" about the consequences of moving left and right. As the net learns the layout of the maze it is able to make accurate predictions about what lies ahead, choosing the greater evaluation between making a left or right turn at the next choice point [Fulcher 89].

A -> B -> C -> D -> E -> F -> G -> H -> **I**

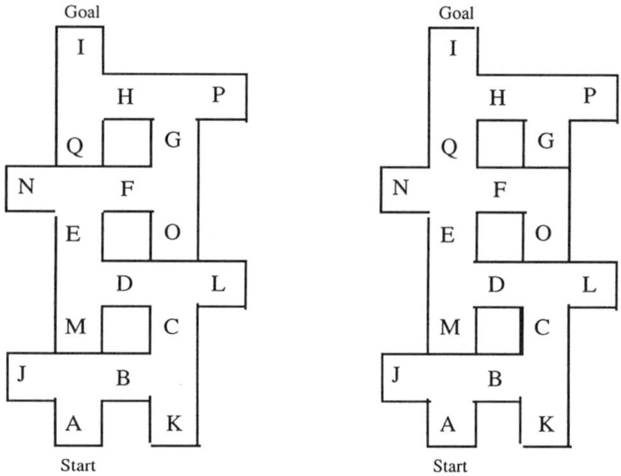

Figure 8.1. Learning in a Maze as a Sequence of States from Start to Goal

Hence, it is possible to learn solution sequence by backward chaining; Assuming that the environment remains relatively stable, it is feasible to incorporate learning into the recognition paradigm to enhance the system adaptivity so that plan could evolve with the changing environment. For instance, given a slightly different layout in the maze indicated on the right hand side of Figure 8.1, if the sequence learned previously had been followed, it would come unstuck at location **F**. However, learning could then be activated to learn about new layout ready for the next attempt. In here, feedback is provided in the form of either a "right" or "wrong" move to complete the learning process, but there is no provision to support fuzzy information such as "most likely" or "probably". In the next section, we will examine the issue of learning on a probabilistic network.

8.2 Learning by Credit Assignment

To take the matter further down the path of learning, the rating of plans and the criteria of choice could be organised in the form of credit assignment, where each plan in the system is weighted with a value learned through a multiple-valued probabilistic logic node (MPLN) network [Myers and Aleksander 1988]. This can be developed into a tree-like structure with credit assigned to each branch of the tree, and in conjunction with an evaluation function, the best routine or plan can be selected probabilistically.

In contrast to the Backward Chaining, the probabilistic model has a striking similarity to the game tree of an A type or B type chess algorithm and evaluation function is activated at every junction of choice to calculate the best possible branch based on credit assignment. Therefore, it is theoretically possible to learn the appropriate value for every branch of a game tree to assist the tactical agent in finding a better move. However, the colossal size of the complete game tree would restrict this type of learning only at the opening or end-game. In comparison between the probabilistic learning and the traditional brute-force search or heuristic search, the major difference is the adaptability of the knowledge acquired and learning would enable the problem solving model to evolve with the environment.

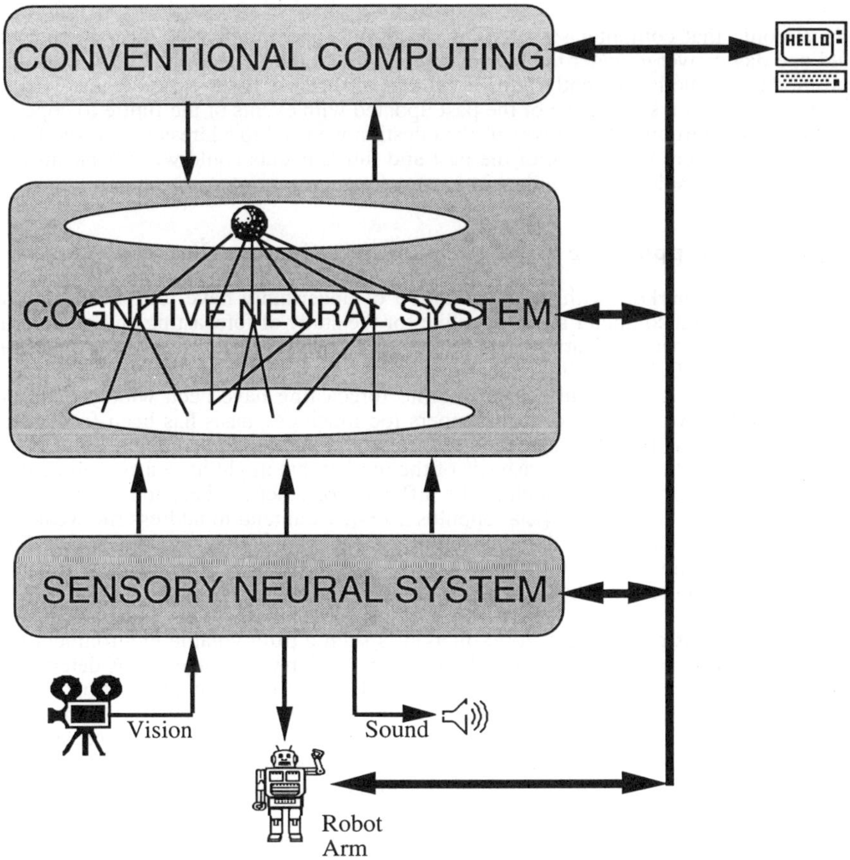

Figure 8.2. A General Neural Architecture from Aleksander and Morton

Being a breed of their own, neural scientists see the cognitive model as a general neural architecture that consists of three major components [Aleksander and Morton 1990]:

a sensory neural level
a cognitive neural level and
a conventional computing level

In here, the sensory neural system is for data fusion to convert electronic signals of all sharps and sizes into information understandable by the cognitive neural system, through video cameras, microphones and other electronic sensors (blackboard/situation map). At the same time, solution and course of actions (plans) generated by the cognitive model are communicated to the outside world through voice synthesizers, graphics screens, or even a robot arm. The conventional computing machinery is included here to provide the usual user interfaces.

It is ironic that computer scientists working on opposite ends of the AI spectrum would one day converge under the banner of cognitive model. Learning and knowledge-based models are both inherently human, whichever end we have started from. Human reasoning is based on knowledge of the past updated with events of the future to cope the ever changing environments. However, the question we need to address here is the frame work required, where knowledge of the past and future events could work hand-in-hand to arrive at a better solution given the circumstances.

8.3 Decision Support for Foreign Exchange System (Forex)

The financial markets with their reputation of uncertainty have long been popular with economists and computer scientists alike for the study of forecasting and prediction. Recent advance in machine learning has further accelerated the excitement to prophesy in financial markets. Being prediction or forecasting, Neural Networks for share prices prediction or Genetic Algorithm for economic forecasting have been widely featured. However, we believe in many of those papers too much emphasis has been focused on events of the past, as if "what happened before would surely happen again", and lesser attention has been placed on other aspects of the market that might have a complimentary impact in medium term; factors such as the influence of other markets and the economic fundamental. In this case study [Liakopoulos 1994], we intend to address the weakness of single track reasoning in a dynamic environment, and investigate the basis where learning could be integrated with knowledge-based system for a better solution in a foreign exchange (Forex) market.

Unlike the chess domain, the Forex market is such a truly volatile environment that event hardly repeats itself entirely, and the movement of the exchange rate is determined by a large number of factors, instead of a single well-defined attacking formation. In this study, we identify four mayor factors that often influence the movement of the exchange rate, i.e. the on-going trends, patterns in the chart, the sentiment in the market, and economic fundamental of a currency. The function of the decision support system is to generate and identify the most appropriate technique at a given time subject to market volatility.

Trends (historical data) + Patterns (historical data) + Market Sentiment + fundamentals ==> Future Event

8.3.1 The Situation Analysis

The Forex market is a typical decentralised environment, where each track of reasoning is driven by "greed and fear" in stimulus-response. However, each track looks at the market movement from its own prospective, and they together enrich the understanding of market behaviour. As far as the situation analysis is concerned, the global database (the blackboard) is the trading screen displaying movements of the major currencies, while each tactical agent has its own situation map to indicate only data that are of interest to them. For instance, the situation map of the trend agent will capture the movement of exchange rate that it is trying to predict, say, the Cable rate (£/$), while the situation map of the market sentiment agent will cover perhaps a range of exchange rates between $ and other majors (Swiss Franc, German Mark ....). Knowledge would be acquired through learning.

8.3.2 The Strategic Agent

Based on the model proposed in the chess domain, the static knowledge bases (the case library, strategic formations, and heuristics) are now replaced by a Time Series model trained with the historical data to capture the patterns and characteristic of the environment, as well as the knowledge of various window sizes to identify the emerging trend in the rate movement. Indication of strength or weakness of a currency could also be detected through the monitoring movement of rate against other major currencies in a grid that registers the relative influence of each currency. At this level, the strategic plan is not a fully connected path linking current situation to the desired situation, but a weighted polynomial equation shown as follows

$$\text{Predicted Rate} = W_1 * \text{Trend\_Agent} + W_2 * \text{Pattern\_Agent} + W_3 * \text{Sentiment\_Agent} + \ldots\ldots$$

This equation could contain an endless list of parameters which may have influence on the rate movement in one way or another. However in the financial market, only close approximation is required to achieve gain and avoid losses, and hence, only predominated factors are included in the model here for prediction. Since each parameter is predicting the movement of rate based on different techniques and assumption, its influences is constantly changing with the movement of the market. For instance, the time series used here for modelling patterns in the market has assumed the environment to be stationary or semi-stationary, and therefore, should feature well in a clam market. But in a very unsettled market, it might be the moving average with a short window size, which will respond more accurately to the market changes. Hence, the strategy here is to train the system to learn the appropriate weight distribution inductively given the market condition, to produce the most accurate result possible.

8.3.3 The Tactical Agents

Like the tactical planning in the chess domain, the actual formulation of solutions are organised at the tactical level, where the knowledge and techniques required are very much different from those of chess and battlefield. In technical forecasting, the predictions are based on time series and moving averages, while market-based forecasting relies on forward rate movement, inter-currency movement and market indicators, such as interest rate, RPI, GDP and other economic numbers to assess the value of a currency. In this investigation, we have combined only three technical approaches to generate solution, and intended to show how each additional technique could help in improving the quality of the solution.

1) **The Time Series Agent**
Traditionally, most time-varying environments are modelled by means of Time Series analysis, techniques such as Autoregression and Moving Average are well established in the field of forecasting. Primarily, the time series learn about the past patterns and behaviour characteristic of the data through training based on the historical data. If we assumed the time series to be stationary, or near stationary, based on the belief that "what happened before would probably happen again", forthcoming events in the same environment could be predicted. However in practice, most time series are non-stationary, and it is necessary to remove non-stationary sources of variation such as trends and seasonal factors in order to fit in a stationary model. Yet non-stationary components, such as trend, may sometimes be of more interest than the stationary residuals, hence a mixed autoregressive moving average model containing p AR terms and q MA, known as ARMA model of order (p,q) is often used.

In our model, we uses a mixed ARMA method in conjunction with an *adaptive filtering* method which contains four parameters, namely the width of the window, the order of the autoregressive process (AR), the order of the moving average process (MA), and the number of cycles needed for adaptive filtering. Generally speaking, these values are set up by the user depending on the problem domain. But in a volatile environment such as the Forex market, different values are needed in different situations, and therefore, it is of fundamental importance to identify a learning algorithm that could adjust these parameters automatically during run-time in order to provide the best possible prediction to the strategic agent; a number of time series models could be set up to run concurrently, with their performances monitored to identify the most suitable set-up according to the market situation, to deliver the best possible prediction to the strategic agent.

In time series, the prediction is based on the observations of the past (**n**) events known as the **window width.**

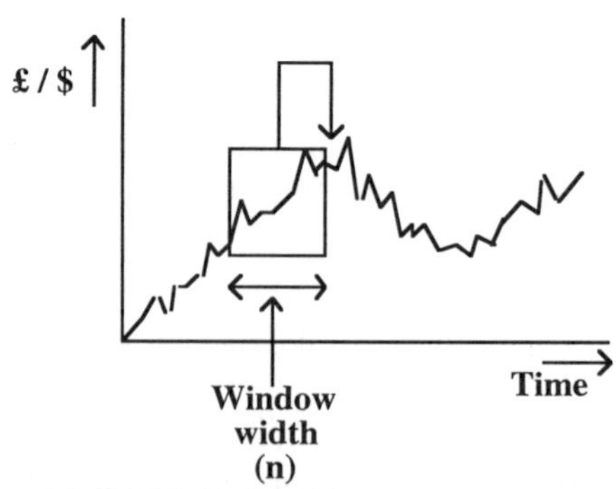

Figure 8.3. The Window Width in Time Series Forecasting

The general form of an **order p** autoregressive process is known as AR(p) model as shown in Equation 8.1:

$$X_t = \phi_1 X_{t-1} + \phi_2 X_{t-2} + \phi_3 X_{t-3} + ... + \phi_p X_{t-p} + e_t \quad [8.1]$$

where the current value of the process is expressed as a weighted sum of past values plus the current shock. The general AR(p) model provides an extremely flexible and versatile form of time series prediction. It represents a general class of mode which is capable of dealing with all types of data by specifying the order p. A typical example is the AR(1) model which weighs past errors in an exponentially decreasing manner.

$$X_t = \phi_1^{n-1} X_{t-n+1} + \phi_1^{n-2} e_{t-n+2} + ... + \phi_1^2 e_{t-2} + \phi_1 e_{t-1} + e_t \quad [8.2]$$

On the other hand, the Equation 8.3 shows the general form of an **order q** moving average process, known as the MA(q) model.

$$X_t = e_1 - \theta_1 e_{t-1} - \theta_2 e_{t-2} - ... - \theta_q e_{t-q} \quad [8.3]$$

However more commonly, a mixed autoregressive moving average model ARMA(p,q) is used, when the two models are combined together into a single equation :

$$X_t = \phi_1 X_{t-1} + \phi_2 X_{t-2} + ... + \phi_p X_{t-p} + e_t - \\ - \theta_1 e_{t-1} - \theta_2 e_{t-2} - ... - \theta_q e_{t-q} \quad [8.4]$$

Furthermore, adaptive filtering can be applied to all of the models described above. The ϕ_i and θ_j parameters are estimated through a non linear square approach by steepest descent. The initial values for these parameters are adjusted by using Equations [8.5] and [8.6] repeatedly for **N cycles** to obtain a set of parameters which would lead to a minimised Mean Square Error.

$$\phi_{i\,t} = \phi_{i\,t-1} + 2K\, e_t\, X_{t-i} \quad [8.5]$$

where $i = 1,2,3,...p$ and $t = p+1,p+2,...N$

$$\theta_{i\,t} = \theta_{i\,t-1} + 2K\, e_t\, e_{t-i} \quad [8.6]$$

where $i = 1,2,3,...q$ and $t = q+1,q+2,...N$

A more detailed discussion of these methods can be found in [Box and Jenkins 1971], and [Makridakis and Wheelwright 1977].

Using the Cable rate between 7/1/80 to 29/5/92, we have initially set up a number of ARMA models to identify the most appropriate one during this period to predict the movement of rate. Since the cable rates are available up to 4 decimal points, i.e. for the rate of £ = $1.7001, the true rate is lying between £ = $1.7002 and £ = $1.7000 with the error in percentage term of just over 0.1% of the average rate, and with the daily movement of data about 0.5% of the exchange rate, the tolerant range would have to be between 0.2% to 0.4% of the average rate. From the test, we have concluded that the ARMA (1,0) model with 0.4% tolerant range produces a hit rate of just over 50%, which we will use here for our investigation.

Table 8.1. The Results of Various ARMA models for the Period Between 7/1/80 and 29/5/92

Tolerant range	AR Order	MA Order	Training Cycles	Window width	Hit rate (%)
0.4% * rate	1	0	200	150	51.532 %
0.4% * rate	1	1	200	150	50.115 %
0.4% * rate	1	2	200	150	50.115 %
0.4% * rate	2	0	200	150	39.621 %
0.4% * rate	1	0	150	135	52.125 %
0.5% * rate	1	0	100	100	59.980 %
0.5% * rate	1	1	100	100	57.429 %
0.4% * rate	1	0	100	100	50.345 %
0.4% * rate	1	1	100	100	48.171 %
0.3% * rate	1	0	100	100	41.039 %
0.3% * rate	1	1	100	100	38.201 %

Operating in a highly volatile environment, it is impossible to find a fixed ARMA model that would function accurately in a Forex market through out the period of observation. We have therefore set up seven ARMA models to be run concurrently, each with different Training Cycle and Window Width as shown in Table 8.2. The best result come from the ARMA model with Training Cycle = 150 and Window Width = 200, which is slightly better than the best result in Table 8.1, and implies that the set-up of training cycle and window width are domain dependent and it is therefore essential to have an adaptive selection scheme that could identify the most appropriate model dynamically subject to market condition. However, the issue of selection is complicated by the assumption of the solution space whether the prediction from each ARMA model is mutually exclusive or partially overlapped? If the solution spaces of all ARMA model were totally overlapping with each other, then the model with the best track record should be selected. On the other hand, if we assumed their solution spaces were only partially overlapped, then the prediction should come from all models in a polynomial of weighted sum.

$$\text{Prediction} = W_1 * \text{ARMA}_1 + \cdots \cdots \cdots + W_7 * \text{ARMA}_7 \qquad [8.7]$$

The weight of each ARMA model is inductively changed through a number of iterations aiming to minimise the error between the actual and the predicted rates, and the best weight distribution that produces the smallest error will be retained to predict the rate for the next day.

Table 8.2. The Hit Rate from the Seven ARMA Models for Data Collected Between 2/1/87 and 4/11/92

AR Order	MA Order	Training Cycles	Window width	Hit rate (%)
1	0	135	135	51.588 %
1	0	200	150	51.453 %
1	0	150	160	51.318 %
1	0	150	170	51.115 %
1	0	150	190	51.656 %
1	**0**	**150**	**200**	**52.197 %**
1	0	170	200	51.588 %

Total Overlapping Solution Space:
Since we do not know which ARMA model will gives us the best prediction, we will examine the hit rate of all seven models in the last five attempts, and the model which emerges with the smallest error will be singled out for consideration. This yields a hit rate of 51.926% (768 hit out of 1479 attempts).

```
- repeat until no more data
  - receive actual rate from the market
  - for all models in the Time Series Agent
     - calculate error for last attempt to replace
       oldest one in the buffer
     - calculate error in past five attempts
  - find agent with minimum error in past five
    attempts
 - for all agents
     - receive and store prediction
 - send the selected prediction to strategic agent
- end repeat
```

Figure 8.4. The Selection Algorithm in an Total Overlapping Solution Space (TO)

Partial Overlapping Solution Space:
However, if we believe each of these seven models has captured part of rate behaviour in one way or another, and collectively they could predict the movement of the rate more accurately based on the weighted polynomial of Equation [8.7]. This yields a hit rate of 51.791% (766 hit out of 1479 attempts).

```
- repeat until no more data
- receive the actual rate from the market
- find the best performing agent in the last
  attempt
- increase respective weight for that agent
  without causing weights of other agents to
  fall below a safety minimum
  (decrease from all other weights is by a
    standard amount)
- apply new weights to yesterday's
  predictions
- while error of the weighted prediction with
   the new weights keeps getting smaller
         (for yesterday)
    - increase respective weight for the
       selected agent in the same manner
    - apply weights to yesterday's predictions
  - end while
```

Figure 8.5. The Algorithm for Integrating All ARMA Outputs in a weighted polynomial (PO)

Although none of model has managed a hit rate as good as the best ARMA model during this period (52.197%), the need for user supervision and intervention has been eliminated. However, further examination of the solution space has unveiled that out of the 51.926 % and 51.791 % hit rates resulted from TO and PO respectively, a large proposition of them were common, which has accounted for 49.636% (734/1479), and only 2.98852% (34/1479) and 2.163624% (32/1479) of the hits are due solely to either TO or PO alone as shown in Figure 8.6. This implies that 54.275% of the events in this environment are predictable, if we could find a way to integrate TO with PO for the generation or prediction of today exchange rate.

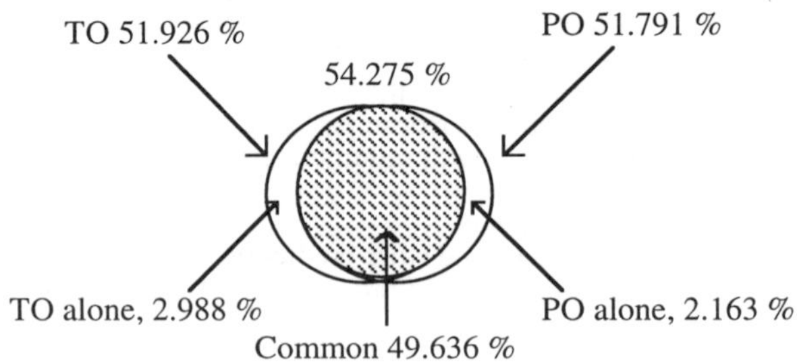

Figure 8.6. The Overlapping Solution Space Between TO and PO Results

The simplest way to achieve this is to integrate the PO prediction into the TO model, where prediction for today is selected from the seven ARMA models, plus an extra one from the weighted polynomial. Using the same selection criteria as before of whichever had scored highest in the past five attempts would be selected has given us the opportunity to capture the 32 events which were previously inaccessible from the TO model. As a result, five extra events have been predicted, making the total hit rate of 772 (734 + 39) out of 1479 events, a 52.265% hit rate compared favourably even to the best result in Table 8.2. This finding also leads us to the conclusion that the volatility of the Forex market can not be served by the simplistic assumption of a either total or partial overlapped solution space and a more sophisticated model would be needed if we intend to improve on the overall hit rate.

2) **The Trends Agent**
The ARMA (1,0) model is designed to learn and capture patterns in the stationary mode, while the influence of non-stationary element such as trend is monitored most by moving averages with different window sizes. It is believed that trends in the market last for approximately three to twenty days [Chau 1992]. Since we can never be sure about the length of the current trend(s), we will set up five MA models, each with different window sizes to study the trends over a different number of days, before combining these proposals to form the final prediction.

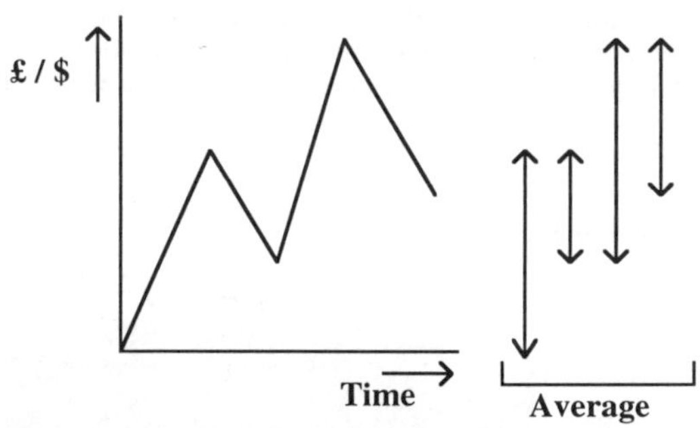

Figure 8.7. The Detection of Trends by Moving Averages

First of all, each moving average model will attempt to capture the current market trends by examining the average daily movement of the rate during the past (n) days (e.g. slope).

$$X_n = (|Rate_{today} - Rate_{today-1}| + |Rate_{today-2} - Rate_{today-3}| + \ldots + |Rate_{today-(n-1)} - Rate_{today-n}|) / n \qquad [8.8]$$

The five window sizes are used here ranging from three, five, ten , fifteen, to twenty day period. These trends provide the indication of forthcoming rate movement in the market, and when combined with the results either the TO or PO of the time series, the agent will enable a prediction for today rate to be formulated. As far as our problem solving methodology is concerned, the strategic solution is made up of two tactical components; the forecasted result from the stationary model (time series) and the expected acceleration resulted from the emerging trends. However, the question here is the manner by which both elements could be combined to generate the best possible prediction. A straightforward merging of both tactical components will result in ten strategic solutions.

- Forecast by PO of Time Series Agent + Trends, from Moving Average Agent
- Forecast by TO of Time Series Agent + Trends, from Moving Average Agent

Alternatively, the outputs from these five window sizes can be combined into only one overall average trend, taking into account both long and short-term trends, before merging it with the results due to either TO or PO model.

$$\text{Average Trend} = (X_{n1} + X_{n2} + X_{n3} + ... + X_{n\,m}) / m \qquad [8.9]$$

where m is the number of agents (five)

This will result in just two strategic solutions; one average trend with the result of either TO or PO model. However, the impact of the newly emerging trend picked up by MA models with shorter window sizes will now be delayed until models with longer window sizes have also picked up the same trend. As a result, the predicted rate from these strategic solutions tend to be less sensitive to new trend, and they are therefore more suitable for less volatile market condition. To compensate for this shortcoming, we have combined the average rates, but not trends of all five models, in a polynomial with yesterday rate to generate the prediction in a slightly different way.

$$\text{Prediction} = W_1*\text{Rate(3 days)} + ... + W_5*\text{Rate(20 days)}\,) + W_{fixed}*\text{Yesterday\_rate} \qquad [8.10]$$

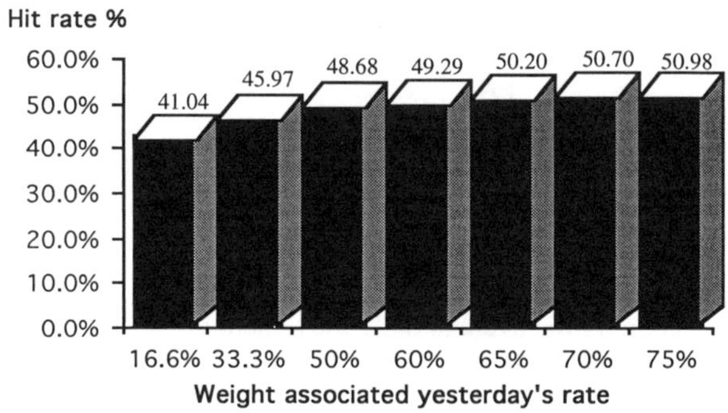

Figure 8.8. The Results of Tests to Identify the Weight for Yesterday's Rate

According to the test conducted on different setting of weight for yesterday rate, it has found that fixing yesterday rate at 75% and distributing the remaining 25% amongst the five moving average models through inductive learning provide the best result, and trend that has a most dominating influence will be given a more significant weight. This is designed to counter-balance the equally weighted average trend (mean) of Equation 8.9, and in a rapidly changing Forex market different consolidation process will be applicable under different circumstances.

3) The Market Sentiment Agent

There are many indicators that one could use to get an idea about where the market is going. As far as the Forex market is concerned, some of the most important factors are the $ exchange rates with other major currencies, forward rates, volume, stock market indices, yields and rates offered by bonds etc. Although it is not difficult to understand why these indicators provide a clue to where the market is heading, after all, what they do is to provide an opinion from their own prospective, and collectively they should create a very clear indication of the sentiment in the market. However in practise, it is very hard to quantify exactly what these correlation is, but with the help of artificial neural network, some kind of association could be established.

Artificial neural networks are modelled on the neuronal process of the brain, which composed of a large number of simple processing units (neurons), each interacts with others via connections with weights, which are modified iteratively to captures the relation between its input(s) and output(s). Although they exist in different topologies and algorithms, some basic components are common to all types of networks :

- **A set of processing units**: although each unit operates independently and has only one output, it can have many inputs.
- **A connectivity graph** or topology of the network that determines how neurons are connected, usually arranged into layers. In multi-layer networks, middle layers are hidden from external input and output, but they receive weighted input.
- **A set of parameters** associated with each unit, normally known as **weights** which indicate the strength of a connection from one neuron to another, are adjusted during learning. Conventionally, weight w_{ij} is related to the connection from unit j to unit i; such that if $w_{ij} > 0$ the connection is excitatory; if $w_{ij} = 0$, there is no connection; and if $w_{ij} < 0$, it is inhibitory.
- **An activation function** associated with each unit that combines the inputs into a scalar value. Usually this function is linear and performs a weighted sum of the inputs as in the case of the McCulloch-Pitts neuron:

$$net_i = \sum w_{ji} o_j \qquad \text{where } o_j \text{ is the output of neuron j}$$

- **An output function** of each unit transforms the activation value into an output, in accordance to the propagation rule and the threshold function, usually a sigmoidal function likes tanh(x).

$$out_i = g(net_i),$$

- **A learning rule** that describes how the parameters within each unit are modified.
- **An environment** in which the learning system must operate.

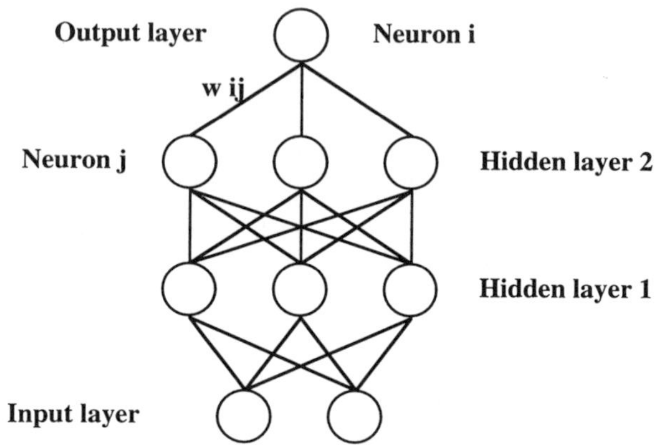

Figure 8.9. A Multi-Layer Feedforward Network

In this investigation, we use a multi-layer feedforward net to correlate between the Cable rate and movement of US dollars with other major currencies trained by backpropagation. Backpropagation involves a forward sweep to generate the output and a corresponding backward sweep to adjust the weights to minimised the error. For a mathematical derivation of backpropagation and a more extensive discussion of the subject, the reader should refer to [Rumelhart et al 86], [Hertz et al 91]. In here, only the correlation between nine major currencies and the Cable rate have been monitored for clue of movement in the market. In practise, many other market indicators could be included to improve the prediction.

US$/DEM, GB£/US$, US$/CHF, US$/FRF, Ecu/US$,
GB£/DEM, DEM/CHF, DEM/FRF, GB£/FRF

where DEM = German Mark, GB£ = British Pound, CHF = Swiss Franc, FRF = French Franc

When learning by error backpropagation, weights between connections are modified to minimise the mean square error (target - output) over a number of input patterns. This involves forward and backward sweeps through the network for all training patterns for a sufficiently large number of iterations. Once learning is complete, the incoming patterns will be presented to the network to generate predictions.

```
- While number of iterations not reached
  and the error has not fallen below required limit
   - for all patterns
      - forward sweep
      - backward sweep (modify weights)
      - add pattern error to overall error
   - end for
- end while
```

Figure 8.10. The Learning Algorithm

Clearly, from time to time the network needs to enhance its knowledge by retraining. Although our preference is to retrain all patterns after each prediction, this is indeed computationally very expensive, and we have therefore opted for a compromise. After the initial training, only a smaller number of iterations will be involved to retrain the network; when the actual rate from the market is taken into account on the following day, patterns can be learned without loosing knowledge of previous patterns.

Table 8.3. The Results of Test from Five Agents with Different Setting

	Run1	Run2	Run3	Run4	Run5
Hidden layers	1	1	2	2	3
Neurons in first layer	30	40	35	30	10
Neurons in second layer	-	-	10	16	31
Neurons in third layer	-	-	-	-	5
Learning rate	0.3	0.3	0.3	0.3	0.3
Momentum	0.8	0.8	0.8	0.8	0.8
No of training patterns	100	100	100	100	100
No of initial iterations	5000	5000	7000	7000	10000
No of patterns after which to re-learn	2	1	1	1	1
No of iterations for re-learning	100	100	100	100	100
Hit rate %	39.7	43.2	48.3	48.4	49.9

To monitor the correlation between the Cable rate and the exchange rates of $ with the nine currencies, we use an input layer of nine neurons to process the nine exchange rates, and use three hidden layers with ten neurons for the first, thirty one for the second and five for the third layer, together to predict the Cable rate (£/$) for tomorrow. This network topology is derived and based on the findings of [Mauree 92] and [Wong 92]. However, because the inputs into the neural net are normalised in the range 0 -> 1 during training, the prediction it generates needs to be scaled back in the following manner:

$$\text{Scaled Target Input} = (\text{Target Input} - \text{Min}_{rate}) / (\text{Max}_{rate} - \text{Min}_{rate}) \quad \text{and}$$
$$\text{Unscaling Output} = (\text{Scaled Output} * (\text{Max}_{rate} - \text{Min}_{rate})) + \text{Min}_{rate}$$

8.3.4 The Selection of Results

In a dream-scenario, a dealer is surrounded by a group of experts from different backgrounds, each watching and predicting the movement of rate as event unfolds on the screen. In a volatile market place, not all of these predictions could be right at all the time, but so long as some of the advice are accurate at some of the time, it is up to the dealer to exercise his/her judgement on which advice to follow. However, how far can we go to trust the machine in decision making? This is the issue which we would like to address in this section, the issue of choice, that has long been associated with Human intelligence ever since the day of Adam and Eve.

According to our observation, the movements of the foreign exchange rates are primarily affected by four types of factors, namely the patterns in the data, on-going trends, market sentiment and changes in political or economic fundamentals coming in the form of news. In a multi-agent model, every tactical agents will study the events as they develop and work out their part of the solution individually before merging it with others to form the strategic solution for consideration. In here, there are seven ways by which a prediction could be formulated.

1. TO prediction from the Pattern Agent:
   The prediction from the most successful ARMA model that has the smallest error in the past five attempts (assuming a total overlapping solution space).

2. TO prediction from the Pattern Agent + Average Trend
   The prediction from the TO model plus the average trend of the past 3, 5, 10, 15 and 20 days, as indicated in Equation 8.9.

   $$\text{Prediction} = \text{Prediction from the best ARMA model} + \text{Average Trend} \qquad [8.11]$$

3. PO prediction from the Pattern Agent:
   The prediction is formed by merging the results of all seven ARMA models in a polynomial of weighted sum, where the best-performed model in the last attempt is given the heaviest weight (assuming a partial overlapping solution space).

   $$\text{Prediction} = W_1{*}ARMA_1 + W_2{*}ARMA_2 + \ldots + W_7{*}ARMA_7 \qquad [8.12]$$

4. PO prediction from the Pattern Agent + Average Trend:
   The prediction is obtained by merging Equation 8.12 with the average trend of the past 3, 5, 10, 15 and 20 days.

   $$\text{Prediction} = W_1{*}ARMA_1 + W_2{*}ARMA_2 + \ldots + W_7{*}ARMA_7 + \text{Average Trend} \qquad [8.13]$$

5. Yesterday rate + Average Rates from the Trend Agent:
   The prediction is generated from yesterday rate and the combination of the average rates from all five moving average models in a polynomial.

   $$\text{Prediction} = W_1{*}\text{Rate(3 days)} + \ldots + W_5{*}\text{Rate(20 days)} + W_{fixed}{*}\text{Yesterday\_rate} \qquad [8.10]$$

6. Yesterday rate + Average Rate and Average Trend from the Trend Agent:
   The prediction of Equation 8.10 plus the mean daily movement of the rate (average trend).

   Prediction=W_1*Rate(3 days)+...+W_5*Rate(20 days)+W_{fixed}*Yesterday_rate+ Average Trend

7. The prediction from the market sentiment agent

As far as the market is concerned, no individual model can be consistently superior to the others, due to his/her limitation in the course of problem solving. Therefore, decision making in a volatile market is best served by a group of agents, each covering different aspects of market condition, and if they could be deployed in parallel, and with an appropriate selection strategy, they will compensate each other in producing a better prediction. Clearly, if more than one models are pointing to the same direction, we may be more confident about them being correct. However, what is the best selection strategy in such a truly volatile environment? How could the machine know which is the most appropriate solution?

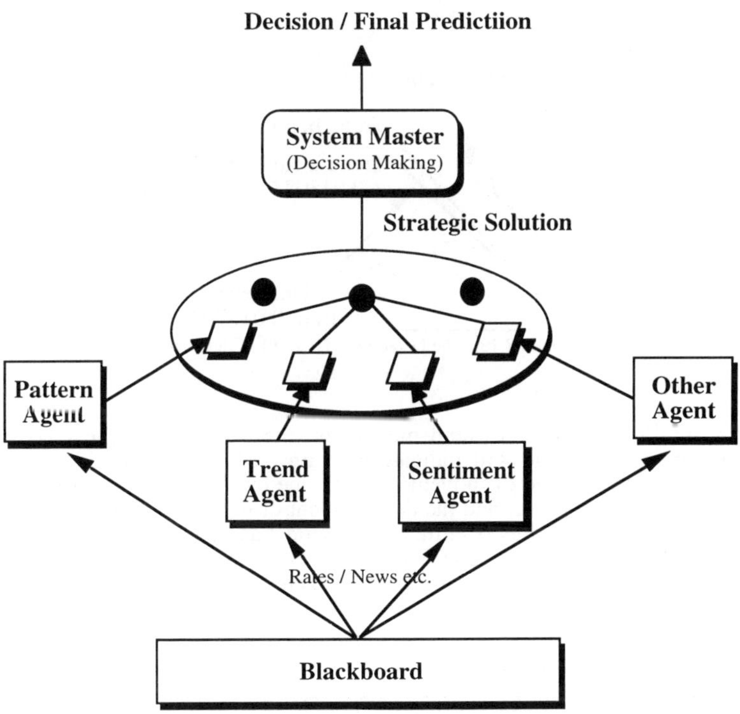

Figure 8.11. The Overview of the Multi-agent Decision Support System

In review of the hit rates of all tactical agents or even their combined strategic solutions presented so far, almost all of them are hopping around the 50% mark and they are neither impressive nor applicable. However given the volatility of the market, we believe that the changes of movement in the market are mainly caused by a new trend emerging in the market, and they could be associated and detected by a certain strategic solution under certain circumstances. Therefore, it would be possible to improve the hit rate significantly by calling upon the right solution at the right time.

To detect the volatility of the market, the system master will examine the trend movement by first obtaining the average trend in the market up to yesterday. Calculated by the Trend agent, this average rate is then measured against the average rate including today's; any differences between the two rates confirm the presence of a new trend; the wider the differences, the stronger the trend. Therefore the correlation between the degree of differences and the performances of all seven strategic solutions could be used as the basis for selection. Since it is very cumbersome to keep track of records for all methods for all points in a continuous space, we have tabulated these correlation in the following ranges:

> the range of average trend movements is from -0.018087 to +0.026774, and
> the range of absolute daily trend changes is between 0 to 0.012797.

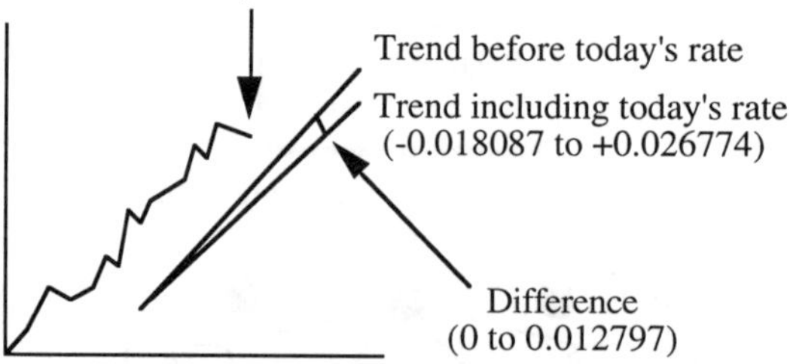

Figure 8.12. The Detection of Volatility in the Market

By examining the average trend movement, the volatility of the market can be tabulated (i.e. a high value will indicate high upward or downward trends), and in conjunction with the degree of movement from one day to another will indicate some inversion of the current trends and the development of new one. Based on just the time series and trends agents, the volatility tabulation has produced some improvement measured by hit rate, from 52.265% hit rate based only on time series models, to 53.887% and 54.969% respectively using a five-agent model (including strategic solution 1, 2, 3, 4 and 5), and a sixth agent model (including strategic solution 1, 2, 3, 4, 5 and 6).

Threshold	0 %	35 %	40 %	50 %
5 Agents	53.887 %	56.227 %	57.014 %	58.035 %
6 Agents	54.969 %	56.579 %	57.426 %	58.395 %

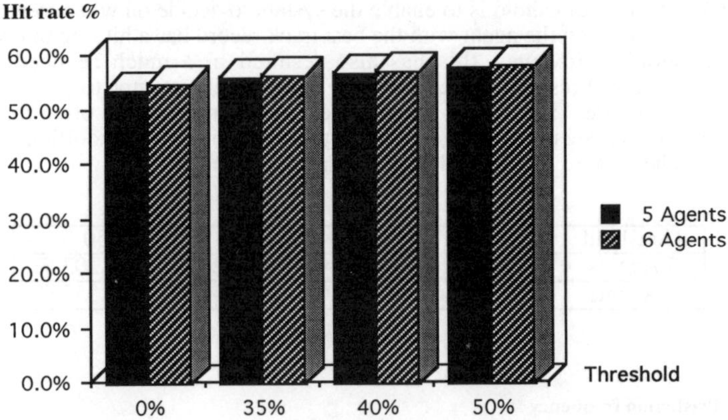

Figure 8.13. The Hit Rates of Both Five- and Six-Agent Models Covering Period from 2/1/87 to 4/11/92

With the adoption of volatility tabulation, every additional agent seems to improve the overall hit rate to a certain extent. However, these results are still nowhere near the 62.5% target that we are looking for, unless the system were allowed to "sit on its hands" and only to offer a prediction whenever it is confidence to do so. In other words, incorporating threshold into the selection process.

```
- while there exists more data
   - receive actual rate from the market
   - for all agents
      - evaluate last prediction
      - update appropriate hit rate
        (for yesterday's position in volatility tabulation)
   - end for
   - update overall hit rate if a prediction was made last time
   - obtain estimated average trend for today
   - subtract it with previous trend estimation to find the difference
   - for all methods
      - receive prediction
   - end for
   - select the best strategic solution based on the tabulation
   - if hit rate of best method > threshold (may be zero)
      - activates the strategic solution as the prediction
   - else
      - no prediction made
   - end if
- end while
```

Figure 8.14. The Algorithm for Selection Strategy

The advantage of threshold is to enable the system to decide on when to predict under the condition only when the agent with the best track record has a hit rate in excess of the pre-set threshold. However, this has also resulted in a much reduced prediction frequency. As the threshold increases, both models will attempt to predict on fewer occasions than before. Yet the six-agent model has attempted more often than the five-agent model, which seems to suggest that with the support of an additional agent, the former is less hesitant to predict and able to achieve a higher hit rate.

Threshold	0 %	35 %	40 %	50 %
5 Agents	100 %	93.914 %	90.128 %	81.203 %
6 Agents	100 %	96.078 %	91.954 %	82.555 %

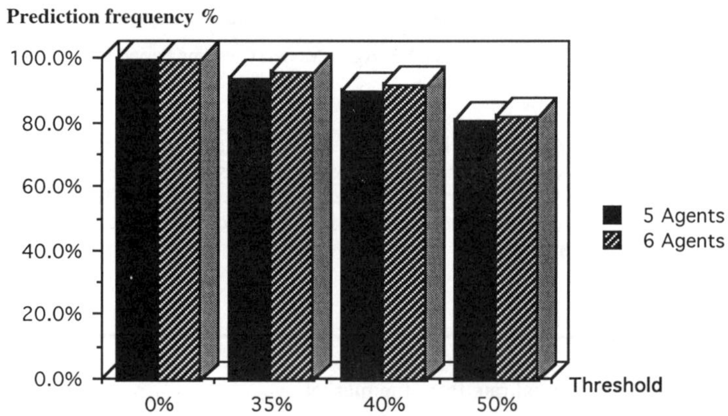

Figure 8.15. The Prediction Frequency of Both Five- and Six-Agent Models

By the same proposition, how far could a seven-agent model go in improving the overall hit rate? We will address this issue by integrating the market sentiment agent with the existing six-agent model. However, the compatible data set of the nine currencies only available between 29/5/87 to 4/11/92, instead of the duration between 2/1/87 to 4/11/92 used in the previous investigation, and we have therefore reduced the data set to cover just the period between 29/5/87 to 4/11/92. Once again, the seven-agent model shows a slight improvement as compared with the results of the six-agent model, and confirms our observation that market sentiment has only a secondary effect towards the movement of the overall rate.

Threshold	0 %	35 %	40 %	50 %
6 Agents	55.5 %	56.8 %	57.5 %	61.5 %
7 Agents	56.2 %	57.4 %	57.8 %	61.7 %

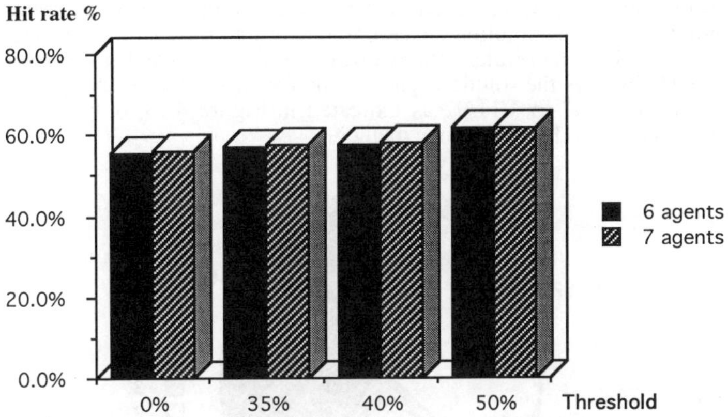

Figure 8.16. The Hit Rates of Both Six- and Seven-Agent Models Covering Period from 29/5/87 to 4/11/92

By comparison, the results from Figure 8.13 and 8.16 seem to suggest that hit rate is environment dependent; using different data sets will result in different hit rates, and either by design or coincidence, our choice of data set that covers and includes events leading to the stock market crash on the 19/10/87 (the black Monday) might unintentionally undermine the performance of our system. In order to verify this hypothesis, we re-run the simulation with the same data set but without the events six months either sides of the black Monday, and the results below confirm our observation by producing a set of hit rates in excess of our target of 62.5%.

Threshold	0 %	35 %	40 %	50 %
6 Agents	54.93 %	57.80 %	57.80 %	63.28 %
7 Agents	55.60 %	58.52 %	58.52 %	63.80 %

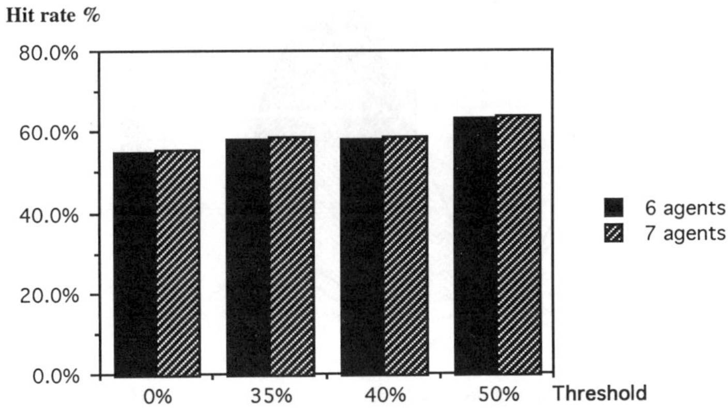

Figure 8.17. The Hit Rates of Both Six- and Seven-Agent Models Covering Period from 31/5/88 to 4/11/92

Furthermore, every additional agent however low its hit rate may be seems alone to have extended area of the solution space previously uncovered by other agents. This finding is supported by the results obtained from the five-, six- and seven-agent models. The Figure 8.16 displays the solution space of the five-agent model in a pie chart, using the data set from 2/1/87 to 4/11/92 as indicated in Figure 8.13, only 62.48 % of the solution space is covered by at least one method.

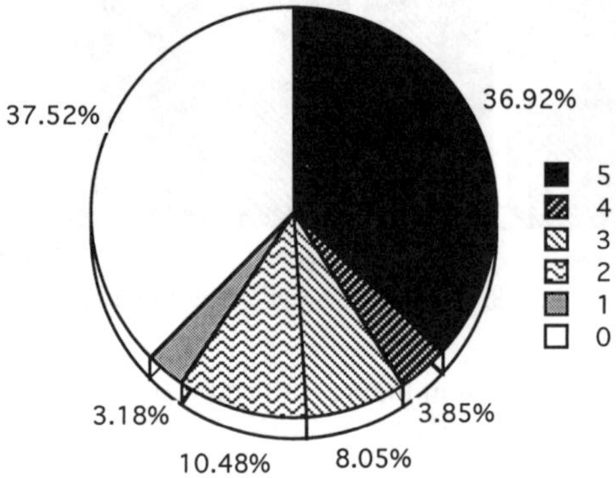

Figure 8.18. The Classification of Solution Space for the Five-Agent Model (from 2/1/87 to 4/11/92)

However, if we are to extend the model to the six- or seven-agent models covering the period of between 31/5/87 to 4/11/92, then once again, the uncovered solution space is further deduced from 37.52% (five-agent) to 35.02% (six-agent) and 32.92% (seven-agent) respectively.

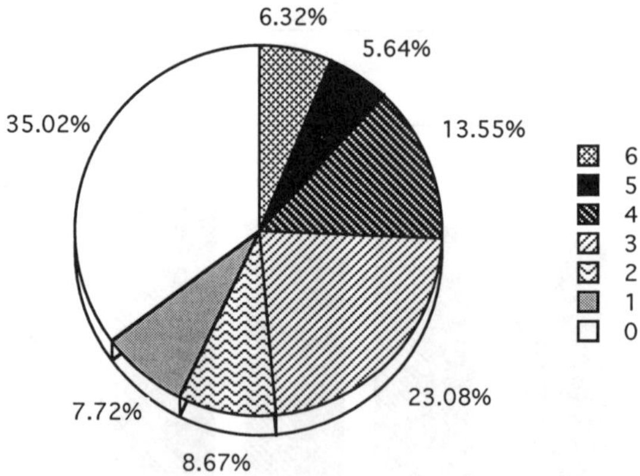

Figure 8.19. The Classification of Solution Space for the Six Agent Model (from 31/5/87 to 4/11/92)

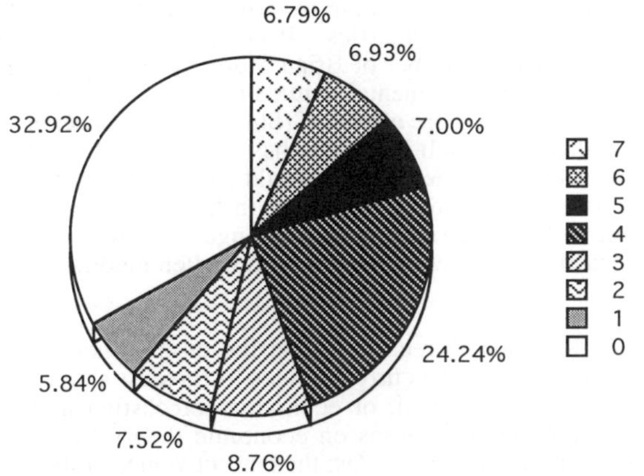

Figure 8.20. The Classification of Solution Space for the Seven-Agent Model (from 31/5/87 to 4/11/92)

Although there is a slight discrepancy between the data set used in the five-agent model and the six- or seven-agent model, the evidence from the six and seven agent models which are based on the same set of data population is so overwhelming that we are in no doubt about the impact and contribution due to additional agent. This implies that if other techniques and market parameters are brought into the decision support system, the uncovered solution space could be cut down in size, particularly in market-based forecasting to correlate the exchange rate movement with the forward rate, and the fundamental forecasting to monitor the influence on rate movement due to balance of payment, relative inflation rate and relative interest rate.

8.3.5 The Activation of Prediction (Command and Control)

Given the prediction selected by volatility tabulation, the task for the command and control is to activate the prediction whenever it feels sure to do so. The prediction which is generated by the cognitive model held inside the decision support system, is subject to uncertainty of the market unknown at the point of prediction. For instance, changes might have taken place because of major political or economical factors not covered by the internal model, and hence, the accuracy of the chosen prediction will now have to be reassessed, or modified to take into account of new development.

The cognitive model used in this investigation is based mainly on technical analysis of historical data. The technical forecaster believes that anything that can possibly affect the exchange rate of a currency is actually reflected in that currency's rate. Some forecasters consider technical analysis as an indirect study of the fundamentals without the need to study of the complicated interrelations amongst the economic factors concerned. Based on the belief (assumption) that history repeats itself, the understanding of the future lies in the study of the past in the form of trends and patterns, and most techniques used in technical analysis are trend-following in nature.

The technical approach is quite simple in terms that there is no need for extensive knowledge of economies or econometrics. It is by this simplicity that the technical approach rises to fame. Brian Marber of Brian Marber & Company says: "Chartists are born, not made. It needs a certain mental attitude to fly in the face of orthodoxy. It's an alternative medicine, but much more effective"[Shireen 88]. However, the main criticism of this approach is that too much emphasis has been placed on the single aspect of historical data as if "what happened before would surely happen again", ignoring other factors that might assist in shedding new light in the movement of rate. In practice though, most technical forecasters use past exchange-rate movements as their baseline technology for forecasting and recommendations are often modified on the basis of other relevant information.

In summary, the technical forecasters treat the environment as a "black box" by extrapolating the past events of the currency rates to forecast about events in the future. On the other hand, the fundamental, or economic forecasting attempt to explain the behaviour of currency movement bases on economic theory by correlating economic variables with movement of exchange rates; the current values of these variables together with their historical impact on a currency's value are studied and used to develop exchange rate projections. However, the choice of these variables and coefficients concerned depends mainly on the economic model used and on the views of the experts who design them [Karidis 91], [Baillie 89].

On the whole, economists believe that like anything sold in the markets, the value of a currency is determined by supply and demand, and any factors that might alter the balance of this equilibrium will provide us with an indication of the future movement of a currency. For example, high inflation in a given country can lead to depreciation in that currency in a foreseeable future. Critical economic factors are the balance of payment position, relative inflation rate (Purchasing Power Parity), relative interest rate (International Fisher Effect), technical factors, and government economic policy and intervention.

However, such economic models, despite their relative success in projecting the direction of possible market movement in medium to long-term, have met with considerable scepticism and criticism. It is particularly believed that as economies change as a result of market condition, or government monetary or fiscal policies, their influence on rate movement should change accordingly. Surely, no one can possibly claim that there exists a model which describes perfectly the relations between different parts of an economy and the movement of a currency. Furthermore, it is difficult to quantify this medium or long-term projection into determining the rate movement on the day. Hence, the consensus in the market is that the fundamental forecasting is to achieve **correct** anticipation of the direction of exchange rate movement, while the technical forecasting is to **accurately** predict the rate of the day. The accuracy is measured by means of deviations between the forecasted rates and the actual rates.

A correct signal is what is needed in establishing the forward rate of a currency, an expectation of the currency's value in the future, and with future and option markets becoming more closely interlocked with the money markets, market-based forecasting has increasingly been monitored to provide a lead to the actual rate movement. Assuming that some traders in the market expect Sterling to appreciate against the US dollar in the near future. This would trigger speculators to buy Sterling with US dollar, and consequently force up the value of Sterling immediately. Conversely, if Sterling were expected to depreciate against the dollar, the speculators would sell off Sterling now and hoping to buy them back later at a lower price. Since the direction of forward rates could be projected by means of fundamental models, such as economic statistics announced in news which might alter the economic equilibrium, the prediction generated by technical forecasting will have to be reassessed.

Has any economic number been changed today?
Please enter the new value:
What was the expected value in the market?
What was the previous value?

Any political event that could affect market sentiment?
How seriously do you think this is going to affect the market?

Figure 8.21. The Sample Dialogues to Capture News That Might Alter the Equilibrium on Exchange Rate

Serafimides studied the effect of news [Serafimides 90] and progressively built up a knowledge base which enable his system to predict the market reactions to certain events e.g. how the drop in interest rates is received in the market in the form of rate movement, and how far the predicted rate should be modified to take into account of the news. Although his investigation is still very primitive, the impact of news is certain to enable his system to extrapolate the impact of past events to modify his prediction.

8.4 Summary

The day when millions change hand in second, what a money trader need is to keep his nerve, as well as a piece of cool-headed and well researched advice on what position to take in this volatile environment. This advice, traditionally coming in the direction where the currency is moving or in a particular range where the currency is expected to trade is projected by economic models or by technical analysis. The movement of forward rate in the future and option markets will also be watched as a source to provide clue to where the currency is heading toward. Since none has been found to be consistently superior to the others, many prefer a mixed forecasting by combining predictions from various techniques in a weighted polynomial. Amongst them, the discriminant analysis is a typical example of this kind.

$Y = b'X$ where Y is a (1 x n) vector of discriminant scores
b' is a (1 x p) vector of discriminant weight, and
X is a (p x n) matrix containing the value of each n individuals on the p independent variables.

Known as classification theory, the discriminant analysis uses multivariate statistical analysis to classify an individual event or a group of individual events into one of several populations on the basis of a list of measurements, ranging from consumer price index, inflation rate, three month forward rate, to money supply figures (M0 and M4). In the simplest case which consists of just two distinct groupings, one group are associated with exchange rate increase from one event (day or month) to another, and the second group identified with exchange rate decrease from one event to another. This analysis enables the forecaster to determine whether the foreign exchange will appreciate or depreciate on the following day. From a machine learning point's of view, this is a form of generalisation to classify the behaviour of event into one group or the other. However, in practice, unless all aspects of influences on rate movement could be covered, this classification technique could only be an approximation to the reality. Furthermore, the volatility on the Forex market, where the driving force behind the short-term rate movement is often difficult to pinpoint, has made it almost impossible to generalise into a working model, and hence, discriminant analysis is more applicable to the medium-term directional forecasting.

In some way, the discriminant analysis is similar to the weighted polynomial used for the AMRA models, which was designed for a stationary environment, and therefore, making it unsuitable for spot rate prediction. The volatility tabulation, on the other hand, adopts a more dynamic selection strategy, switching tactical agent according to emerging trend, and as a result, yields a better hit rate. However, a day is a long time in the Forex market, and prediction generated on the closing rate of yesterday could easily be knocked sideways by all sorts of news filtering through the market. The presence of the command and control in modifying the prediction is as relevant in Forex environment as in the battlefield. In this book, we have studied problem solving in both domains, and the adoption of the Standard Operating Procedure has enabled us to deal with a complex issue unparalleled to the "blocks world" problem. Although at the tactical level, there is little common ground that we could generalise into the platform and the tactics and skill needed in playing chess are incompatible to predicting exchange rate movement in the Forex market, the strategic structure of the SOP has provided us with a framework to formulate, consolidate, select, and execute solution in a highly dynamic environment.

In this chapter, we have assessed the impact of learning in coping with the volatility in market, and its ability to make and change decision in such a highly dynamic environment. From these studies, we are convinced that although there is still long way to go in designing "operated-by-wire" decision support systems, it is certainly feasible to incorporate Standard Operating Procedure to enhance the machine capability in dealing with complex applications in a changeable environment, and it is a matter of time before we would have to work alongside them in shaping our destiny.

REFERENCES

Adelson-Velskiy, G. M., Arlazarov, V. L., Bitman, A. R., Zhivotovskiy, A. A., and Uskov, A. V. (1970). *Programming a Computer to Play Chess.* Russian Math. Surveys, 25, pp. 221-262.

Agre, P. E. and Chapman, D. (1987). *Pengi: an implementation of a theory of activity.* In: Proceedings of AAAI-87, pp. 268-272, Morgan Kaufmann.

Aleksander I. & Morton H (1990). *An Introduction to Neural Computing.* Chapman and Hall.

Ambros-Ingerson, J. and Steel, S. (1988). *Integrating Planning, Execution and Monitoring.* In: Proceedings of AAAI 1988.

Avouris, N. M. and Gasser, L. (1992). *Distributed Artificial Intelligence: Theory and Praxis.* Kluwer Academic Publishers.

Bell, M. (1984). *The ADX - An Expert System Framework for Air Defence.* Proc. IKBS defence seminar, RSRE, Malvern, UK.

Berliner, H. (1973). *Some Necessary Conditions for a Master Chess Program.* Proc. Third International Joint Conference on Artificial Intelligence, pp. 77-85.

Berliner, H. (1979). *The B* Tree Search Algorithm: A Best-First Proof Procedure.* Artificial Intelligence 12, pp. 23-40.

Berliner, H. and Ebeling, C. (1989). *Pattern Knowledge and Search: The SUPREM Architecture.* Artificial Intelligence 38, pp. 161-198.

Bernstein, A., Roberts, M. de V., Arbuckle, T., and Belsky, M. A. (1958). *A Chess Playing Program for the IBM 704.* Proc. Western Joint Computer Conference, pp. 157-159.

Baillie, R. (1989). *The Foreign Exchange Market - Theory and Econometric Evidence,* Cambridge University Press.

Bonasso, R. P. (1988). *What AI Can Do for Battle Management: A Report of the First AAAI Workshop on AI Applications to Battle Management.* AI Magazine, Fall, pp. 77-83.

Bond, A. H. and Gasser, L. (1988). *Readings in Distributed Artificial Intelligence,* Morgan Kaufmann Publishers, Inc.

Box, G. E. P. and Jenkins, G. M. (1971). *Time Series Analysis, Forecasting and Control,* Holden-Day, San Francisco.

Brooks, R. and Connel, J. H. (1986). *Asynchronous Distributed Control System for a Mobile Robot.* SPIE, Vol. 727 Mobile Robots.

Chau, C. (1992). *Trend Following in the Foreign Exchange Markets,* MSc Dissertation, Dept. of Computing, Imperial College, London.

Church, R. M. and Church K. W. (1977). *Plans, Goals, and Search Strategies for the Selection of a Move in Chess.* Chess Skill in Man and Machine, Frey, editor, Springer-Verlag, pp. 131-156.

Clark, K. L. and Gregory, S. (1986). *PARLOG*: Parallel Programming in Logic. In: ACM Trans. on Programming Languages and Systems, 8 (1), pp. 1-49.

COMBAT-SIM, (1989). Perceptronics, INC., USA.

Connah, D. (1991). *Why we need a new approach to the design of agents.* AISBQ, Vol. 76.

Conte, R., Miceli, M. and Castelfranchi, C. (1991). *Limits and Levels of Cooperation: Disentangling Various Types of Prosocial Interaction.* In: Distributed AI 2, Demazeau and Muller (Eds.), North-Holland.

Craig, I. D. (1989). *The Cassandra Architecture: Distributed Control in a Blackboard System,* Ellis Horwood Limited.

Currie, K. and Tate, A. (1989). *O-PLAN: The Open Planning Architecture.* AIAI-TR-67, AIAI, University of Edinburgh, 80 South Bridge, Edinburgh, UK.

Demazeau, Y. and Muller, J. P. (1991). *From Reactive to Intentional Agents.* Decentralised AI 2, pp. 3-14, North-Holland.

Donnelly, T. (1974). HSIANG *CH'I*: The Chinese Game of Chess. A Wargames Research Group Production.

Doran, J., Palmer, M. and Gilbert, N. (1992). *The EOS Project: Modelling Upper Palaeolithic Social Change.* In: Proceedings of Simulating Societies, Gilbert (Ed.), Guildford, U. K.

Durfee, E. H. and Lesser, V. R. (1987a). *Using Partial Global Plans to Coordinate Distributed Problem Solvers.* In: Proceedings of the 1987 International Joint Conference on Artificial Intelligence, pp. 875-883.

Durfee, E. H., Lesser, V. R. and Corkill, D. D. (1987b). *Coherent Cooperation Among Communicating Problem Solvers.* IEEE transactions on Computers, Vol. C(36), pp. 1275-1291.

Engelmore, R. and Morgan, T. (1988). *Blackboard Systems.* Addison-Wesley.

Ferber, J. (1989). *Eco Problem Solving: how to solve a problem by interactions.* In: Proceedings of Ninth Workshop on Distributed Artificial Intelligence, Seattle.

Ferber, J. and Drogoul, A. (1992). *Using Reactive Multi-Agent Systems in Simulation and Problem Solving.* In: Distributed Artificial Intelligence: Theory and Praxis, Avouris and Gasser (Eds.), pp. 53-80, Kluwer Academic Publishers.

First Battle, (1987). *First Battle: BN-CORPS.* The US Army Command and General Staff College.

Fulcher, E. (1989). *BARNABUS: A Neural Net Which Learns Sequences by Backward Chaining,* Neural Systems Engineering Internal Report, Imperial College EF1/89.

Gasser, L., Braganza, C. and Herman, N. (1987). *MACE: a Flexible Testbed for Distributed AI Research.* In: Distributed Artificial Intelligence, Huhns (Ed.), pp. 119-152, Pitman.

Giles, L. (1985). *Sun Tzu on the Art of War,* Tunhwang Press, Taiwan.

Gillies, D., Gabbay, D., Hunter, A., Muggleton, S., Ng, Y. and Richards B. (1992). *The Rule-Based System Project: Using Confirmation Theory and Non-monotonic Logic for Incremental Learning.* In: Inductuve Logic Programming (eds. Muggleton), Academic Press.

Greenblatt, R. D., Eastlake III, D. E., and Crocker, S. D. (1967). *The Greenblatt Chess Program.* Proc. AFIPS Fall Joint Computer Conference, 31, pp. 801-810.

Gregory, S. (1987). *Parallel Logic Programming in PARLOG: The Language and its Implementation,* Addison-Wesley.

Guderian, H. (1952). *Panzer Leader,* New York.

Harris, L. R. (1974). *The Heuristic Search under Conditions of Error.* Artificial Intelligence 5, pp. 217-234.

Harris, L. R. (1977). *The Heuristic Search: An Alternative to the Alpha-Beta Minimax Procedure.* Chess Skill in Man and Machine, Frey, editor, Springer-Verlag, pp. 157-166.

Hertz. J., Krough, A. and Palmer, R. G. (1991). *Introduction to the Theory of Neural Computing,* Addison-Wesley.

Jagannathan, V., Dodhiawala, R., and Baum, L.S. (1989). *Blackboard Architecture and Applications,* Academic Press.

Karidis, J. (1991). *Directional Foreign Exchange Rate Forecasting,* MBA Dissertation, Management School, Imperial College, London.

Klahr, P. and Waterman, D. A. (1986). *Expert Systems: Techniques, Tools, and Applications.* Addison-Wesley.

Lai, C. K. (1987). *Chinese Chess: An Introduction to the Openings.*

Lai, C. K. (1990). *Chinese Chess: The Endgame Technique.*

Lai, C. K. (1991a). *Checkmate in Two: One Hundred Chinese Chess Problems for Beginners.*

Lai, C. K. (1991b). *Victories All the Way.*

Lai, C. K. (1992). *Fifty Games of GM Li Laiqun with Tactical Analysis by Li Laiqun.*

Lakin, W. L. and Miles, J. A. H. (1987). *An AI Approach to Data Fusion and Situation Assessment. Advances in Command, Control and Communication Systems,* Peter Peregrinus, pp. 339-377.

Lakin, W. L., Miles, J. A. H. and Byrne, C. D. (1986). *Intelligent Data Fusion for Naval Command and Control, Controller,* HMSO, London. (Also Published in: Blackboard Systems, Robert Engemore and Tony Morgan, editors, pp. 443-458, Addison-Wesley, 1988.)

Liakopoulos, C. (1993). *A Multi-agent Decision Support System for the Foreign Exchange Market,* MEng Dissertation, Dept. of Computing, Imperial College.

Liebowitz, J. (1990). *The Dynamics of Decision Support Systems and Expert Systems.* The Dryden Press.

Lo, S. T. (1991). *Sun Tzu on the Art of War,* Dawn Press, Taiwan.

Makridakis, S. and Wheelwright, S. (1977). *Adaptive Filtering: An integrated Autoregressive Moving Average Filter for Time Series Forecasting.* Operational Research Quarterly.

Marty, J. P. (1982). *KOMPASS: A Computer-Based War Game.* International Defense Review 4.

Mauree, V. (1992). *A Neural Net Based System for Forecasting Foreign Exchange Rates,* MSc Dissertation, Dept. of Computing, Imperial College, London.

Mayers, C. & Aleksander, I (1988). *Learning Algorithm for Probabilistic Logic Nodes,* Abstracts of INNS First Annual Meeting, p.205.

Middleton, S. (1987). *Air Defence Threat Assessment. Advances in Command, Control and Communication Systems,* Peter Peregrinus, pp. 378-398.

Newell, A., Shaw, J. C., and Simon H. A. (1958). *Chess Playing Programs and the Problem of Complexity.* IBM Journal, Oct., pp. 320-335.

Newell, A. and Simon, H. A. (1972). *Human Problem Solving.* Prentice-Hall, Englewood Cliffs, N. J.

Nii, H. P. (1986). *Blackboard Systems: The Blackboard Model of Problem Solving and the Evolution of Blackboard Architecture.* AI Magazine, 7(2), pp. 38-53.

Palay, A. J. (1983). *Searching with Probabilities.* Ph.D. thesis, Department of Computer Science, Carnegie-Mellon University, Pittsburgh, USA.

Rees, D. (1964). *KOREA: The Limited War.* Macmillan and Company Limited.

Rice, J. P. (1984). *MXA - A Framework for the Development of Blackboard Systems,* Proc. IKBS Defence Seminar, RSRE, Malvern, UK.

Rumelhart, D. E., Hinton, G. E. and Williams, R. J. (1986). *Learning Representations by Back-Propagating Errors,* Nature 323, pp. 533-536.

Sacerdoti, E. D. (1974). *Planning in a Hierarchy of Abstraction Spaces.* Artificial Intelligence, vol. 5, No. 2, pp. 115-135.

Sacerdoti, E. D. (1975a). *A Structure for Plans and Behaviour.* SRI Technical Note 109, Menlo Park, CA.

Sacerdoti, E. D. (1975b). *The Nonlinear Nature of Plans.* Advance Papers IJCAI-75, Tbilisi, USSR, pp. 206-214.

Serafimides, S. (1990). *Exchange Rate Forecasting System,* BSc Dissertation, Dept. of Computing, Imperial College, London.

Shannon, C. E. (1950a). *Programming a Computer for Playing Chess.* The Philosophical Magazine, Vol. 41, Mott, editor, Taylor & Francis, Ltd., pp. 256-275.

Shannon, C. E. (1950b). *A Chess-Playing Machine.* Science American, vol. 182, No. 2, pp. 48-51.

Slate, D. J. and Atkin, L. R. (1977). *Chess 4.5 - The Northwestern University Chess Program.* Chess Skill in Man and Machine, Springer-Verlag, pp. 82-118.

Steeb, R., Cammarata, S., Hayes-Roth, F. A., Thorndyke, P. W. and Wesson, R. B. (1981). *Architectures for Distributed Intelligence for Air Fleet Control.* Technical Report R-2728-ARPA, Rand Corporation, Santa Monica, CA, U. S. A.

Steels, L. (1989). *Cooperation between distributed agents through self organisation.* Journal of robotics and autonomous systems, Vol. 6.

Tailor, A. (1988). *MXA - A Blackboard Expert System Shell. Blackboard Systems,* Robert Engemore and Tony Morgan, editors, pp. 315-333, Addison-Wesley.

Turing, A. M. (1950). *Computing Machinery and Intelligence. Computers and Thought,* McGraw-Hill Book Company, Feigenbaum and Feldman, editors, pp. 11-35.

Turing, A. M. (1953). *Digital Computers Applied to Games. Faster than Thought,* Bowden, editor, Sir Issac pitman & Sons, Ltd., pp. 286-310.

Von Neumann, Jr. and Morgenstern, O. (1944). *Theory of Games and Economic Behavior,* Princeton.

Wavish, P. R. and Connah, D. M. (1990). *Representing Multi-Agent Worlds in ABLE* (Technical Note No. TN2964). Philips Research Laboratories.

Wilkins, D. (1980). *Using Patterns and Plans in Chess.* Artificial Intelligence 14, pp. 165-203.

Wohl, J. G. (1981). *Force Management Decision Requirements for Air Force Tactical Command and Control,* IEEE Trans. SMC-11 (9).

Wong, M. (1992). *Forecasting Exchange Rates Using Neural Networks,* MSc Dissertation, Dept. of Computing, Imperial College, London.

Zanconato, R. (1988). *BLOBS - An Object-Oriented Blackboard System Framework for Reasoning in Time. Blackboard Systems,* Robert Engemore and Tony Morgan, editors, pp.335-345, Addison-Wesley.

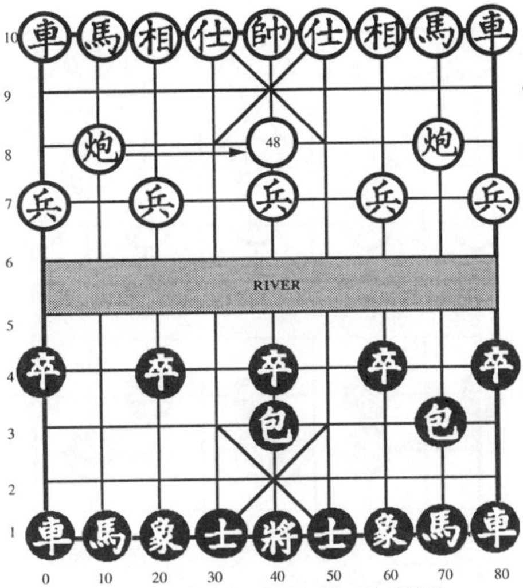

Case 1: Move (10, 18, 48, 6000)

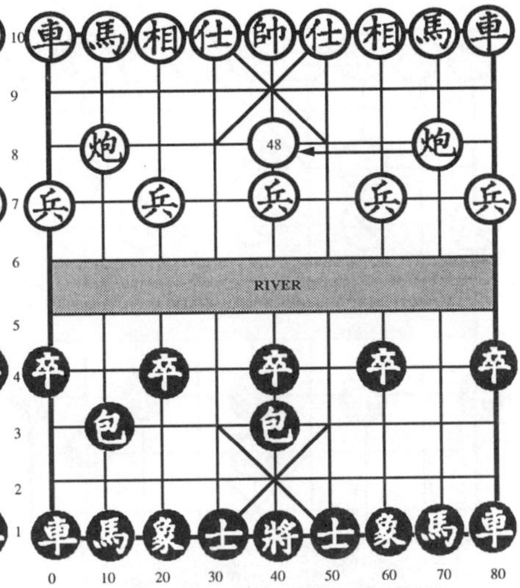

Case 2: Move (11, 78, 48, 6000)

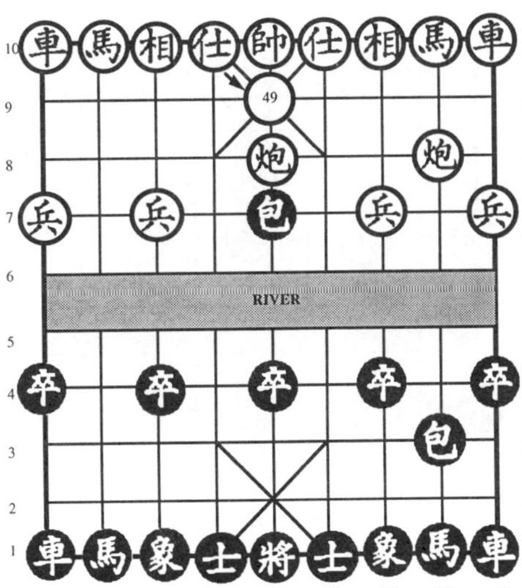

Case 3.1: Move (2, 40, 49, 6000)

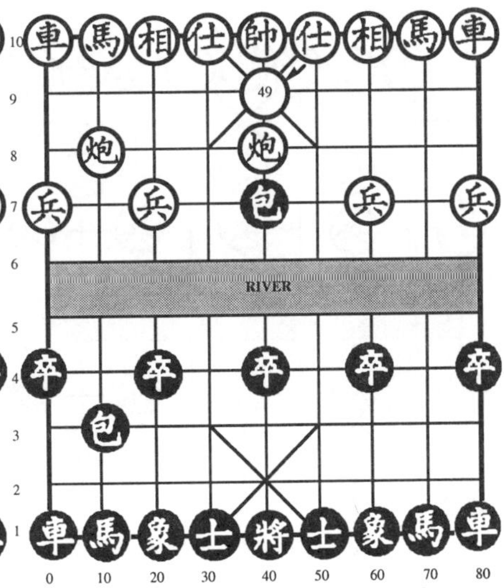

Case 3.2: Move (3, 60, 49, 6000)

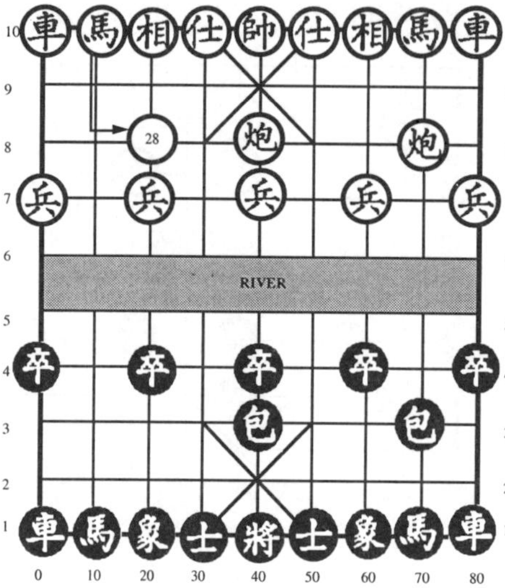

Case 4: Move (8, 20, 28, 6000)

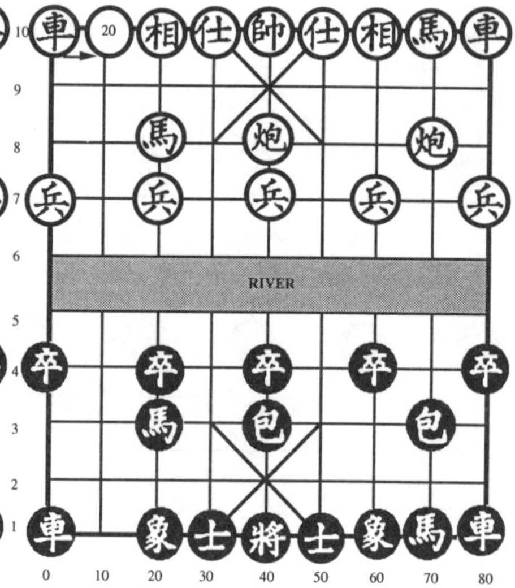

Case 5: Move (6, 10, 20, 6000)

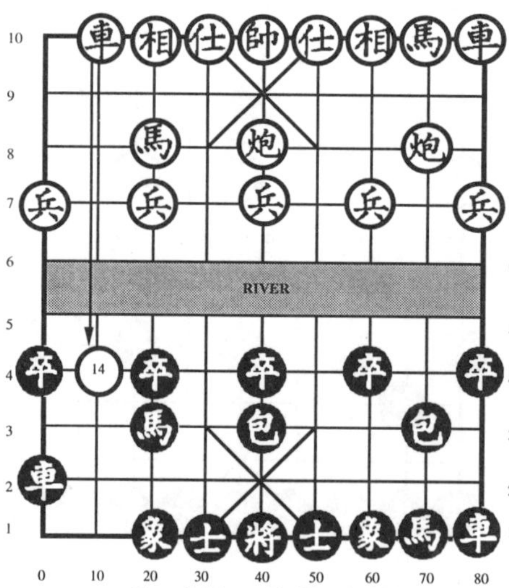

Case 6: Move (6, 20, 14, 6000)

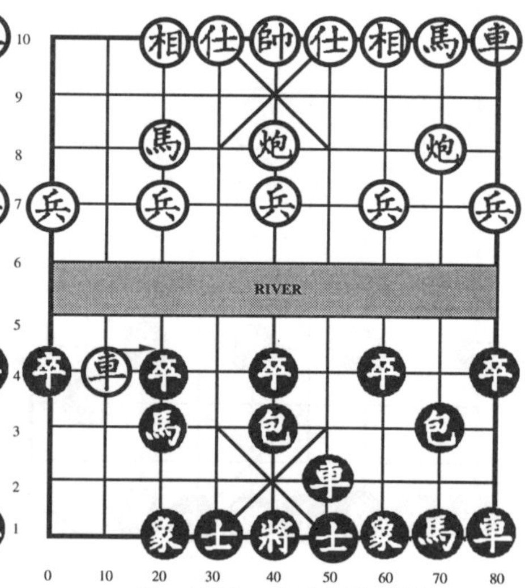

Case 7: Move (6, 14, 24, 6000)

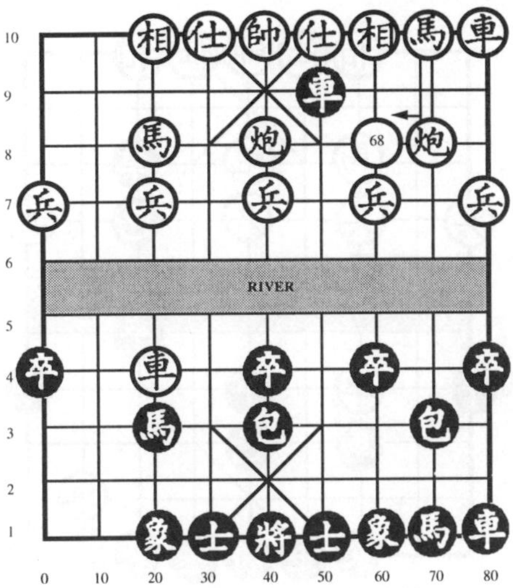

Case 8: Move (9, 80, 68, 6000)

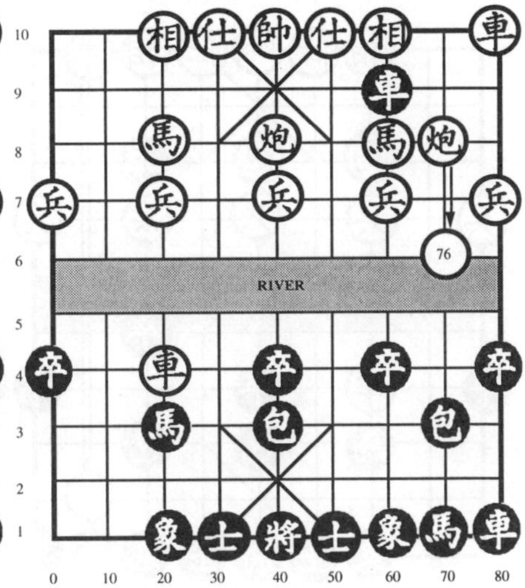

Case 9: Move (11, 78, 76, 6000)

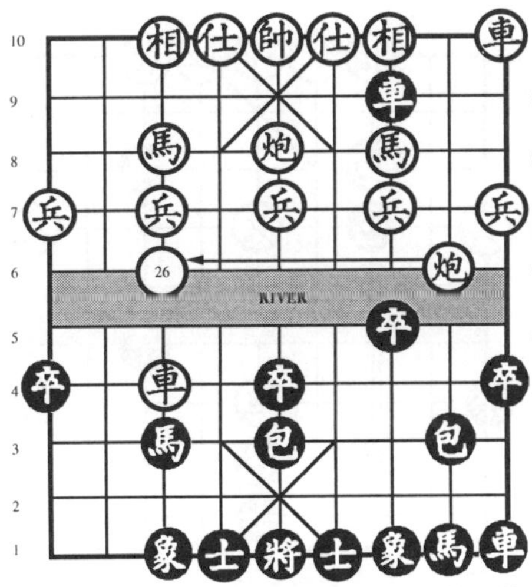

Case 10: Move (11, 76, 26, 6000)

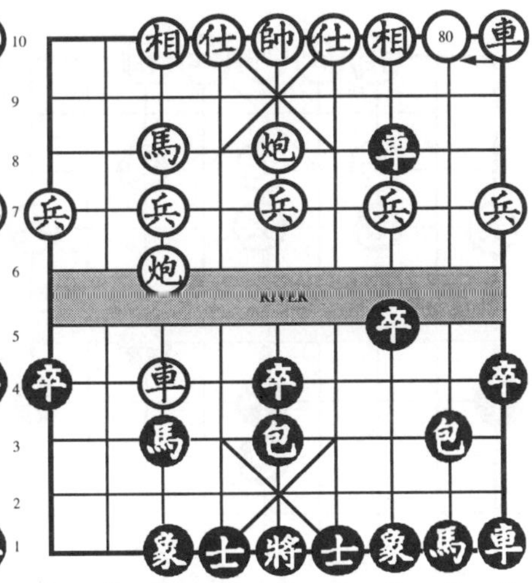

Case 11: Move (7, 90, 80, 6000)

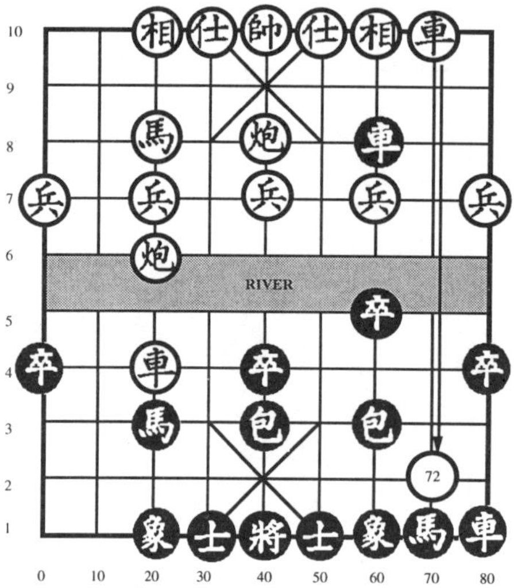

Case 12: Move (7, 80, 72, 6000)

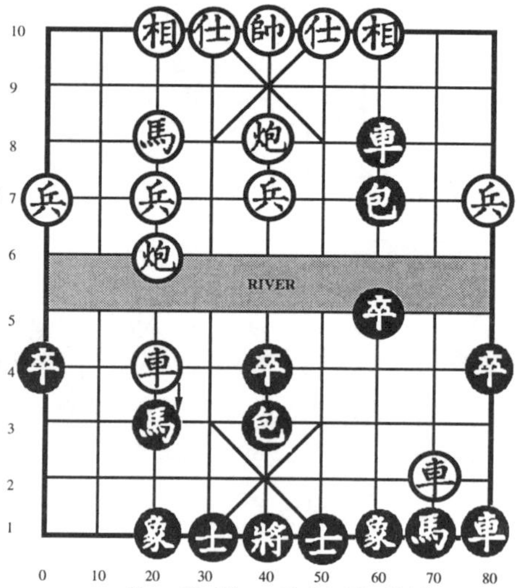

Case 13: Move (6, 24, 23, 6000)

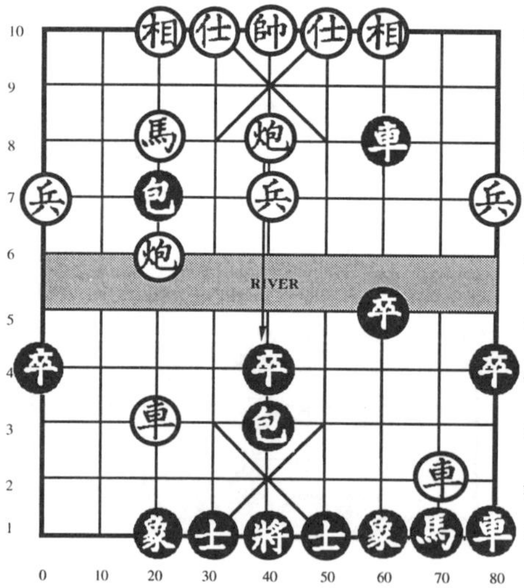

Case 14: Move (10, 48, 44, 6000)

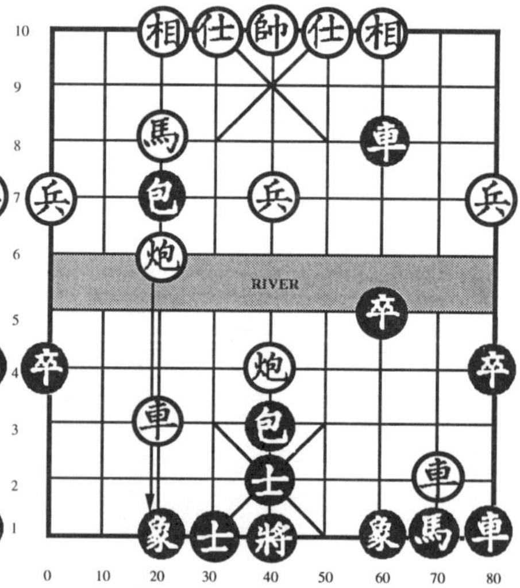

Case 15: Move (11, 26, 21, 6000)

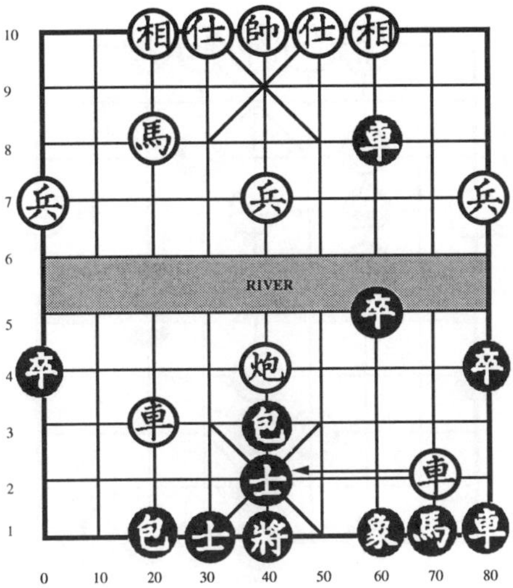

Case 16: Move (7, 72, 42, 6000)

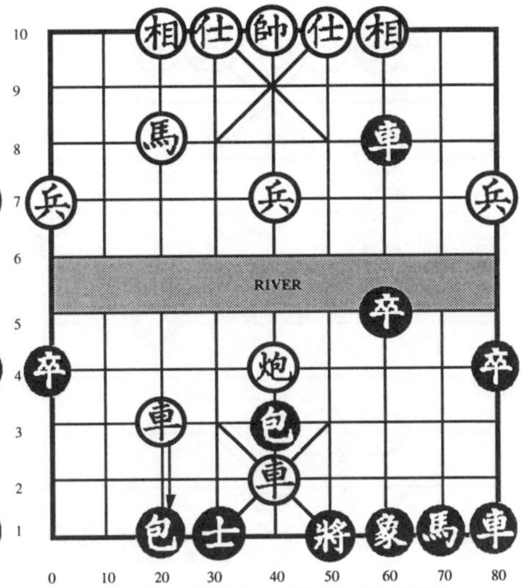

Case 17: Move (6, 23, 21, 6000)

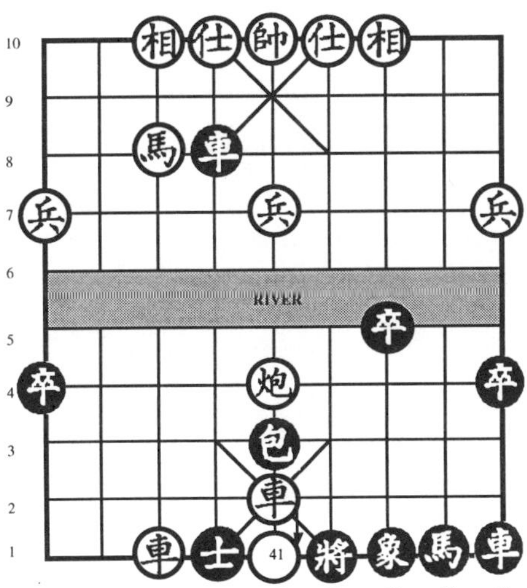

Case 18: Move (7, 42, 41, 6000)

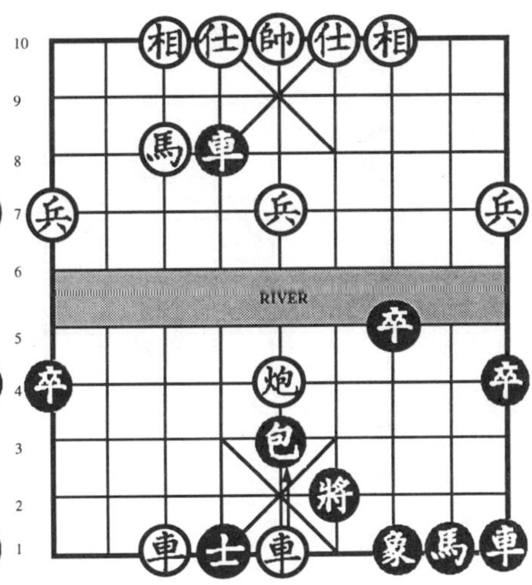

Case 19: Move (7, 41, 43, 6000)

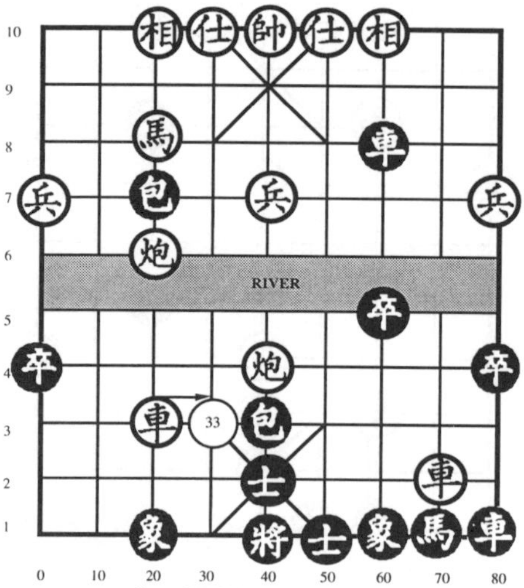

Case 20: Move (6, 23, 33, 6000)

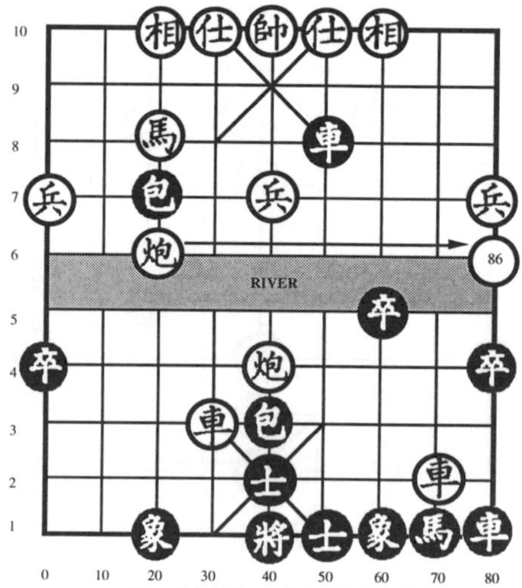

Case 21: Move (11, 26, 86, 6000)

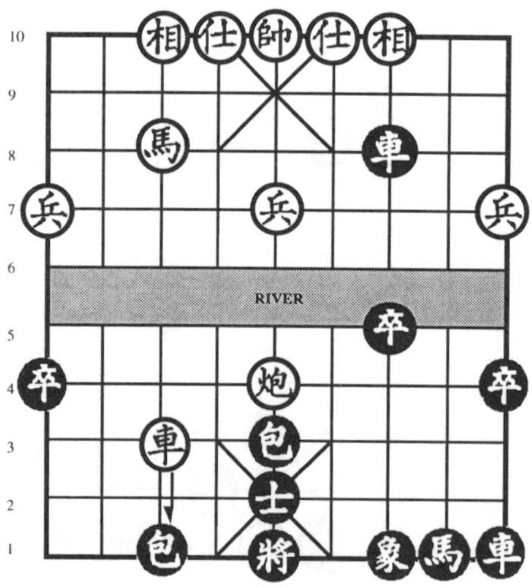

Case 22: Move (6, 23, 21, 6000)

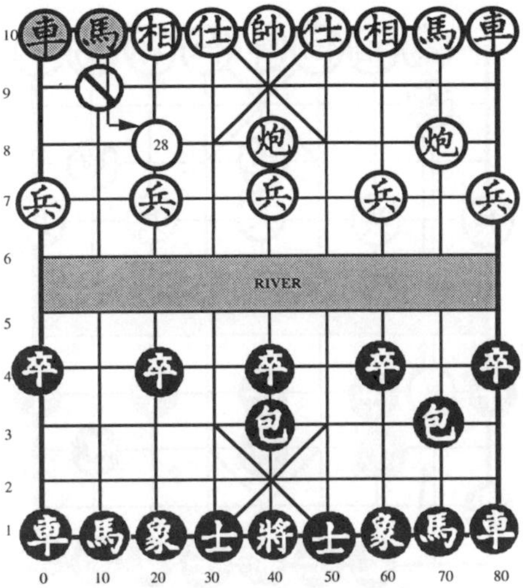

Pattern 1: Move (8, 20, 28, 100)
At (8, 20, Position), At (6, 10, Position),
No_piece (19, Board),
Safe (28, Colour),
Legal (8, 28, Legal_moves): ture;

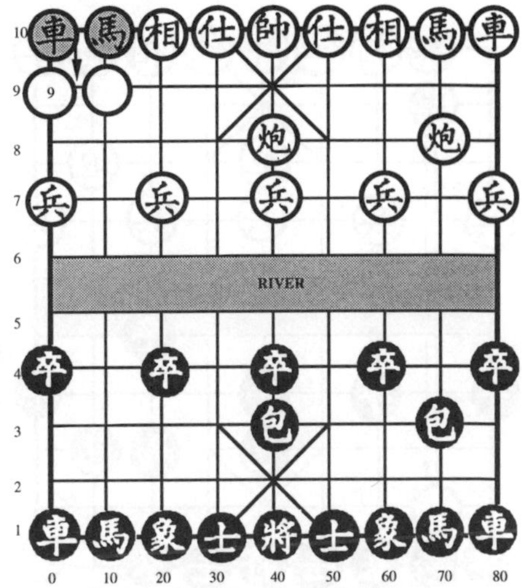

Pattern 2: Move (6, 10, 9, 100)
At (8, 20, Position), At (6, 10, Position),
Piece (19, Board),
Safe (9, Colour),
Legal (6, 9, Legal_moves): ture;

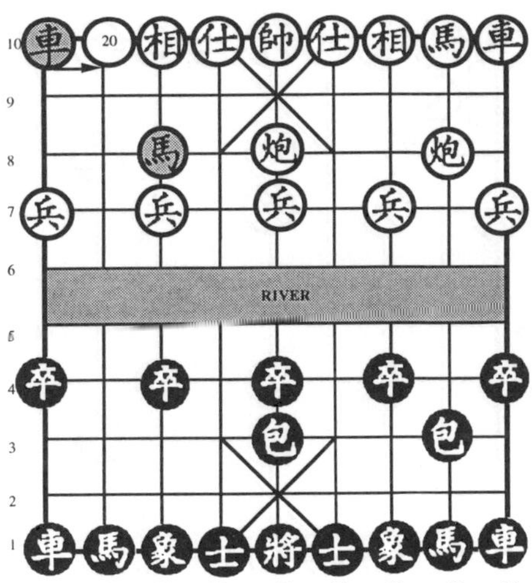

Pattern 3: Move (6, 10, 20, 100)
At (8, 28, Position), At (6, 10, Position),
Safe (20, Colour),
Legal (6, 20, Legal_moves): ture;

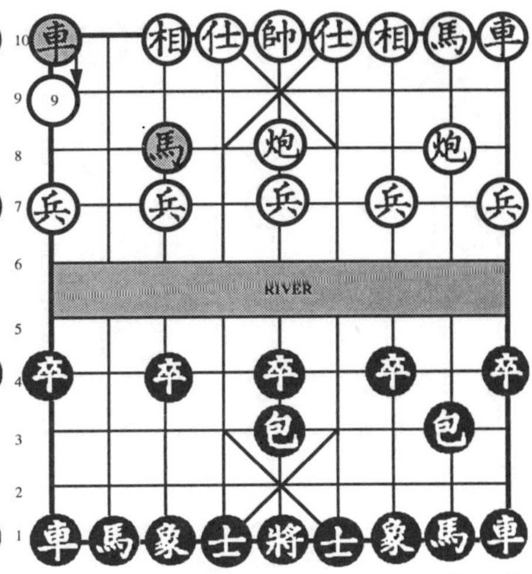

Pattern 4: Move (6, 10, 9, 100)
At (8, 28, Position), At (6, 10, Position),
Safe (9, Colour),
Legal (6, 9, Legal_moves): ture;

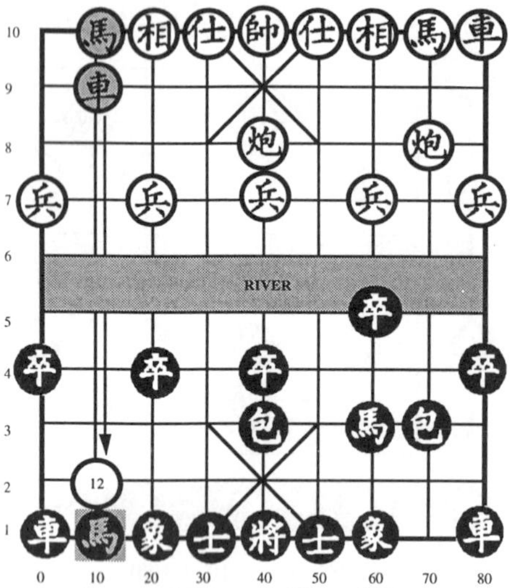

Pattern 5: Move (6, 19, 12, 100)
At (8, 20, Position), At (6, 19, Position),
At (24, 11, Position),
Safe (12, Colour),
Legal (6, 12, Legal_moves): ture;

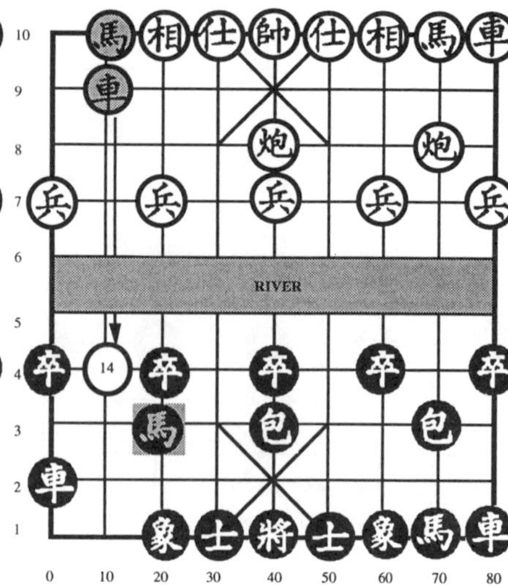

Pattern 6: Move (6, 19, 14, 100)
At (8, 20, Position), At (6, 19, Position),
At (24, 23, Position),
Safe (14, Colour),
Legal (6, 14, Legal_moves): ture;

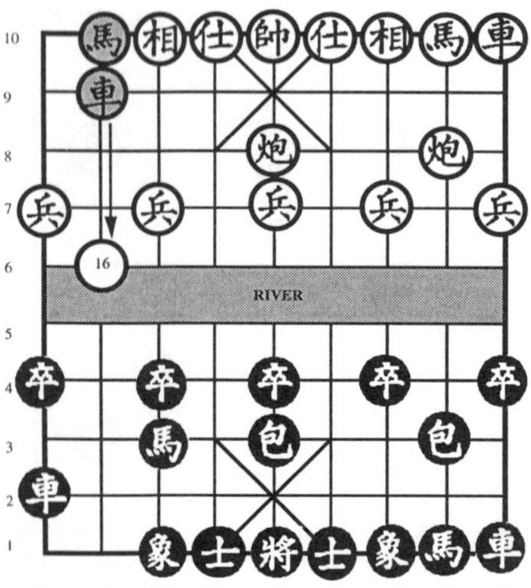

Pattern 7: Move (6, 19, 16, 100)
At (8, 20, Position), At (6, 19, Position),
Safe (16, Colour),
Legal (6, 16, Legal_moves): ture;

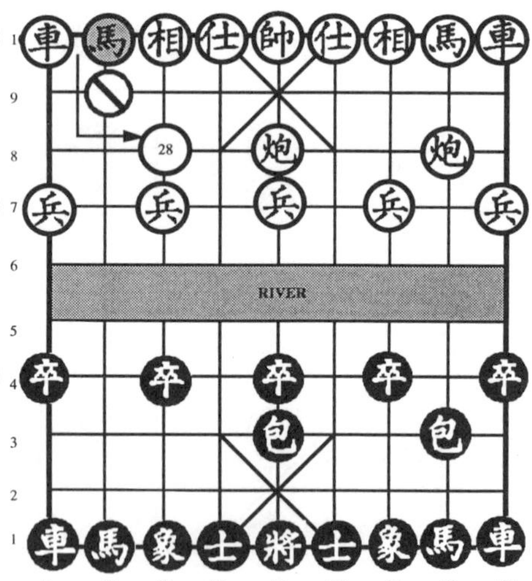

Pattern 8: Move (8, 20, 28, 100)
At (8, 20, Position), No_piece (19, Board),
Safe (28, Colour),
Legal (8, 28, Legal_moves): ture;

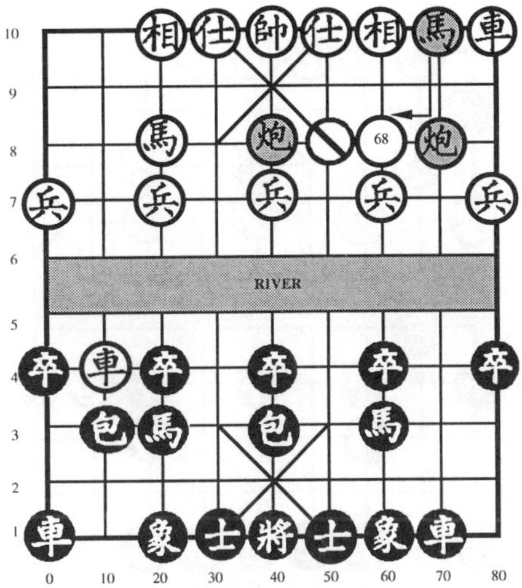

Heuristic 1: Move (9, 80, 68, 300)
At (11, 78, Position), Danger (78, Position),
At (10, 48, Position), At (9, 80, Position),
No_piece (68, Board), No_piece (58, Board),
Safe (68, Colour),
Legal (9, 68, Legal_moves): ture;

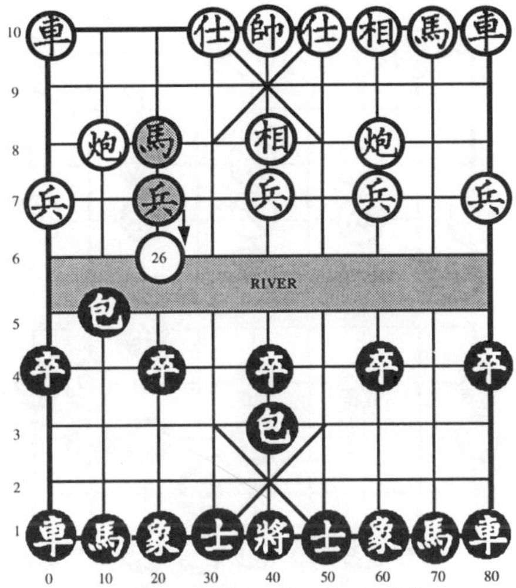

Heuristic 2: Move (13, 27, 26, 15)
At (13, 27, Position),
At (8, 28, Position),
Safe (26, Colour),
Legal (13, 26, Legal_moves): ture;

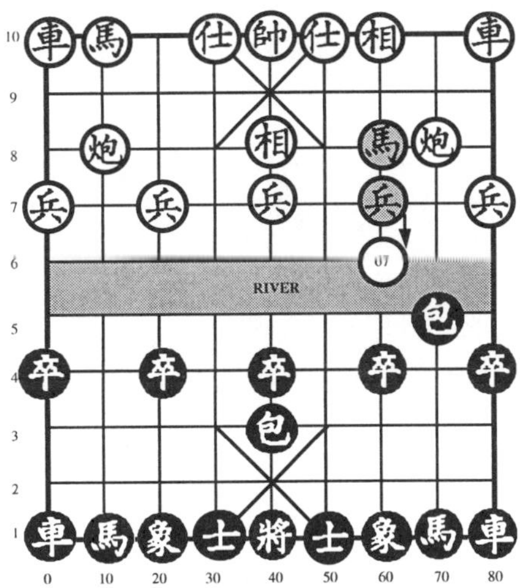

Heuristic 3: Move (15, 67, 66, 15)
At (15, 67, Position),
Alive (9, Position), Safe (66, Colour),
Legal (15, 66, Legal_moves): ture;

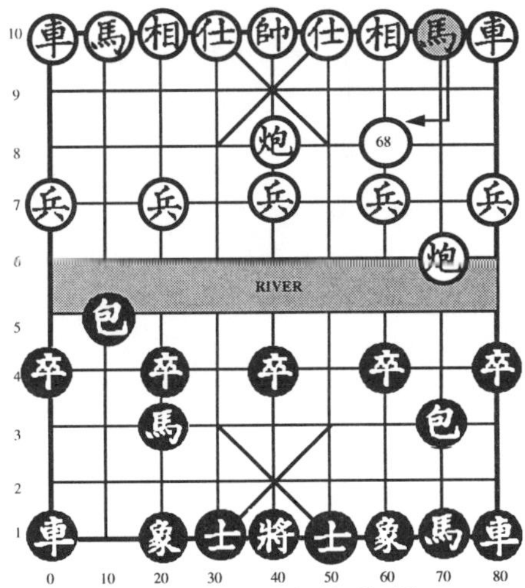

Heuristic 4: Move (9, 80, 68, 15)
At (9, 80, Position),
Safe (68, Colour),
Legal (9, 68, Legal_moves): ture;

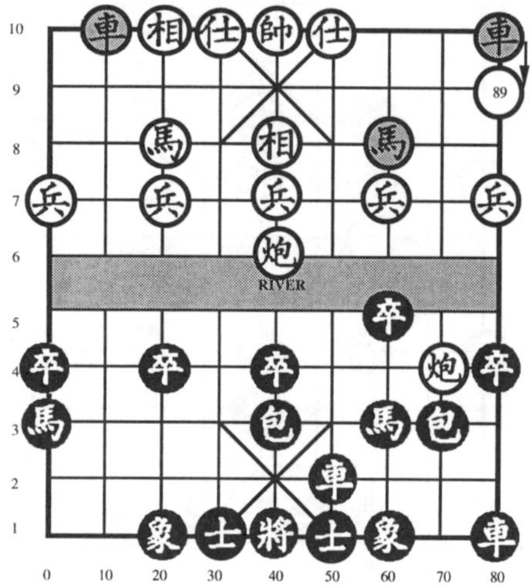

Heuristic 5: Move (7, 90, 89, 15)
At (7, 90, Position), At (6, 20, Position), Not_at (9, 80, Position), Safe (89, Colour), Legal (7, 89, Legal_moves): ture;

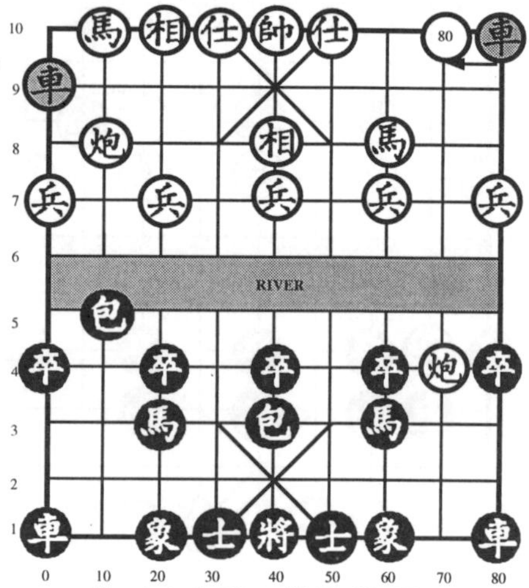

Heuristic 6: Move (7, 90, 80, 15)
At (7, 90, Position), At (6, 9, Position), Safe (80, Colour), Legal (7, 80, Legal_moves): ture;

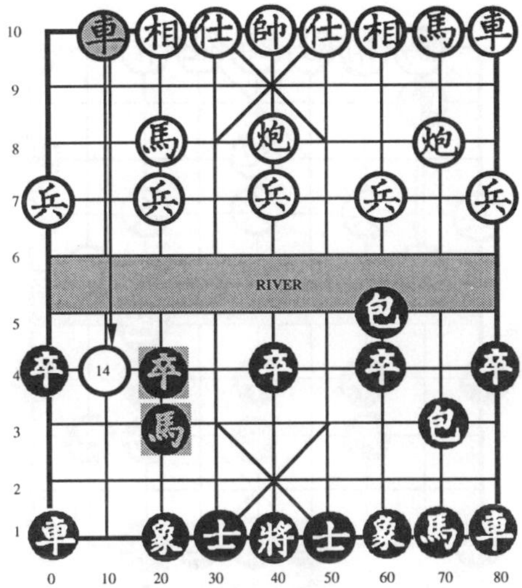

Heuristic 1: Move (6, 20, 14, 100)
At (6, 20, Position), At (24, 23, Position),
At (29, 24, Position),
Safe (14, Colour),
Legal (6, 14, Legal_moves): ture;

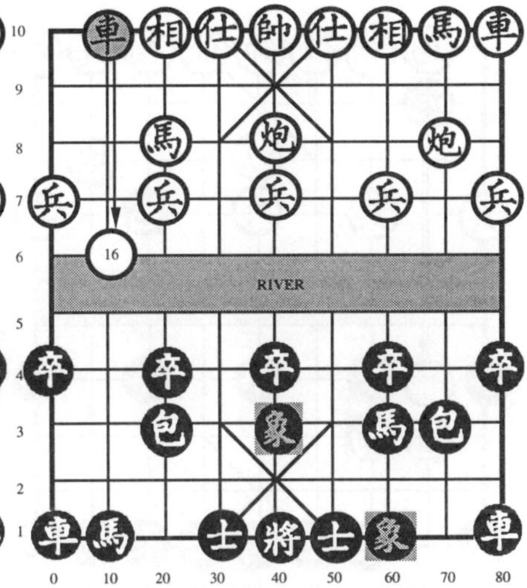

Heuristic 2: Move (6, 20, 16, 100)
At (6, 20, Position),
Or ([20, 21], 43, Position),
Safe (16, Colour),
Legal (6, 16, Legal_moves): ture;

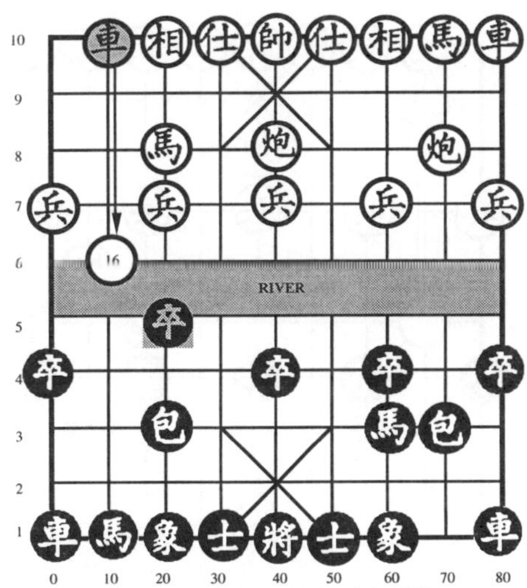

Heuristic 3: Move (6, 20, 16, 100)
At (6, 20, Position), At (29, 25, Position),
Safe (16, Colour),
Legal (6, 16, Legal_moves): ture;

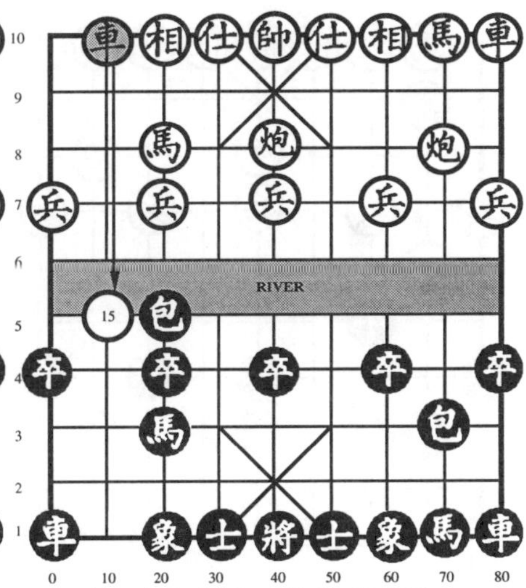

Heuristic 4: Move (6, 20, 15, 100)
At (6, 20, Position),
Safe (15, Colour),
Legal (6, 15, Legal_moves): ture;

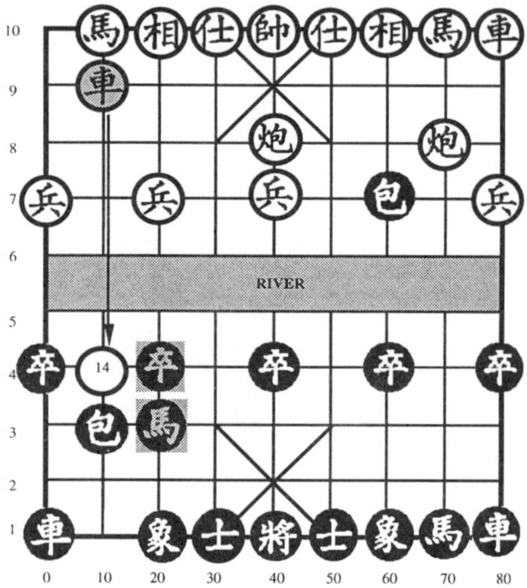

Heuristic 5: Move (6, 19, 14, 100)
At (6, 19, Position), At (24, 23, Position),
At (29, 24, Position),
Safe (14, Colour),
Legal (6, 14, Legal_moves): ture;

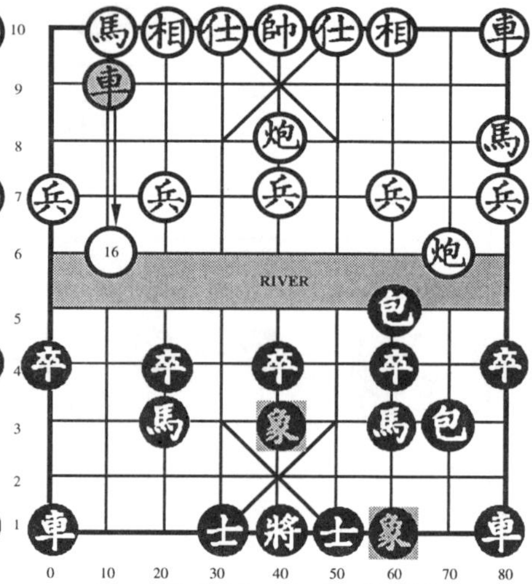

Heuristic 6: Move (6, 19, 16, 100)
At (6, 19, Position),
Or ([20, 21], 43, Position),
Safe (16, Colour),
Legal (6, 16, Legal_moves): ture;

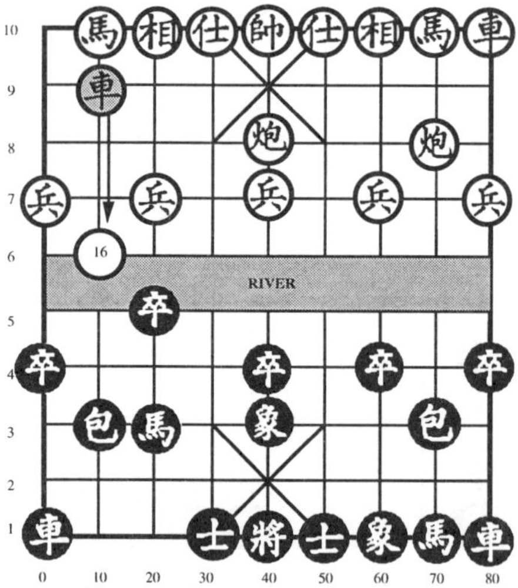

Heuristic 7: Move (6, 19, 16, 100)
At (6, 19, Position), At (29, 25, Position),
Safe (16, Colour),
Legal (6, 16, Legal_moves): ture;

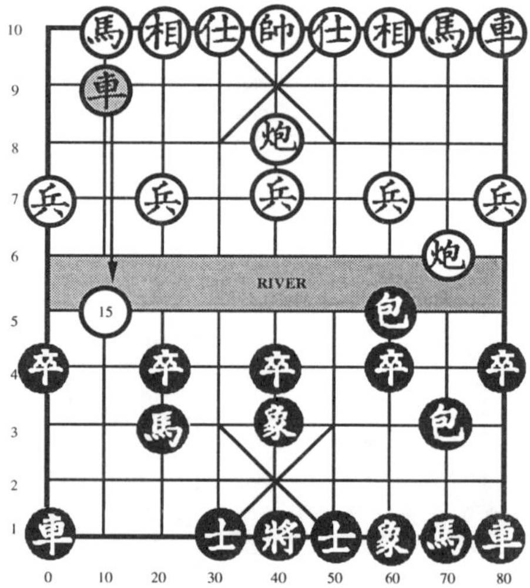

Heuristic 8: Move (6, 19, 15, 100)
At (6, 19, Position),
Safe (15, Colour),
Legal (6, 15, Legal_moves): ture;

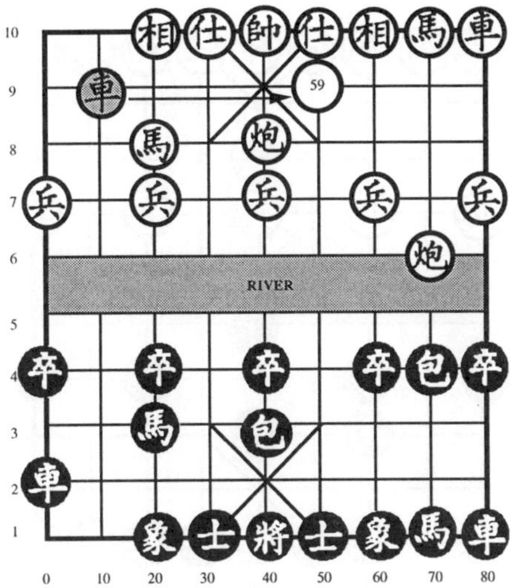

Heuristic 1: Move (6, 19, 59, 100)
At (6, 19, Position),
Safe (59, Colour),
Legal (6, 59, Legal_moves): ture;

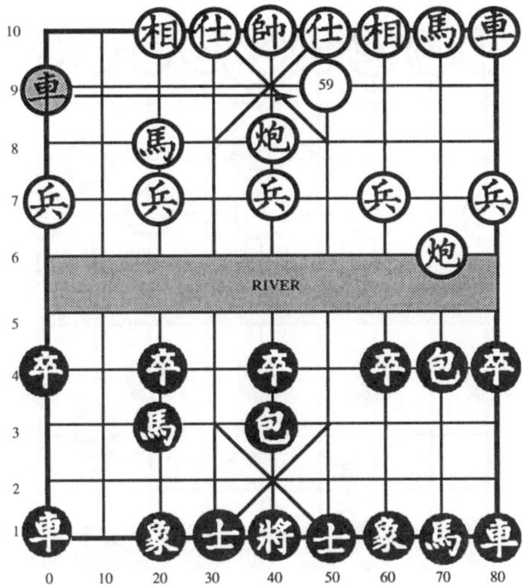

Heuristic 2: Move (6, 9, 59, 100)
At (6, 9, Position),
Safe (59, Colour),
Legal (6, 59, Legal_moves): ture;

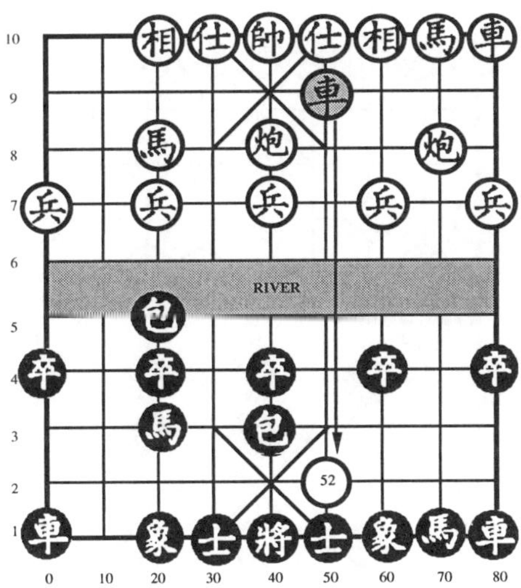

Heuristic 3: Move (6, 59, 52, 100)
At (6, 59, Position),
Safe (52, Colour),
Legal (6, 52, Legal_moves): ture;

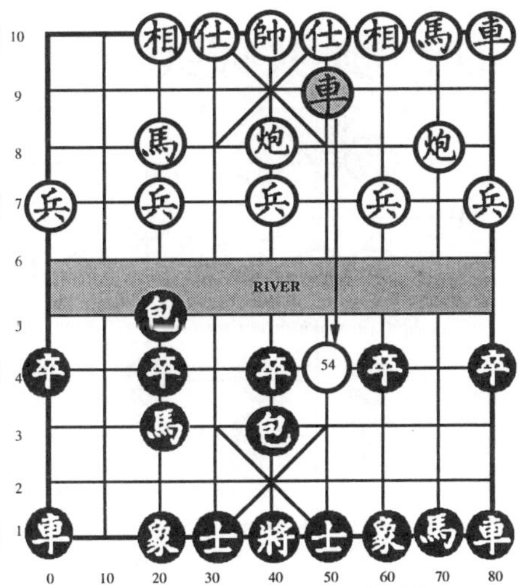

Heuristic 4: Move (6, 59, 54, 100)
At (6, 59, Position),
Safe (54, Colour),
Legal (6, 54, Legal_moves): ture;

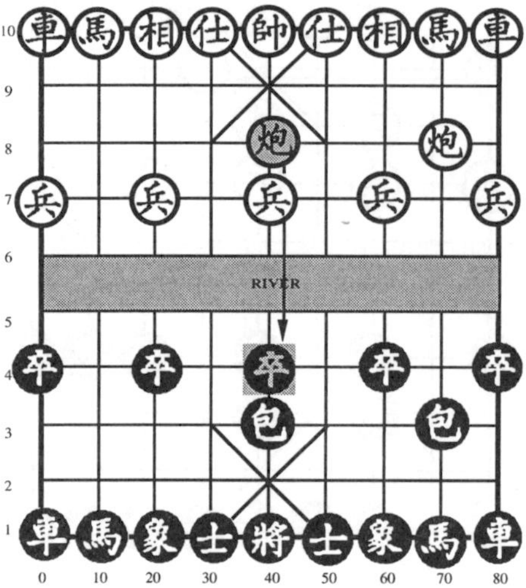

Heuristic 1: Move (10, 48, 44, 100)
At (10, 48, Position), At (30, 44, Position),
Safe (44, Colour),
Legal (10, 44, Legal_moves): ture;

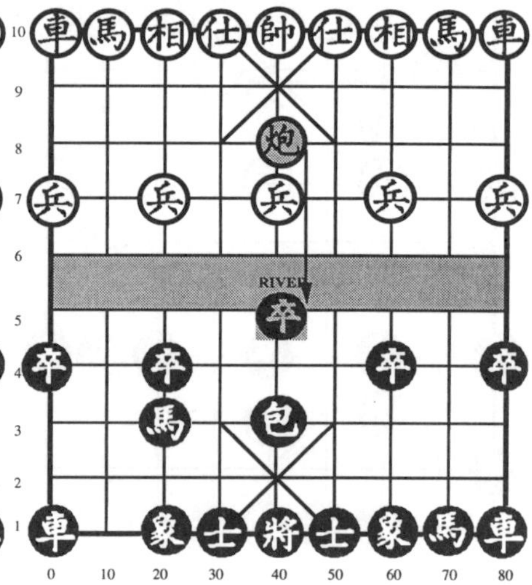

Heuristic 2: Move (10, 48, 45, 100)
At (10, 48, Position), At (30, 45, Position),
Safe (45, Colour),
Legal (10, 45, Legal_moves): ture;

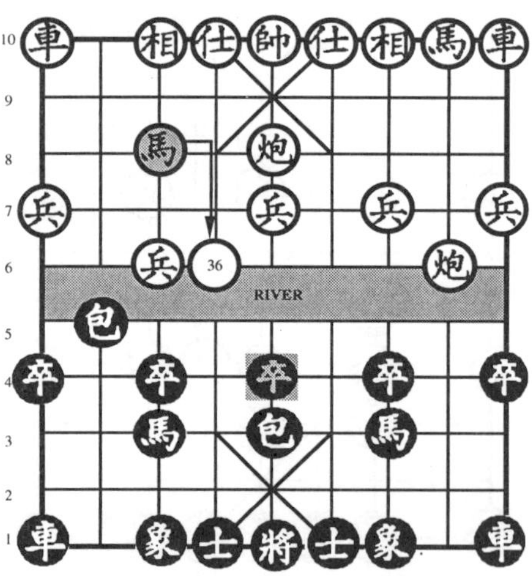

Heuristic 3: Move (8, 28, 36, 100)
At (8, 28, Position), At (30, 44, Position),
Safe (36, Colour),
Legal (8, 36, Legal_moves): ture;

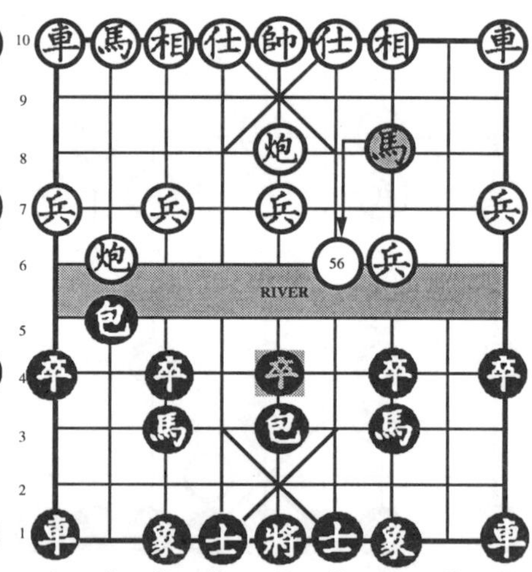

Heuristic 4: Move (9, 68, 56, 100)
At (9, 68, Position), At (30, 44, Position),
Safe (56, Colour),
Legal (9, 56, Legal_moves): ture;

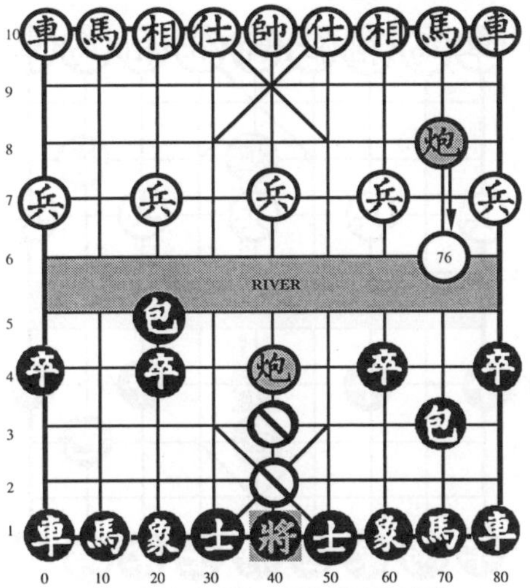

Heuristic 1: Move (11, 78, 76, 700)
At (10, 44, Position), At (11, 78, Position),
At (17, 41, Position), Safe (76, Colour),
No_piece(42, Board), No_piece(43, Board),
Legal (11, 76, Legal_moves): ture;

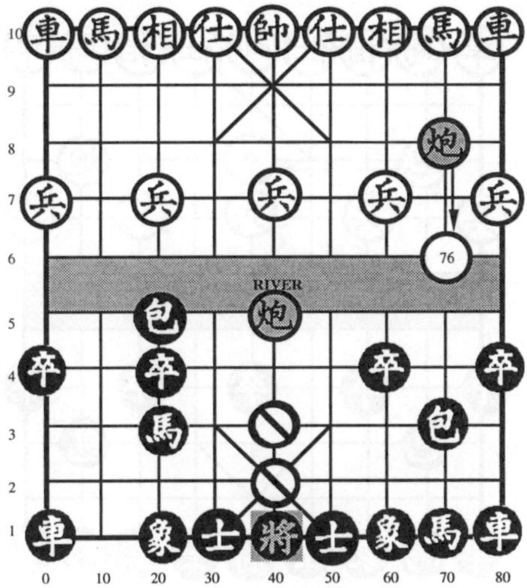

Heuristic 2: Move (11, 78, 76, 700)
At (10, 45, Position), At (11, 78, Position),
At (17, 41, Position), Safe (76, Colour),
No_piece(42, Board), No_piece(43, Board),
Legal (11, 76, Legal_moves): ture;

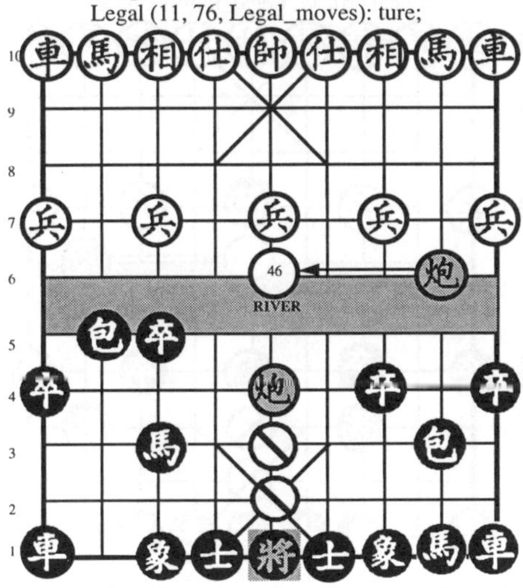

Heuristic 3: Move (11, 76, 46, 700)
At (10, 44, Position), At (11, 76, Position),
At (17, 41, Position), Safe (46, Colour),
No_piece(42, Board), No_piece(43, Board),
Legal (11, 46, Legal_moves): ture;

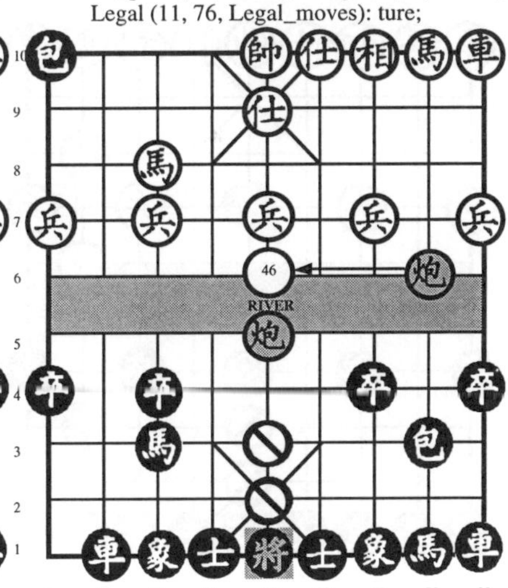

Heuristic 4: Move (11, 76, 46, 6000)
At (10, 45, Position), At (11, 76, Position),
At (17, 41, Position), Safe (46, Colour),
No_piece(42, Board), No_piece(43, Board),
Legal (11, 46, Legal_moves): ture;

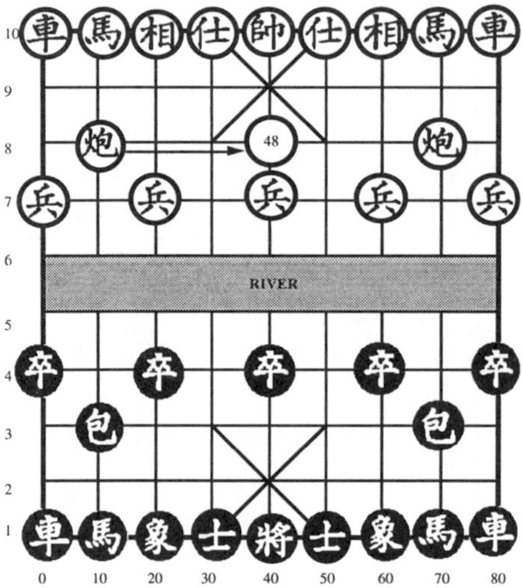

1st Move --> Move (10, 18, 48, 6000)
Cannon Opening Case 1:

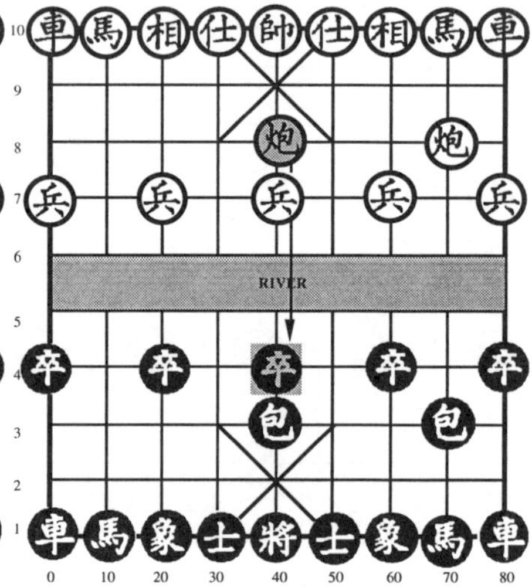

2nd Move --> Move (10, 48, 44, 100)
Central Attack Heuristic 1: Safe (44, Colour), At (10, 48, Position), At (30, 44, Position), Legal (10, 44, Legal_moves): ture;

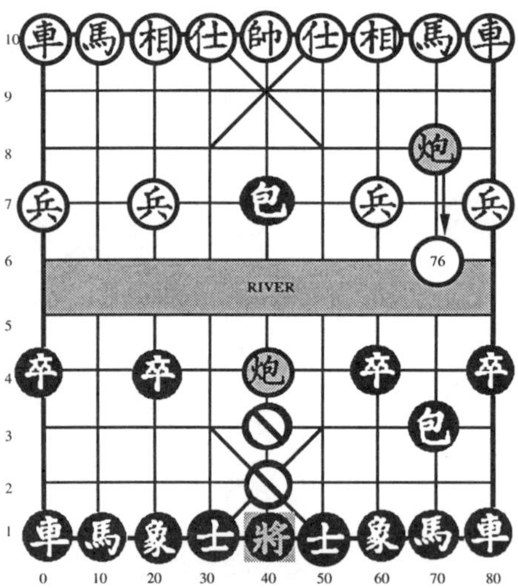

3rd Move --> Move (11, 78, 76, 700)
Double Cannons Heuristic 1:
At (10, 44, Position), At (11, 78, Position), At (17, 41, Position), Safe (76, Colour), No_piece(42, Board), No_piece(43, Board), Legal (11, 76, Legal_moves): ture;

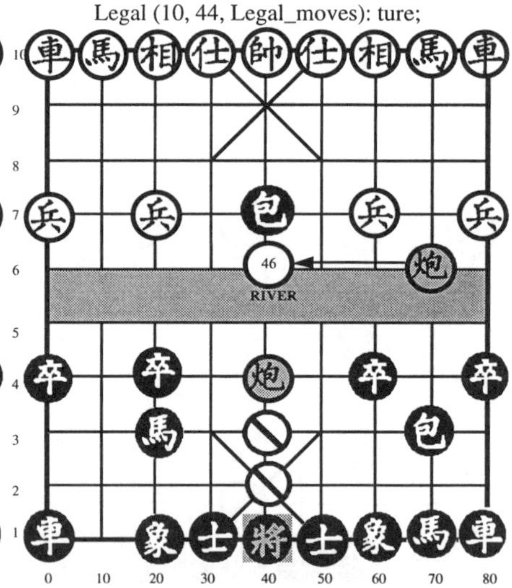

4th Move --> Move (11, 76, 46, 700)
Double Cannons Heuristic 3:
At (10, 44, Position), At (11, 76, Position), At (17, 41, Position), Safe (46, Colour), No_piece(42, Board), No_piece(43, Board), Legal (11, 46, Legal_moves): ture;

Table D1: Positional Value of Red Rook
Both rooks are valued at (-2)

	0	10	20	30	40	50	60	70	80
10	車	10	6	14	12	14	6	10	車
9	8	4	8	16	8	16	8	4	8
8	4	8	6	14	12	14	8	8	8
7	6	10	8	14	14	14	8	10	6
6	12	16	14	20	20	20	14	16	12
					RIVER				
5	12	14	12	18	18	18	12	14	12
4	12	18	16	22	22	22	16	18	12
3	12	12	12	18	18	18	12	12	12
2	16	20	18	24	26	24	18	20	16
1	14	14	12	18	16	18	12	14	14

Table D2: Positional Value of Blue Rook
Both rooks are valued at (-2)

	0	10	20	30	40	50	60	70	80
10	14	14	12	18	16	18	12	14	14
9	16	20	18	24	26	24	18	20	16
8	12	12	12	18	18	18	12	12	12
7	12	18	16	22	22	22	16	18	12
6	12	14	12	18	18	18	12	14	12
					RIVER				
5	12	16	14	20	20	20	14	16	12
4	6	10	8	14	14	14	8	10	6
3	4	8	6	14	12	14	8	8	8
2	8	4	8	16	8	16	8	4	8
1	車	10	6	14	12	14	6	10	車

Table D3: Positional Value of Red Horse
Both horses are valued at (-4)

	0	10	20	30	40	50	60	70	80
10	0	馬	0	0	0	0	0	馬	0
9	0	2	4	4	-2	4	4	2	0
8	4	2	8	8	4	8	8	2	4
7	2	6	8	6	10	6	8	6	2
6	4	12	16	14	12	14	16	12	4
					RIVER				
5	6	16	14	18	16	18	14	16	6
4	8	24	18	24	20	24	18	24	8
3	12	14	16	20	18	20	16	14	12
2	4	10	28	16	8	16	28	10	4
1	4	8	16	12	4	12	16	8	4

Table D4: Positional Value of Blue Horse
Both horses are valued at (-4)

	0	10	20	30	40	50	60	70	80
10	4	8	16	12	4	12	16	8	4
9	4	10	28	16	8	16	28	10	4
8	12	14	16	20	18	20	16	14	12
7	8	24	18	24	20	24	18	24	8
6	6	16	14	18	16	18	14	16	6
					RIVER				
5	4	12	16	14	12	14	16	12	4
4	2	6	8	6	10	6	8	6	2
3	4	2	8	8	4	8	8	2	4
2	0	2	4	4	-2	4	4	2	0
1	0	馬	0	0	0	0	0	馬	0

Table D5: Positional Value of Red Cannon
Both Cannons are valued at (0)

	0	10	20	30	40	50	60	70	80
10	0	0	2	6	6	6	2	0	0
9	0	2	4	6	6	6	4	2	0
8	4	炮	8	6	10	6	8	炮	4
7	0	0	0	2	4	2	0	0	0
6	-2	0	4	2	6	2	4	0	-2
					RIVER				
5	0	0	0	2	8	2	0	0	0
4	0	0	-2	4	10	4	-2	0	0
3	2	2	0	-10	-8	-10	0	2	2
2	2	2	0	-4	-14	-4	0	2	2
1	6	4	0	-10	-12	-10	0	4	6

Table D6: Positional Value of Blue Cannon
Both Cannons are valued at (0)

	0	10	20	30	40	50	60	70	80
10	6	4	0	-10	-12	-10	0	4	6
9	2	2	0	-4	-14	-4	0	2	2
8	2	2	0	-10	-8	-10	0	2	2
7	0	0	-2	4	10	4	-2	0	0
6	0	0	0	2	8	2	0	0	0
					RIVER				
5	-2	0	4	2	6	2	4	0	-2
4	0	0	0	2	4	2	0	0	0
3	4	包	8	6	10	6	8	包	4
2	0	2	4	6	6	6	4	2	0
1	0	0	2	6	6	6	2	0	0

Table D7: Positional Value of Red Soldier
Distribution of values are (0, -2, 4, -2, 0)

	0	10	20	30	40	50	60	70	80
10	0	0	0	0	0	0	0	0	0
9	0	0	0	0	0	0	0	0	0
8	0	0	0	0	0	0	0	0	0
7	兵	0	兵	0	兵	0	兵	0	兵
6	2	0	8	0	8	0	8	0	2
					RIVER				
5	6	12	18	18	20	0	18	12	6
4	10	20	30	34	40	34	30	20	10
3	14	26	42	60	80	60	42	26	14
2	18	36	56	80	120	80	56	36	18
1	0	3	6	9	12	9	6	3	0

Table D8: Positional Value of Blue Soldier
Distribution of values are (0, -2, 4, -2, 0)

	0	10	20	30	40	50	60	70	80
10	0	3	6	9	12	9	6	3	0
9	18	36	56	80	120	80	56	36	18
8	14	26	42	60	80	60	42	26	14
7	10	20	30	34	40	34	30	20	10
6	6	12	18	18	20	0	18	12	6
					RIVER				
5	2	0	8	0	8	0	8	0	2
4	卒		卒		卒		卒		卒
3	0	0	0	0	0	0	0	0	0
2	0	0	0	0	0	0	0	0	0
1	0	0	0	0	0	0	0	0	0

INDEX